Ethics after Wittgenstein

Also available from Bloomsbury

Beauty and the End of Art, by Sonia Sedivy
Portraits of Wittgenstein, edited by F. A. Flowers III and Ian Ground
Wittgenstein on Internal and External Relations, by Jakub Mácha
Wittgenstein, Religion and Ethics, edited by Mikel Burley

Ethics after Wittgenstein

Contemplation and Critique

Edited by
Richard Amesbury and Hartmut von Sass

BLOOMSBURY ACADEMIC
LONDON • NEW YORK • OXFORD • NEW DELHI • SYDNEY

BLOOMSBURY ACADEMIC
Bloomsbury Publishing Plc
50 Bedford Square, London, WC1B 3DP, UK
1385 Broadway, New York, NY 10018, USA
29 Earlsfort Terrace, Dublin 2, Ireland

BLOOMSBURY, BLOOMSBURY ACADEMIC and the Diana logo are trademarks of
Bloomsbury Publishing Plc

First published in Great Britain 2021
This paperback edition published in 2022

Copyright © Richard Amesbury, Hartmut von Sass and Contributors 2021

Richard Amesbury and Hartmut von Sass have asserted their right under the Copyright,
Designs and Patents Act, 1988, to be identified as Editors of this work.

For legal purposes the Acknowledgments on p. vii constitute an extension
of this copyright page.

Cover image: Extreme-Photographer/iStock

All rights reserved. No part of this publication may be reproduced or transmitted in any
form or by any means, electronic or mechanical, including photocopying, recording, or
any information storage or retrieval system, without prior permission in writing from the
publishers.

Bloomsbury Publishing Plc does not have any control over, or responsibility for, any third-
party websites referred to or in this book. All internet addresses given in this book were
correct at the time of going to press. The author and publisher regret any inconvenience
caused if addresses have changed or sites have ceased to exist, but can accept no
responsibility for any such changes.

A catalogue record for this book is available from the British Library.

A catalog record for this book is available from the Library of Congress.

ISBN: HB: 978-1-3500-8714-9
PB: 978-1-3502-1455-2
ePDF: 978-1-3500-8715-6
eBook: 978-1-3500-8716-3

Typeset by Deanta Global Publishing Services, Chennai, India

To find out more about our authors and books visit www.bloomsbury.com and sign up for
our newsletters.

Contents

Preface — vi

Introduction: Doing Ethics after Wittgenstein *Richard Amesbury and Hartmut von Sass* — 1

Part One   Ethics and Wittgenstein

1 Ethics as We Talk It *Lars Hertzberg* — 13
2 Wittgenstein, Ethics, and Fieldwork in Philosophy *Nora Hämäläinen* — 28
3 The Texture of Importance: Ethics after Cavell and Diamond *Sandra Laugier* — 50

Part Two   Wittgenstein, Ethics, and Metaethics

4 Three Wittgensteinian Interventions in Current Metaethical Debates *Julia Hermann* — 75
5 Wittgensteinian Anti-Anti-Realism: One "Anti" Too Many? *Hans-Johann Glock* — 99
6 Wittgenstein and Moral Realism: The Debate Continues *Sabina Lovibond* — 128
7 Does It Pay to Be Good? On D. Z. Phillips Having a Theory about Not Having a Theory in Ethics *Hartmut von Sass* — 147

Part Three   After Wittgenstein

8 "A Certain Purity of Attention to the World": The Ethical Demands of Wittgensteinian Philosophizing *Mikel Burley* — 173
9 Wittgenstein and Political Theology: Law, Decision, and the Self *Richard Amesbury* — 194
10 Wittgenstein Does Critical Theory *Alice Crary* — 214

Notes on Contributors — 249
Index — 251

Preface

This volume owes its origins to a 2016 international conference on ethics in the light—or the shadow?—of Ludwig Wittgenstein, hosted jointly by the University of Zurich's Institute for Social Ethics, directed by Richard Amesbury, and the Collegium Helveticum, an institute for transdisciplinary research at which Hartmut von Sass served as deputy director. We would like to thank both institutions for their generous support and to recognize Christoph Ammann, the event's third co-organizer. None of this would have been possible without generous funding from the Swiss National Science Foundation.

We have collected here significantly revised versions of the papers given at the conference and would like to thank all contributors, first, for their willingness to write and substantially rewrite their papers for this collection and, second, for their patience, since it has taken some time to make the finished product accessible to a wider public here.

We have added three papers to those initially presented in Zurich. These are the ones by von Sass, Hans-Johann Glock, and Amesbury. We would like to thank Peeters for permission to print Glock's essay, an earlier version of which appeared in *Ethical Perspectives* 22:1 (2015), 99–129, and Brill for permission to print Amesbury's essay, an earlier version of which was published in the *Journal of Law, Religion and State* 6:1 (2018), 49–67. An important discussion of Wittgenstein's relation to realism and anti-realism, Glock's essay also provides context for Lovibond's essay. A version of Crary's essay will be published roughly concurrently to this volume in *Crisis and Critique: Philosophical Analysis and Current Events: Proceedings of the 42nd International Wittgenstein Symposium*, edited by Anne Siegetsleitner, Marie-Luisa Frick, and Andreas Oberprantacher. We are grateful to two anonymous peer reviewers for their feedback on earlier drafts of each chapter. Finally, our special thanks go to our editor at Bloomsbury, Becky Holland and Arun Rajakumar, for their help in realizing this volume.

Introduction

Doing Ethics after Wittgenstein

Richard Amesbury and Hartmut von Sass

1 Locating the Debate

Widely regarded as one of the most important philosophers of the last century, Ludwig Wittgenstein (1889–1951) helped to reshape philosophical thinking in fields such as epistemology, philosophy of language, and philosophy of mind. However, the ethical import of his work remains a topic of considerable debate. Depending on how one reads Wittgenstein, either he had relatively little to say about ethics or the whole of his work had an ethical point—and of course there are various positions in between, such as the view that his philosophical writings, though not generally focused on ethics, nevertheless contain insights that shed light on the topic. Though clearly absorbed with ethical questions throughout his life, Wittgenstein's explicit philosophical remarks about the subject—among which must be included not only his "Lecture on Ethics", but also his claim (in a letter to publisher Ludwig von Ficker) that his *Tractatus Logico-Philosophicus* should be understood as having an ethical point—do not easily lend themselves to facile summation or theorizing. Although many philosophers in the field of ethics cite the influence or inspiration of Wittgenstein, there is little agreement about precisely what it means to do ethics in the light of Wittgenstein.

Given his well-known opposition to "theorizing," Wittgenstein is not easily classified—for example, as either a realist or a nonrealist—and his approach to philosophical questions—variously described as "therapeutic" or "contemplative"—cuts across the grain of much contemporary moral theory. Among thinkers influenced by Wittgenstein, several broad "schools" of interpretation have arisen, including those associated with Stanley Cavell, John McDowell, D. Z. Phillips, Cora Diamond, and Sabina Lovibond, with disagreement on some fundamental questions: What does it mean for ethics to say (as Wittgenstein did) that philosophy "leaves everything as it is"? What light does Wittgenstein cast on the role and character of the person doing ethics? What does Wittgenstein's thought contribute to understandings of political themes like justice, authority, and community? Is the Wittgensteinian tradition essentially conservative, or can it accommodate radical social critique? Is ethics characterized chiefly in terms of a special vocabulary, or can any concept function ethically? Is it important to distinguish ethical reasons from other kinds of reasons, and if so, on what does such a distinction depend? How much weight should an account of ethics assign to norms, judgments, and formal arguments? What role is played by pictures, stories, and gestures? Is morality best understood in terms of "grammar"? Is it in some sense inexpressible? How apt is the metaphor of visual perception? This volume brings together an international cohort of leading scholars in this field to address these issues in service of the general question of what it means to do ethics *after Wittgenstein*.

These chapters do not resolve these debates, but they move them forward. Taken together, they advance a conception of philosophical ethics characterized by an attention to detail, meaning, and importance, the pursuit of which itself makes ethical demands on its practitioners: moral philosophy is a moral endeavor. Working in conversation with literature and film; engaging deeply with anthropology, critical theory, and political theory; and addressing contemporary problems and examples, these thinkers reclaim Wittgenstein's legacy as an indispensable resource for ethics. While ambivalent about the term "realism," the account of ethics developed here is generally hostile to anti-realism and moral relativism, and to readings of Wittgenstein commonly taken to support the latter positions in ethics.

2 This Volume: An Overview

This volume is loosely divided into three parts. The first comprises chapters directly concerned with Wittgenstein's philosophy and, especially, with methodological as well as moral questions. The second part deals with metaethical topics, more precisely with Wittgensteinian reactions to contemporary debates in metaethics, in particular with the prospects of moral realism. The third part puts the stress on doing ethics *after* Wittgenstein. The texts compiled in this final section bring current social debates into dialogue not only with Wittgensteinian philosophers such as Stanley Cavell, Peter Winch, and D. Z. Phillips, but also with the Frankfurt School of critical theory and the field of critical legal thought known as *political theology*. Wittgensteinian philosophy has often been characterized as inherently conservative or politically quietist. These latter chapters suggest otherwise, arguing that it can contribute to social critique. The very distinction between ethics and politics is, of course, contested, but several of the chapters in this volume suggest that it would be a mistake to draw a sharp boundary between them.

2.1 Ethics and Wittgenstein

As its title suggests, Lars Hertzberg's opening chapter, "Ethics as We Talk It," posits ethics as an integral part of ordinary communication and interaction. Hertzberg argues that Wittgenstein's early "Lecture on Ethics" shows that, contrary to the *Tractatus*, it is possible to talk about (talk about) ethics. A realm of the unsayable and of mystical silence is left behind here, in order to attend to the diversity of everyday ethical and moral locutions: expressions of commitment, objects of contemplation, and reminders of things we take to be important. Hertzberg underlines the fact that it would be awkward to consider these expressions—"ethics as we talk it"—as being *informative* in the sense of importing concerns that are alien to the person contemplating moral issues. This is particularly shown in reference to morally significant constellations depicted by literature. Hertzberg specifically relies on a novel by Karl Ove Knausgaard and a short story by Hemingway in order to plumb the moral depths of the breakdowns in our communication that call for ethical attention.

A similar interest in the relation between ethics and literature is shown in Nora Hämäläinen's chapter "Wittgenstein, Ethics, and Fieldwork in Philosophy." For her, as for many other philosophers influenced by Wittgenstein, the most fruitful version of post-Wittgensteinian accounts of moral philosophy circles around philosophical debates about narrative literature. To deepen this approach, Hämäläinen proceeds in three steps. First, she gives a helpful overview concerning Wittgenstein's descriptive "methodology," in particular in his *Philosophical Investigations*: not delivering theories, leaving everything as it is in describing, rather than explaining it (away), etc. Second, she discusses three interrelated themes—thinking for ourselves, seeing aspects, and discovering what we did not know we knew—as easily connectable to the chain of remarks by Wittgenstein presented before. Accordingly, moral philosophy is work on our own understanding, on different ways of looking at things that are so close to us that we often tend to neglect them. Third, philosophical work on and in dialogue with literature meets these themes in illuminating ways. Hämäläinen reminds us of the danger of philosophically dismissing empirical inquiry. Philosophical description itself might call for or at least involve research on or empirical attention to the ways in which "we" live in and with language. This could be an important part of what Austin called "*field work* in philosophy" (emphasis in original).

By drawing on Wittgenstein's thought, the work of Stanley Cavell and Cora Diamond offers—among many other things—a redefinition of ethics: it transforms our view of the way ethics and knowledge bear on our ordinary lives. In her chapter "The Texture of Importance," Sandra Laugier shows how Cavell's work on film—in the way he draws our attention to gestures, particulars, details of our ordinary lives—is the basis of such a transformation of ethics and of a different approach to moral reflection. This is an ethics of perception and sensitivity, of attention to what our moral life "looks like," and an ethics of importance. The importance of film lies in its power to make what is important, what matters, emerge: "to magnify the sensation and meaning of a moment." Attention to particulars is this specific attention to the invisible importance of things and moments, the importance of what is "covered over" in our ordinary life. To redefine ethics by starting from what is important, and its connection with the vulnerability of our experience, as Cavell and Diamond do, provides the basis for an ethics of the *particular*. Our capacity for attention is the result of the development of a perceptive capacity: to be able to see a detached detail, or gesture, against its background. Here the importance is in details. Moral philosophy, Laugier argues, must change its field of study from the examination of general concepts to the examination of particular visions, of individuals' "configurations" of thought: attention to detail, to forms of life.

2.2 Wittgenstein, Ethics, and Metaethics

Julia Hermann's "Three Wittgensteinian Interventions in Current Metaethical Debates" opens the second section with a Wittgensteinian appraisal of three topics in current analytic metaethics. The first topic is moral objectivity. First, she criticizes a Platonist conception of objectivity and argues that objectivity in ethics is not weaker than objectivity in science, but different. A Wittgensteinian conception of objectivity is deflationary and more faithful to the actual uses of the concept.

The second Wittgensteinian intervention is directed at the "ideally coherent Caligula." Discussions of this curious philosophical character, she argues, contain several flaws. First, they are based on a false dichotomy between two unhappy alternatives, which reveals an implausibly individualistic picture of what constitutes a normative reason to act. Second, participants fail to see, for example, that the moral wrongness of torturing people for fun constitutes a moral certainty. They assume that there have to be *reasons* for people to refrain from grossly immoral actions, and that it makes sense to say that someone has the most normative reason not to, for instance, torture people for fun. Third, the question "Should Caligula be moral?" is misguided. Fourth, the arguments put forward by realists and anti-realists draw on our intuitions about "far-fetched, imaginary cases," whereas it is impossible for us to have clear intuitions about such cases, since ideally coherent eccentrics are just too remote from actual human beings.

Finally, Hermann addresses moral error theory. Advocates of that theory implicitly deny the central functions that moral norms and practices have in human societies, and they assume that morality is something that we could simply decide to get rid of. Hermann argues that error theorists underestimate how deep we would have to dig if we wanted to eradicate morality. Humans are moral beings all the way down. That in the absence of moral reasons there would still be prudential reasons is cold comfort, given that prudence cannot fulfill the functions morality has in human societies.

Hans-Johann Glock's chapter, "Wittgensteinian Anti-Anti Realism—One 'Anti' Too Many?," focuses on the much debated question of Wittgenstein's relation to moral realism. Glock reminds us that Wittgenstein attached overarching personal importance to questions of moral value. Yet, Wittgenstein's written treatments of ethics are brief and obscure, while his views on language have had a strong, albeit intermittent and diffuse, influence on analytic moral philosophy. His remarks on ethics seem to be totally at odds with realist and cognitivist accounts. On Glock's reading, both the *Tractatus* and "A Lecture on Ethics" maintain that ethics transcends linguistic expression, and the later remarks seem to point in the direction of a variant of expressivism and relativism. Nevertheless, in the 1980s Wittgenstein's philosophy of language was invoked by Oxford philosophers like John McDowell and Sabina Lovibond against the still prevailing noncognitivist mainstream. These "anti-anti-realists" (a term coined by McDowell) maintained that from a Wittgensteinian perspective, all indicative sentences, including moral ones, make claims to truth. Glock's chapter discusses this proposal, historically, exegetically, and substantively. Anti-anti-realism (AAR) chimes with Wittgenstein's deflationary account of truth. But that account is not committed to the conclusion that all propositions that can be called "true" or "false" have the same semantic status. Indeed, Glock argues that

AAR is at odds with Wittgenstein's view that the similarity in linguistic form disguises logical differences between moral and descriptive propositions.

In her contribution, "Wittgenstein and Moral Realism: The Debate Continues," Sabina Lovibond responds to Glock's objections, particularly as the latter related to her 1983 book *Realism and Imagination in Ethics*, which Glock took to exemplify the so-called "anti-anti-realist" approach. Lovibond's chapter defends her earlier book as faithful in spirit to the later Wittgenstein's view of language as integrated into a wider nexus of activity and seeks to reconstruct the motivation for a "seamless or homogeneous" conception of language, as proposed there (the conception which, according to Glock, threatens to lead one astray). In particular, an attempt is made to reactivate the idea of "intellectual authority-relations" that mediates in the 1983 discussion between (1) nonfoundational epistemology in the analytical tradition and (2) a more general-purpose kind of critical theory. This, it is suggested, is the context in which we can hope to do justice both to the legitimate diversity of our evaluative concerns and to the implicit commitment to correctness—or "getting things right"—which shapes much of our thinking. Realism, about morals or anything else, calls upon us to maintain that commitment even in the face of discursive difficulty or stalemate, and it is not obligatory to think that a full appreciation of Wittgenstein's later philosophy will lead us to exchange this attitude for one based on "communitarian" principles.

Alluding, in the title, to D. Z. Phillips's criticism of Phillipa Foot, Hartmut von Sass's chapter "Does It Pay to Be Good?" turns to the question of whether Phillips's "contemplative" approach to ethics is internally consistent. Von Sass begins by giving an account of Phillips's contemplative philosophy—developed in debates about genuine faith and existential orientations in life—about different, but equally vivid possibilities for understanding religious practices. This descriptive and, later on, contemplative endeavor was also applied and worked out in the field of ethics as clarification of how *not* to *do* ethics. Here, however, things start to turn problematic, since in order to defend a descriptive or contemplative ethics, von Sass contends, a methodological metaethics is required. Phillips does, in fact, have such a general method, and this, von Sass argues, is precisely the problem: to present his case for a contemplative ethics—as an ethical demand on the philosopher—he refers to a metaethics that suffers crucially from a lack of contemplation that would have to be applied to itself. If contemplation opens the conceptual and hermeneutical space to appreciate divergent ways of dealing with a (ethical or philosophical) problem, the metaphilosophical question of how to philosophize itself calls for contemplation. Von

Sass suggests that this might imply that contemplation is only one possibility within what Rush Rhees called the "hubbub of (philosophical) voices."

Unfortunately, von Sass contends, it is one of the major difficulties with Phillips's work that it does not apply contemplation to itself, that is, a self-reflective contemplation. In other words, Phillips had a theory about not having a theory and presented (or sometimes presupposed) a generalized metaethics concerning ethics without any generalizations. Hence, von Sass argues, this proto-program is unsuccessful due to a deep inconsistency in Phillips's "system." By "system" von Sass means Phillips's far-reaching semantic assumptions concerning the formation of our concepts and, combined with it, the relation between beliefs and the practices in which these beliefs have their context.

Offering a critical evaluation of D. Z. Phillips's philosophical approach, von Sass's chapter brings together two different issues: Phillips's meta-philosophical claim according to which philosophy has to be descriptive or contemplative and his semantic claim that an expression's meaning is the consequence it makes practically. The critique is twofold: it seeks to show, first, in which sense the meta-philosophical claim about description and contemplation is itself neither descriptive nor contemplative; and second, that Phillips's contemplative dismissal of consequentialist thinking in ethics is at odds with his "theory" of meaning, which involves a consequentialist semantics.

2.3 After Wittgenstein

Continuing in a similar vein, Mikel Burley's chapter focuses on the "Ethical Demands of Wittgensteinian Philosophizing" by elaborating on the idea of descriptive purity, not only in Wittgenstein but also in the work of some of his followers, such as Phillips. Phillips's way of adopting the methods of Wittgenstein and his student Rhees was in terms of the mode of philosophizing that Phillips termed "contemplative." Burley's chapter examines that mode with regard to its ethical implications. In particular, it considers what it means to say, as Phillips did, that a contemplative inquiry "makes ethical demands of the enquirer." Phillips is not alone in proposing that an approach influenced by Wittgenstein makes such demands, but what do the demands amount to, how do they relate to the idea of "a certain purity of attention to the world," and are they demands that can feasibly be met? In addressing these questions, the concern is not merely the exegetical one of clarifying what Phillips means by declaring that contemplative philosophizing places ethical demands upon the philosopher. Rather, Burley asks what a contemplative approach to philosophy allows and enables us to say about ethically relevant topics, and especially about forms of life that, in certain respects, the inquirer finds morally troubling or repulsive. In fact, Burley contends, there are not two completely distinguishable tasks here, since examining Phillips's meaning necessarily involves examining examples of contemplative philosophizing in practice.

The chapter begins by explicating the debate between Phillips and other philosophers influenced by Wittgenstein over the question of how the philosophical and the personal are related. The debate is complicated because although Phillips wants to defend a distinction between these elements in one respect, there is another respect in which he acknowledges that philosophical and personal aspects of a philosopher's life cannot be separated. Second, purity of attention is placed alongside the imperative to "do conceptual justice" to one's philosophical subject matter and examine the significance of these methodological impulses for contemplative philosophy. Third, the chapter turns to instances of contemplative philosophizing in action, principally from the work of Wittgenstein and Rhees, which Phillips held to be exemplary. By focusing on the thought of these philosophers in relation to what is "deep and sinister" in human life, Burley seeks to elucidate the role of emotional and moral response in philosophical reflection. In conclusion, he proposes that the ethical demands of Wittgensteinian philosophizing are a complex matter, involving not a relinquishing of one's emotional and moral responses but a careful integration of those responses into one's philosophical reflections.

Richard Amesbury's contribution, "Wittgenstein and Political Theology: Law, Decision, and the Self," offers a Wittgensteinian intervention into ethico-legal theory, addressing the decisionism taken by Carl Schmitt to be characteristic of political sovereignty. Once a respected German jurist and philosopher, Schmitt cast his lot with National Socialism, and in the postwar period, his work fell into deserved disrepute. In recent decades, however, it has been selectively rehabilitated, particularly by philosophers on the political left (such as Derrida, Agamben, and Paul Kahn) seeking to provide alternatives to liberal accounts of law and the state, a project sometimes known—following the title of one of Schmitt's best-known works—as *political theology*. But whereas Schmitt located sovereignty in the decision-making power of an executive, some contemporary practitioners of political theology lay more stress on the role of the judiciary. According to this account, the interpretation of law depends upon judicial decisions that serve to impose meaning on otherwise semantically indeterminate norms.

Whereas the liberal model treats legal norms as, in Wittgenstein's phrase, "rails laid invisibly to infinity," the decisionist account holds that track is constantly being put down, as the decisions of judges confer meaning. Amesbury's chapter brings this Schmittian analysis of law into conversation with the work of Schmitt's contemporary, Wittgenstein, in an effort to resist the choice between liberal "reason" and decisionistic "will." When it comes to law, Amesbury argues, one need not choose between reason and will, between an abstract rule that "applies itself" and a will that heroically, if arbitrarily, decides. A third possibility is to understand law within the contexts of its use, to view it as, among other things, a cultural practice.

Alice Crary's contribution, "Wittgenstein Does Critical Theory," turns to the relation between Wittgenstein and critical theory and aims to illuminate the distinctive challenges of liberating social criticism. The chapter's primary concern is an account of the nature of critical social thought that, while intuitively attractive, goes missing in many institutionally central philosophical conversations about such thought. This is because the account presupposes a heterodox conception of rationality that often is not even registered as a legitimate possibility, much less seriously discussed. Yet the relevant conception of rationality informs influential philosophical treatments of liberating social criticism, including, for instance, some notable contributions to critical theory. It is possible to mount a defense of this conception, Crary argues, thereby providing support for the appealing conception of critique it brings within reach, by reconstructing—with some substantial criticisms and additions—an argument from mid-twentieth-century Anglo-American philosophy of the social sciences, namely, the argument that forms the backbone of Peter Winch's *The Idea of a Social Science*. Winch draws his guiding insights from the later philosophy of Wittgenstein, and one payoff of reevaluating Winch's work against the backdrop of congenial work in critical theory is that this makes it possible not only to decisively contest the deeply ingrained idea that Wittgenstein's later thought has a politically conservative bent but also, more positively, to demonstrate the great value of his thought for emancipatory criticism. The larger payoff of this ecumenical method, she argues, is nothing more and nothing less than advancing the enterprise of critique.

Collectively and individually, these chapters seek to invite readers into the rich debate over the implications for moral philosophy of Wittgenstein's approach to philosophy, to move that debate forward in philosophically substantive ways, and to extend the resulting insights into new domains and debates.

Part One

Ethics and Wittgenstein

1

Ethics as We Talk It

Lars Hertzberg

1 Are Ethical Judgments Nonsense?

Wittgenstein's reticence concerning questions in moral philosophy is a famous theme. It is often linked to the remarks in Wittgenstein's only sustained treatment of ethical issues, the "Lecture on Ethics," where he makes the claim that the attempt to put absolute value into words is a violation of the conditions of sense.[1] However, the idea that there is a direct connection between these two matters is not unproblematic. For one thing, if the idea of the nonsensicality of judgments of absolute value precluded his writing or speaking about ethics, the lecture itself ought not to have come about. Or put it like this: in giving the lecture he showed that he thought one could talk about talk *about* ethics—and there's no reason why he should have abstained from doing that in the future, in analogy with talking *about* talk about the mind, meaning, etc.

For another thing, his views about nonsense certainly changed during his career; so, whatever would have constituted a reason for not talking about ethics in the period up until 1930 would not have stayed the same during the 1930s and 1940s.

It is also very hard to know what to make of his claim, in the "Lecture," that absolute value judgments cannot be made. He imagines two dialogues. In the first, someone is told his tennis game is not much good; he shrugs off the criticism by saying that he does not care about playing any better—in which case, supposedly, the critic will say, "Ah, then that is all right." In the second dialogue, someone says, "You're behaving like a beast," and the other person answers, "I know I behave badly, but then I do not want to behave any better." According to Wittgenstein, it would here be out of the question for the first person to respond by saying that in that case it is all right. Rather, he suggests, the first person's response would be: "Well, you *ought* to want to behave better."

There is, of course, a distinction to be made between telling a person there is something she has to do *if* she wants to bring about certain results and telling her there is something she has to do regardless of her goals. I am not sure whether that is a good way of marking off the ethical. Anyway, the conversations imagined by Wittgenstein are rather stilted, not to say weird. Be that as it may, Wittgenstein makes the important claim that the speaker who says, at the end of the latter conversation, "You *ought* to want to behave better," is making an absolute judgment of value. In other words, he is suggesting that a sensible thing, indeed the only sensible thing, to say in the course of a (supposedly) more or less normal piece of human interaction is something that, by his own lights, makes no sense. This raises the question of how Wittgenstein's use of the concept of nonsense is to be taken.

There is a strange duality in the rhetoric surrounding the talk of nonsense in the lecture. On the one hand, Wittgenstein is putting the distinction between sense and nonsense in fairly straightforward, restrictive terms: nonsense, he says, is whatever is not factual (he also contrasts nonsense with "true propositions" and "true scientific propositions"—here, he might rather have talked about propositions with truth-value). But on the other hand, he speaks about the distinction in more dramatic, or shall we say romantic, terms: nonsense is an abuse of language; it is an absolutely hopeless running against the walls of the cage of language (which he then immediately paraphrases with the less radical claim that ethics can be no science). At the same time, he expresses his deep respect for our tendency to speak in these ways.

Well, what is the force of Wittgenstein calling certain uses of words nonsense? Does Wittgenstein mean that we ought to resist the temptation to speak in these ways, or is he actually encouraging us to indulge in it? Is telling the guy who says he's OK with behaving like a beast he *ought* to want to behave better also a case of running—hopelessly?—against the walls of the cage?

Does Wittgenstein simply mean to make us aware that there are other ways of speaking than reporting facts? Of course, people do things like asking questions, giving orders, etc. To characterize these ways of speaking as "running one's head against the walls of a cage" seems overly dramatic. Besides, Wittgenstein shows no interest at this stage in exploring what is involved in calling a judgment factual, simply taking it for granted as an unambiguous notion—this, on the other hand, is a problem that he does address in his later work.

Or is Wittgenstein, rather, making some deeper point about *ethical* discourse in particular? Is he, perhaps, gesturing toward the fact that our ways of speaking about ethical issues run counter to assumptions commonly made about what takes place in human conversation? Or differently put, is he thinking of some particular way in which the attempt to get a clear view of ethical talk lends itself to philosophical misunderstanding? The problem, on this account, would lie, not in the ways we talk, but in the ways philosophers are inclined to construe our talk. The cage in question, then, would be that of the philosopher's presumptions, not of human language as actually spoken. Wittgenstein's use of the word "nonsense," on this reading, is ironic: "if you are right, then you will have to discard all this as nonsense—which we all agree would be absurd." I am putting this forward as a possible reading of Wittgenstein's lecture—I don't know how plausible it is.

2 A Restricted View of Meaningful Talk

Be that as it may, Wittgenstein, in the *Tractatus* as well as in the "Lecture on Ethics," is expressing what we might call a diminished or restricted view of meaningful speech; similar views recur in different forms in much twentieth-century analytic philosophy. What I have in mind are views according to which only *some* of the forms of what we are used to thinking of as normal speech are genuine or meaningful or rational ways of speaking; in a milder version, certain forms of speaking are held to be *paradigmatic* of what it is to speak meaningfully or rationally. In the *Philosophical Investigations*, the idea of such a diminished view—or rather, a variety of diminished views—recurs, but now as a source of philosophical temptation. I shall try to articulate some of the characteristics of such views and also try to spell out what might make them attractive to philosophers. I shall then point out some aspects of ordinary conversation that tend to get neglected in the diminished view. Finally I shall present some cases of what might be considered everyday conversations addressing ethical concerns, and suggest what might tempt us to think of them as falling outside the limits of meaningful speech, even though there seems to be nothing obscure or untoward in what the speakers are saying.

On one version of the diminished view, to speak genuinely is to assert that something is the case. As Wittgenstein says (*Tractatus* 4.5), "The general form of a proposition is: This is how things stand." The truth of an assertion is to be assessed by comparing how it represents things with the way things really are. If a listener trusts the speaker's judgment, she will take him to be in a position to decide that the assertion accords with the facts, and if she believes him to be sincere, she will take herself to have reason to believe what is said. Accordingly, the assertion is apt to contribute to, or to make her modify, her conception of how things stand in the world.

On this account, the giving and receiving of assertions can be construed as a straightforward form of rational interaction, involving determinate criteria of success. Now, I am not arguing that the attempt to make communication intelligible played any explicit role in Wittgenstein's thinking in writing the *Tractatus*—such mundane matters did not concern him at that time. I am, however, trying to sketch out a background, often unspoken and maybe unconscious, which helped shape much thought about language among analytic philosophers during the twentieth century.

Commands, it seems, can easily be brought under the same heading as assertions. In case the speaker has a call on the addressee's obedience, his issuing a command provides the addressee with a reason for acting accordingly. What constitutes obedience is determined by the state of affairs represented as what is required in the formulation of the command.

In §§ 22 and 23 of *Philosophical Investigations*, Wittgenstein addresses the diminished view of speaking. In § 22 he discusses Frege's idea that each assertion can be thought of as consisting of an assumption prefixed with an assertion sign. Wittgenstein suggests that the "assumption" could be thought of as a sentence-radical, which can then be put to different uses: to say how things *are*, to order a person to *make* something the case, or to *ask* whether it is the case. That is to say, it might be thought that these ways of speaking either are or could easily be brought under the purview of what in the lecture (and in the *Tractatus*) is represented as senseful language. In each case, representation remains at the core of sense. Here we have the diminished view of speaking in essence. In the next paragraph, Wittgenstein asks, "But how many kinds of sentence are there? Say assertion, question, and command?" and then he goes on to say, by way of contrast with the diminished view,

> There are *countless* kinds; countless different kinds of use of all the things we call "signs," "words," "sentences." And this diversity is not something fixed, given once for all; but new types of language, new language-games, as we may say, come into existence and others become obsolete and get forgotten.[2]

He then lists some twenty examples of different language games; it is important to note that none of his examples would seem to fit under the description of moral discourse as traditionally conceived (i.e., involving words like "ought," "right/wrong," "good/evil").

Wittgenstein ends the section by writing,

> It is interesting to compare the diversity of the tools of language and of the ways they are used, the diversity of kinds of words and sentence, with what logicians

have said about the structure of language. (This includes the author of the *Tractatus Logico-Philosophicus*.)[3]

I read Wittgenstein here as (among other things) trying to release us from a philosophical straightjacket: from the idea that what constitutes meaningful speech is what could be characterized, perhaps, as effective speech: that is, uttering words in situations where the addressee has reason to accommodate what the speaker is saying (by believing or obeying him), and the speaker reckons with the addressee having a reason to do so.

3 Varieties of Talk

Now there certainly are numerous cases in which assertions and commands would seem to fulfill the criteria of effective speech at least to some degree. (Even where the conditions are fulfilled, the result may not come about: for instance, a person may be unable to take in information that is too distressing or runs counter to strongly held convictions.) Human conversation may take many different forms, however. If we limit verbal interchanges to instances of effective speech, we end up with quite a schematic picture of the ways in which human beings interact with words. What Wittgenstein is reminding us of in § 23 is that the purposes of speaking are not to be laid down *a priori*. Even what might be called assertions and commands (as defined by the syntactic form of what is said) are not clearly circumscribed categories. Consider a few examples:

(1) A sister and brother are looking out the window, watching their father work in the garden. The sister says, "Just look at him! He's *old*!" The response she is seeking is not obedience: she is not ordering her brother to turn his gaze in a certain direction; rather, she is asking him to focus his attention in a certain way. The assertion that their father is old is not meant to convey new information, nor is she invoking any determinate criteria of what it means to be old. Perhaps she is *suddenly struck* by their father having aged, or maybe she is trying to persuade her brother to be more considerate of him. The attitude she is expressing is, of course, bound up with thoughts about his age, his being weak or tired or confused, etc. But what the sister is saying is not reducible to those facts. Her brother may come to see what she sees, or he may reject her claim, saying perhaps, "I don't think he's old," "He's always looked that way," or "You know, the other day he actually he took the stairs in three bounds." There is no method for resolving such a disagreement: reasons won't settle the issue. We might say of the sister, echoing Wittgenstein, "Her attitude is a proof of her attitude."

(2) "Mind your own business!" Jim tells his friend Samantha, who has been urging him to see a doctor about his backache. Though his words have the form of telling her to do something, their intent is rather to make her abstain from doing what she is doing. He is not ordering her, rather telling her how he feels. "I can't stand your meddling in my affairs!" he might have said, much to the same effect. To characterize something as "meddling" is, normally, to represent it as something that ought not to be done. But is she actually meddling? That is a matter they had best try to settle between themselves.

(3) "You've done a terrific job!" Julia's boss is encouraging her after she's organized a big art exhibition and is despondent because some of the reviews were pretty critical. Is he informing her of a fact? The criteria of "terrific job" aren't well-defined. However, the force of his words has to do with his being someone who knows what he is talking about, and especially so if Julia knows he wouldn't say such a thing unless he meant it. Also, his wanting to tell her this in itself gives her a reason for cheering up. But even if she admits she has good reasons for cheering up, it isn't something she can simply decide to do: she may still be miserable.

(4) "But I don't *want* to go to college!" Jessica plans to go looking for work right after high school. No doubt she feels a genuine revulsion against the idea of continuing to go to classes for four more years. She wants her parents to leave her alone. For them, what's at stake here is not just the veracity of an introspective report. They may either try to make her take up a different attitude toward her revulsion, to think of it as a passing phase, or alternatively try to give her reasons to change her mind.

(5) "You're just being jealous." Jack and Jill go to a philosophy conference together. Jill's ex-husband gives a talk, which has Jill enthusiastic. Jack doesn't think much of it: there was nothing new really, just elegant rhetoric. Jill is baffled by his response, and puts it down to his jealousy. Or maybe she is unsure about her own opinion (might she still have a weak spot for her ex-husband?) and tries to fend off Jack's criticism by invoking emotional bias.

These cases are chosen more or less at random. What they have in common is the fact that while they have the grammatical form of assertions or commands, they are neither reports of facts nor orders in any straightforward sense; and yet they are perfectly familiar, indeed banal, ingredients of everyday conversation. In many cases, conversations that totally lacked elements of this kind would strike us as barren, nearly robotic. Are these lines "rational?" They do not fit the criteria of effective speech. On the other hand, we would not consider them *irrational*. What do they achieve? In some cases, they may just be a way of touching the other, making her laugh, insulting her, or helping lift her spirits, etc.[4] But very often they will be ways of channeling the conversation: starting it up or putting an end to it, changing its focus, or the like. In doing philosophy, in reflecting on the linkup between the things people say and the reality they are talking about, it seems, we tend to focus on "one-off interchanges," that is, on situations constituted by, and limited to, the speaker informing the addressee or issuing a command, then noting the addressee's response (whether one of belief or disbelief, of obedience or of failure to obey, etc.). In many cases of actual conversation, however, the linkup between the words spoken and the wider concerns within which the conversation is taking place is much less direct: the bearing of what is said on those wider concerns is mediated by the whole conversational mesh in which the particular words are embedded.

4 Ethical Talk: First Example

Next, I want to take a look at two pieces of conversation from literature. The speakers in them, it appears, are trying to come to terms with ethical issues.

Suppose it is asked how representative these conversations are, coming as they do from literary texts. In response, it should be noted that they are not offered as empirical evidence, as a way of proving: "This is how we talk." They are rather to serve as reminders, and they will only function that way if the reader/listener recognizes them as examples of ethical discourse. The hope is that the fullness of literary examples will help us to relate to them as something we may or may not be able to identify with.

My first example is from Karl Ove Knausgaard's autofictive novel *My Struggle*. Fresh out of high school, at the age of eighteen, the protagonist takes a job as a primary school teacher in a small fishing village in Northern Norway. The school, lying in a remote area with several months without daylight in the winter, has had difficulties recruiting teachers. Karl Ove's predecessor in the job quit in the middle of the school year.

After some time, Karl Ove, too, finds his existence there a struggle. As the autumn term is winding down, Karl Ove is seriously tempted to quit. The idea of quitting first comes up in the following internal monologue:

I could just stop teaching
Who said I couldn't?

Who said so?

Everybody said so, but who said I had to listen to them?

No one could stop me handing in my notice, could they? I didn't even need to hand it in, all I had to do was stay down south after Christmas, just not return. I would be putting the school in a predicament, but who said I couldn't do that?

After this, he calls his mother to tell her about his qualms:

> "Nothing has changed here, but the job's beginning to weigh me down. I can only get out of bed in the morning with the greatest of difficulty. And it struck me today that I could just hand in my notice. I'm really not enjoying it at all. I haven't been trained for this either. So I wondered about studying after Christmas instead."
>
> "I can understand you being frustrated and that it's tough going," she said. "But I think you should sleep on it before you decide. Christmas is around the corner, and you'll be able to unwind and relax lying on the sofa here if you like. I think everything will look different then, when you go back up."
>
> "But that's exactly what I don't want!"
>
> "Work goes through patches. There was a time when you thought it was a lot of fun. It's quite normal for you to have a down period now. I'm not saying you shouldn't quit. That's up to you to decide. But you don't need to make up your mind right now, that's all I'm saying."
>
> "I don't think you understand what I'm telling you. It won't get any better. It's just a huge drag. And for what?"
>
> "Life is a drag at times," she said.
>
> "That's what you always say. Your life may be a drag, but does mine have to be?"
>
> "I was only trying to give you some advice. In my opinion, it's good advice."
>
> "OK," I said. "The odds are I'll give up the job, but you're right, I don't need to make a decision now."[5]

What KO is expressing, above all, is the sudden, daunting discovery of freedom. The freedom theme is brought out in his repeatedly asking the rhetorical question, "Who said?" This discovery—we might also call it the discovery of conscience—must be particularly poignant in the case of someone like KO who has grown up under the tutelage of a stern and controlling father: in the past, his feelings of guilt were inseparable from the fear of being found out by his father.

KO feels he must call his mother to ask for her blessing (absolution), but she refuses to give it. But neither does she criticize him. She also invokes the "who says" theme, saying, "I can't say you can't quit." Whether she were to support or to oppose his desire to quit, she would be indulging his wish to load the responsibility for his decisions onto someone else.

One striking thing about this bit of conversation is that while KO evidently finds it hard to make up his mind to quit, the reasons *against* quitting are hardly brought to the fore. Most of KO's arguments are in favor of giving up the job. Neither KO nor his mother tries to formulate any moral injunction, such as "One has to honour one's commitments" and the like. The wrongness of letting the school down, we might say, is what gives shape to the conversation, rather than part of what is being talked about.

If the mother were to formulate the injunction, it would show her to be deaf to what he was trying to say, since without the moral consideration he would not be in a conundrum in the first place. Suppose, on the other hand, KO himself were to thematize the moral rule: doing so, I suggest, might signal a readiness to relativize the requirement, to put it under scrutiny. It would open the door to going either way.

I am here reminded of a point made by Peter Winch in his salient essay "Moral Integrity." He discusses Tolstoy's story "Father Sergius." The main character of the story is a hermit with a reputation for holiness. On one occasion, he resists a woman's attempt to seduce him, but on a later occasion he succumbs to the lure of a peasant girl. Winch writes,

> Marie's [the girl's] question "What does it matter?" invited a judgment explaining why religious purity is more important than the satisfaction of lust, a comparison, as it were, between two different objects. And no such judgment was possible. I do not mean that earlier, at the time of his strength, Sergius *could* have answered the question; the point is that, from that earlier perspective, the question did not arise for him.[6]

I don't wish to deny that we sometimes articulate moral injunctions, couched in specifically moral language, in addressing moral issues. Various cases can be thought of. We do so, for instance, in admonishing a child: "One has to keep one's promises." In that case, we may imagine, these words are part of trying to get the child to understand what promising is. What I am arguing, on the other hand, is that for a conversation to revolve around a moral concern is not dependent on the use of moral vocabulary. Sabina Lovibond makes a related point in her *Ethical Formation*:

> moral thought—much of the time at any rate—is like irony or humour in being identifiable not by the occurrence of any special vocabulary, but only through a more holistic appreciation of the spirit of an utterance.[7]

In fact we will often, for various reasons, *avoid* explicitly moral formulations. We may not wish to seem to moralize, to come across as pretentious, to put ourselves at a distance from those we are speaking to, to lay ourselves open to a charge of hypocrisy. On the other hand, we may have a sense of moral vocabulary as eroded, may feel that in using it we will be succumbing to cliché. In short, we may shun moral language now for its force, now for its triteness.

Moral injunctions may be put forward as expressions of commitment, or as objects of contemplation, or as reminders of things we hold important. It would be weird to think of them as being *informative* in the sense of importing concerns that are new to the person reflecting on the issue. It would certainly be a caricature of moral seriousness to construe our grappling with a moral problem on the model, say, of trying to find the relevant passage in an instruction manual.

Lt. Col. Stuart Couch, a US military lawyer, was assigned to prosecute the detainee Mohamedou Ould Slahi in Guantánamo in 2003. As he was preparing for the case, he came to suspect that Slahi's confessions had been extracted through torture. He writes,

> it was at the end of this, hearing all of this information, reading all this information, months and months and months of wrangling with the issue, that I was in church this Sunday, and we had a baptism. We got to the part of the liturgy where the congregation repeats—I'm paraphrasing here, but the essence is that we respect the dignity of every human being and seek peace and justice on earth. And when we spoke those words this morning, there were a lot of people in that church, but I could have been the only one there. I just felt this incredible, alright, there it is. You can't come in here on Sunday, and as a Christian, subscribe to this belief of dignity of every human being and say I will seek justice and peace on the earth, and go on with the prosecution using that kind of evidence. And at that point I knew what I had to do. I had to get off the fence.[8]

In consequence, Couch withdrew from the case. One should note that he said *you can't* say these words and then go on prosecuting a case based on torture. In one sense that is not true. One can imagine Couch or others involved in the prosecution or interrogation of detainees having said these words on several occasions, and either not attending to the words at all or nodding agreement yet having no sense of a conflict between the words they were saying and the work they were doing. Couch's feeling that he might have been the only one in the church goes with his sense that the words were spoken directly to him: on that particular day, he was truly open to the meaning of the words.

5 Ethical Talk: Second Example

My second example comes from Ernest Hemingway's short story "Hills Like White Elephants."[9] Two people, referred to as "the man" and "the girl," are waiting for a train somewhere on the railway station between Barcelona and Madrid. The man is trying to persuade the girl to undergo some procedure; she is unwilling to do it. One gradually comes to surmise (though it is not made explicit) that they are talking about an abortion. The girl does not respond at all to begin with, then she turns passive-aggressive:

> "Then I'll do it. Because I don't care about me."
> "What do you mean?"
> "I don't care about me."
> "Well, I care about you."
> "Oh, yes. But I don't care about me. And I'll do it and then everything will be fine."
> "I don't want you to do it if you feel that way."

Then comes a key passage:

> The girl stood up and walked to the end of the station. Across, on the other side, were fields of grain and trees along the banks of the Ebro. Far away, beyond the river, were mountains. The shadow of a cloud moved across the field of grain and she saw the river through the trees.
> "And we could have all this," she said. "And we could have everything and every day we make it more impossible."
> "What did you say?"
> "I said we could have everything."
> "We can have everything."
> "No, we can't."
> "We can have the whole world."
> "No, we can't."
> "We can go everywhere."
> "No, we can't. It isn't ours any more."
> "It's ours."
> "No, it isn't. And once they take it away, you never get it back."
> "But they haven't taken it away."
> "We'll wait and see."
> "Come on back in the shade," he said. "You mustn't feel that way."
> "I don't feel any way," the girl said. "I just know things."
> "I don't want you to do anything that you don't want to do—."

For the man, it all comes down to preferences. He is trying to make the girl see the attractions of his proposal. On the one hand, he points to the simplicity of the procedure (within the scope of a short dialogue he says once that the operation is "awfully simple, not really an operation at all," twice that it is "perfectly simple," once that it is "perfectly natural"). On the other hand, he tells her that if she goes through with the operation, he will be in a better mood, since this (the pregnancy) is the only thing that worries him. In short, a childless life is a trouble-free life. He claims he won't force her to go through with the procedure if she doesn't want to, yet obviously, if he does not want the child, the prospect of their starting a family life is doomed. That is why his telling her she can do what she likes sounds to her like bitter irony.

For her, however, the decision is not a matter of what she prefers, as when she says, "I don't feel any way . . . I just know things" (one can hear the scare quotes around "feel"). The matter is not up to her: the problem is that by getting rid of their child, they would be losing the world. This is a remarkable thought. I take her to mean that in having the abortion, they would lose their innocence, they would be sacrificing an incipient life to their life of aimless meandering. Earlier, when they had ordered a new drink, she had said, "That's all we do, isn't it—look at things and try new drinks?" Perhaps she has looked forward to having a child to care for as something that would give them an anchor in the world, as something that would rescue them from "the unbearable lightness" of their current state of being.

But this is precisely what the man cannot see. For him, having the baby would prevent their having a good time: "We can go anywhere." "No, we can't. It isn't ours any more. . . . And once they take it away, you never get it back" (the world? the unborn child?). And when he objects, "But they haven't taken it away," she replies, "We'll wait and see," suggesting that he too may come to realize the loss once it is too late.

"We won't have the world any more" has the form of an assertion, but of course she is not informing the man of a fact, expecting him to credit it on her authority. It is something you either see or do not see.

6 The Precariousness of Ethical Talk

Near the end of the story, it says of the man, "He looked at the people. They were all waiting reasonably for the train." In a purely descriptive text, this is the only subjective line, conveying the man's perspective. Clearly, he is frustrated that he should be stuck with the only unreasonable being in the station (as he considers her to be). Because he cannot share the girl's perspective, her reluctance to terminate the pregnancy comes across to him as sheer pig-headedness. That is also why he cannot understand why his "I don't want you to do it if you don't want to" is just empty words to her.

She no longer sees meaning in the life he is envisaging for them. Her problem is that she feels unable to make him share her perspective. She tried a metaphor: "the world won't be ours any more." It didn't work. She might try others. They may or may not open his eyes to how she sees things. However, it seems there is no assured path from his view of things to hers; there is no point at which she could say, "if you understand my words, then you have to admit."

Nor can she say, "Trust me, I know." She needs him to see for himself, or there is no point in her effort. He appears to be ready to humor her, but again, that is not what she wishes for.

We could say: it is where communication becomes precarious that the ethical calls on our attention.

There is an analogy here with the other cases I have been considering. In each of them, a person views, or has viewed, his life from two incompatible perspectives. There seems to be no assured path from one to the other. Father Sergius has lost his earlier perspective on things and seems to have no way of retrieving it. Lt. Col. Stuart Couch has gained a perspective to which, before, he was blind. The new perspective suddenly strikes him; there was no path of thought that took him to it. (In the case both of Sergius and of Couch, of course, a long series of experiences forms the background to the changes of perspective.) Karl Ove faces two different perspectives at once and is daunted by his inability to decide which is the right one. "Is it really up to me to choose? How frightening!"

There is nothing to be said in these situations that would fit the philosophers' notion of effective speech. A change of heart is required, and it will either occur or not occur. Obviously, no appeal to moral precepts is by itself going to bridge the gap between perspectives. Conceivably, the fact that moral insights may not open themselves to being communicated effectively may have contributed to Wittgenstein's inclination, in his *Lecture on Ethics*, to call the attempt to express them nonsensical.[10]

Notes

1 For Wittgenstein's lecture as well as commentary, see Ludwig Wittgenstein, *Lecture on Ethics*, ed. with commentary by Edoardo Zamuner, Ermelina Valentina Di Lascio and D. K. Levy (Chichester: Wiley Blackwell, 2014).

2 Ludwig Wittgenstein, *Philosophical Investigations* (Chichester: Blackwell, 2009), § 22.
3 Ibid., § 23.
4 John L. Austin's category of "behabitives" seems to have some relation to these kinds of expression. See his *How to Do Things with Words* (Cambridge, MA: Harvard University Press, 1975), 160–1.
5 Karl Ove Knausgaard, *My Struggle, Book Four*, trans. Don Bartlett (Brooklyn, NY: Archipelago Books, 2015), 408–9.
6 In Peter Winch, *Ethics and Action* (London: Routledge and Kegan Paul, 1972), 188–9.
7 Sabina Lovibond, *Ethical Formation* (Cambridge, MA: Harvard University Press, 2002), 38. This passage is a response to Cora Diamond's essay "Wittgenstein, Mathematics and Ethics," in *The Cambridge Companion to Wittgenstein*, ed. Hans Sluga and David Stern (Cambridge: Cambridge University Press, 1996), in which she in turn is commenting on Lovibond's earlier book, *Realism and Imagination in Ethics*. Diamond is arguing that what characterizes ethical talk is not its being *about* a specific subject, about ethical reality as it were, but the *ways* in which things are being talked about. She compares ethical talk to mathematical talk in this respect: mathematical talk, too, is a way of talking, rather than talk about a certain subject matter (about "mathematical reality"). Lovibond, in the passage quoted, seems to signal her agreement with Diamond's point—which was, in fact, a major source of inspiration for the present chapter.
8 Larry Siems, "Introduction," in Mohamedou Ould Slahi, *Guantánamo Diary* (New York: Little, Brown and Company, 2015), xli. On a related point: the pharmaceutical firm Pfizer recently announced its decision not to manufacture drugs for use in executions. The reason stated was: "Pfizer makes its products to enhance and save the lives of the patients we serve" (http://www.theguardian.com/world/2016/may/13/pfizer-blocks-drugs-lethal-injections). Evidently, this principle had been adopted a long time ago; what was new was the thought that it actually prevented the company from assisting in executions.
9 In Ernest Hemingway, *Men without Women* (New York: Charles Scribner's, 1927).
10 I wish to thank Aurelia Armstrong, David and Maureen Meehan, and Merete Mazzarella for helpful comments.

Works Cited

Austin, John L., *How to Do Things with Words*, Cambridge, MA: Harvard University Press, 1975.

Diamond, Cora, "Wittgenstein, Mathematics and Ethics," in Hans Sluga and David Stern (eds.), *The Cambridge Companion to Wittgenstein*, Cambridge: Cambridge University Press, 1996.

Hemingway, Ernest, *Men without Women*, New York: Charles Scribner's, 1927.
Knausgaard, Karl Ove, *My Struggle, Book Four*, trans. Don Bartlett, Brooklyn, NY: Archipelago Books, 2015.
Lovibond, Sabina, *Realism and Imagination in Ethics*, Oxford: Blackwell, 1983.
Lovibond, Sabina, *Ethical Formation*, Cambridge, MA: Harvard University Press, 2003.
Siems, Larry, "Introduction," in Mohamedou Ould Slahi, *Guantánamo Diary*, New York: Little, Brown and Company, 2015.
Winch, Peter, *Ethics and Action*, London: Routledge and Kegan Paul, 1972.
Wittgenstein, Ludwig, *Tractatus Logico-Philosophicus*, London: Routledge & Kegan Paul, 1961.
Wittgenstein, Ludwig, *Philosophical Investigations*, Chichester: Blackwell, 2009.
Wittgenstein, Ludwig, *Lecture on Ethics*, ed. with commentary by Edoardo Zamuner, Ermelina Valentina Di Lascio, and D. K. Levy, Chichester: Wiley Blackwell, 2014.

2

Wittgenstein, Ethics, and Fieldwork in Philosophy

Nora Hämäläinen[1]

1 What Is Ethics after Wittgenstein?

It is no secret that post-Wittgensteinian moral philosophy is a home or a resting place for people who are uncomfortable with contemporary mainstream analytic moral philosophy, that is, for people who do not think that normative moral theory, metaethics, analytic moral psychology, or the like contain the most helpful kinds of philosophical inquiry into morals. Most people who end up doing philosophy "after Wittgenstein" have some training in analytic ethics and may, in fact, have quite different ideas about what its central flaws or shortcomings are. D. Z. Phillips's central objection was that it is unduly generalizing.[2] Peter Winch held that its idea of philosophical normativity in ethics is misguided: "philosophy can no more show a man what he should attach importance to than geometry can show a man where he should stand."[3] Philosophers like Cora Diamond and Alice Crary have voiced objections against the conception of rationality, reason, and thinking, emblematic for analytic philosophy: one that (in spite of important exceptions like Nussbaum) at least up to recently has given little room for different sensibilities and perspectives.[4]

But the experience that draws people from mainstream analytic moral philosophy to post-Wittgensteinian ethics is, I think, a general notion that moral theory and metaethics, etc., as contemporary disciplines of inquiry, are dead to many the interesting complexities of moral life, and thus unable to help one understand them better. Wittgensteinian moral philosophy, in contrast, is seen as concerned precisely with these, and with the complexities of how we speak of good, evil, and morality. The Wittgensteinian inheritance is felt more open to an investigation of the very terms by which we talk about morality and to an intensified dialogue between moral philosophy and moral experience. Familiarly this investigation is often conducted by means of examples, around which the philosopher builds his or her reflections. For me, as for many others, the most attractive form of post-Wittgensteinian work in moral philosophy centers around philosophical discussions on narrative literature.[5] In these discussions, the literary text performs a number of interlinked functions.

First, an outline of or a scene from a literary narrative is presented, along with an ethical problematization, which the literary text addresses, explicitly or implicitly.

Second, the shortcomings of some standard theoretical (or generalizing or explanatory) way of addressing the issue are discussed. The literary piece is put to work to engage our imagination in a represented human situation: not to judge, generalize, or explain, but to single out what is distinctive and ethically interesting about it.

Third, usually some more general critical point or moral, philosophical, or methodological lesson is extrapolated from the discussion as well. These lessons can be of quite various kinds, some directed at mainstream moral philosophy, some at tendencies in our everyday thinking, some at interesting conceptual confusions.[6]

In these discussions, the literary work is brought forth as a site for the renegotiation of understanding. Conversation over a piece of literature or a reading of a piece of literature is seen to offer a place for seeking a common understanding of the lives depicted, the moral questions, goods and evils exposed, as well as the concepts involved.

This chapter is concerned not only with the promises of this practice but also with where we may discover its limitations. I discuss some aspects of its particular capacity to illuminate "our lives in language" or what Raimond Gaita has called "the realm of meaning,"[7] and then move on to consider some common restrictions to how this kind of inquiry is understood that seem to me both problematic and unnecessary. More specifically, I am interested in the idea of these inquiries as conceptual investigations, but I am bothered by a certain tendency to articulate their point and purpose in contrast to empirical investigations and the search for and introduction of new knowledge. Since this tendency springs from some central methodological remarks made by Wittgenstein, it is a persistent one, and constitutive for many Wittgensteinian philosophers' understanding of their own method.

2 Wittgenstein's Method?

Before moving on to characterize ethics after Wittgenstein, I will remind us of some of Wittgenstein's central methodological notes in the *Philosophical Investigations*.[8]

A philosophical problem has the form: "I do not know my way about." (PI § 123)

> Philosophy may in no way interfere with the actual use of language; it can in the end only describe it. / For it cannot give it any foundation either. / It leaves everything as it is. (PI § 124)

> Philosophy simply puts everything before us, and neither explains nor deduces anything.—Since everything lies open to view there is nothing to explain. For what is hidden, for example, is of no interest to us.

> One could also give the name of "philosophy" to what is possible before all new discoveries and inventions. (PI § 126)

> The work of the philosopher consists in assembling reminders for a particular purpose. (PI § 127)

> If one tried to advance *theses* in philosophy, it would never be possible to debate them, because everyone would agree to them. (PI § 128)

> The aspects of things that are most important for us are hidden because of their simplicity and familiarity. (One is unable to notice something—because it is always before one's eyes.) (PI § 129)

Philosophy, thus, does not bring us new knowledge but, rather, helps us recover and reorganize what we already know or in some sense have before our eyes. Some further aspects of this idea of philosophy can be found a few pages earlier:

> It was true to say that our considerations could not be scientific ones. . . . And we may not advance any kind of theory. There must be nothing hypothetical in our considerations. We must do away with all *explanation*, and description alone must take its place. And this description gets its light, that is to say its purpose, from the philosophical problems. These are, of course, not empirical problems; they are solved, rather, by looking into the workings of our language, and that in such a way as to make us recognize those workings: *in despite of* an urge to misunderstand them. The problems are solved, not by giving new information, but by arranging what we have always known. Philosophy is a battle against the bewitchment of language. (PI § 109)[9]

In spite of dramatic words like "battle" and "bewitchment," these paragraphs evoke an image of the philosopher as carefully and calmly laying a puzzle out of pieces that are already spread out on the table before him. It is, however, useful to observe that several different methodological lessons can be derived from these passages:

1. Philosophy is not science.
2. Philosophy does not uncover anything hidden.
3. Philosophy does not advance theses.
4. Philosophy does not present theories.
5. Philosophy does not answer empirical questions.
6. Philosophy does not seek solutions by empirical means.
7. Philosophy reorganizes what we already know in order to attain clarity.
8. Philosophy is a descriptive endeavor.
9. Philosophy is concerned with our uses of language.

Thus, the work of the philosopher is carefully circumscribed, distinguished from the jobs of other seekers of knowledge and severed from many traditional jobs of philosophy, but the remarks do not give a systematic formula for philosophical work, and different emphases among them are possible, resulting in different practices. Much depends on where the followers of Wittgenstein have perceived the most important dangers to the integrity of the philosophical endeavor, and to their own particular interests.

3 What Does "Arranging What We Have Always Known" (§ 109) Mean?

Let me try a generalization for heuristic purposes. I suggest that post-Wittgensteinian discussions of literature navigate a space that is defined by Wittgenstein's methodological instructions and yet constantly tend to escape them, much because neither literature nor the work of philosophy is easily contained by method or by pregiven aims. Moreover, the latter is all for the good.[10]

I will here look at three interrelated and intertwined themes in ethical investigations conducted by means of literature in post-Wittgensteinian philosophy, and how they comply to Wittgenstein's idea of philosophical work as previously described. I have selected these three themes because I think they all bring forth something particularly attractive in ethics after Wittgenstein but they also exhibit at the same time a tendency toward an unhelpfully narrow understanding of what philosophical work could or should be.

3.1 Thinking for Ourselves

The first theme I want to draw attention to is a certain emphasis on the importance of thinking for oneself: of not accepting moral dogmas or views second hand, but arriving at a perspective through reflective work of one's own. This is the central though somewhat covert theme of Cora Diamond's paper "Having a Rough Story of What Moral Philosophy Is," where she draws out the transformative potential of literature for moral thought.[11] She notes, "Lawrence spoke of *the novel* as a great discovery: 'It won't let you tell didactic lies; it shows them up, shows you up if you try to put them in.'"[12] One of the things she gestures at here is the holistic and Socratic aspect of literature and philosophy: the ways in which they are concerned with our way of looking rather than with distinctive normative contents. The tricky thing about ways of looking is that they cannot be handed over to the interlocutor in argumentative discourse, but require complex engagement and attention to the world from each person engaged in the inquiry. The benefit of the novel, if Lawrence is right, is that it gives the lie to busybody moralizing and presses both writer and reader to think.

The theme is also crucial to "Anything but argument,"[13] where Diamond counters Onora O'Neill's insistence on arguments in rational philosophical conviction with transformative experiences of attention.[14] In such experiences, the thinker or philosopher changes her way of looking, prompted by proper attention to the realities she is confronted with. In the examples given by Diamond imaginative sympathy plays the central role, but it would be a mistake to believe that she wants to exchange an ethics of reason for an ethics of sympathetic imagination. At stake here is rather the question of what serious moral thinking is like.

A similar idea of the lesson not being in the arguments, but in the independent transformation of one's way of looking, is also prominent in Peter Winch's classical discussion of the parable of the Good Samaritan, where he highlights the inconclusive nature of Jesus's injunction in the parable.[15] The form of Jesus's advice forces the man to think for himself and to come to interpret the situation in a new way. The edge of these discussions is not only to prompt people to think for themselves but also to reconsider what such thinking involves, and why explicit argument may be unhelpful for inducing it.

No doubt, learning to think for oneself is both difficult and adventurous. But there is something comfortingly simple to the post-Wittgensteinian procedure, as it has been developed in the footsteps of Diamond and others: when doing philosophy we are not in the business of being told something new or on the lookout for facts that could add to our understanding. We are rather rethinking for ourselves, in our own way, what was already before us.

3.2 Seeing Aspects, Seeing As?

A second theme, also present in Diamond's discussion, is the theme of seeing aspects and "seeing as." This theme links to Wittgenstein's discussion of Gestalt shifts in the second part of the PI (the duck-rabbit),[16] but it also springs naturally from other considerations that philosophers like Diamond, Cavell, and Gaita bring to bear on their uses of literary texts. In a literary text or in the telling of a story, the world is never presented to us as such, but always represented in one way rather than another. Similarly, understanding a situation (real or fictional) is not merely about seeing the facts of the situations, but essentially about seeing the situation in a certain light, as a certain kind of situation, rather than another. For analytic moral philosophy, focused on conclusive lines of argument from supposedly neutral facts and distinct values, attention to our ways of seeing, or modes of attention, has been philosophically uninteresting. For the Wittgensteinian moral philosophers they, to the contrary, appear as an essential part of what philosophy is about. In post-Wittgensteinian moral philosophy, attention to how we see things takes a central role: what is it to see another person as a fellow human or as a "neighbor" in the biblical sense? What would it be to see an animal as a companion? What would it mean to attend to a child as person with a distinctive perspective on the world? And what would it be to move from one mode of perception to another: animals as cattle or animals as fellow creatures. These Gestalt shifts are more than transitions between different ways of ordering the facts and something other than facts garnished with evaluation. They are shifts between different ways of engaging the world.

This theme is also prominent in Diamond's discussion of J. M. Coetzee's *Elizabeth Costello*, where the protagonist is deeply troubled by the human use of animals as food, and equally troubled by the way she cannot share her experience with people around her. Costello sees the eating of animals as horrid, potentially "a crime of stupefying proportion," comparable to the mass torture and slaughter of fellow humans.[17]

Diamond emphasizes that Elizabeth Costello does not share the common ground from which to enter an animal rights debate. This would require that she could compare humans and animals, state her reasons for respecting animals, addressing her interlocutor as reasonable creatures. But the distance she perceives between herself and them is too great. There is no common ground from which to begin an argument: there is just her own exposure to evil done by humans to animals. She cannot see the matter as they see it, the Gestalt of the matter has shifted for her irrevocably: she is not of the opinion that it is a horror: it just is so.

This theme of "seeing as" is not the topic of the paper (which is more specific and idiosyncratic), but it is a central, though tacit part of Diamond's toolkit here. It is also highlighted by Stanley Cavell, in his discussion of Diamond's paper. He notes, "The variation of attitudes that Diamond's discussion stresses between the horror of individuals and the indifference of most of society considers moments in which the variation of response seems one between visions of the world, between how its practices are regarded, or seen, or taken to heart, or not."[18] The theme of "seeing as" is also prominent in Cavell's own work, for example, his discussions of Shakespeare's drama, in the shift between seeing the loved one through the skeptical lens as an uncertain object of knowledge, or seeing her *as* a loved one and an acknowledged other.[19]

What is distinctive to the Gestalt shift idea, when transferred from line drawings to complex human situations, is that it easily carries along a simplified picture of what happens at the tipping point, where one picture becomes the other. "First there was a rabbit, but now I cannot but see the duck, although the lines on the pages are identical." Similarly, we may say, "There is no difference in the facts known by Elizabeth Costello and her academic interlocutors: the difference lies in how these facts appear to them." This fits well with Wittgenstein's idea that philosophy is work on what we already knew. This idea draws a circle around those shifts of vision that do not seem to involve new information, and presents these as particularly interesting from the point of view of philosophy. (Because we know that philosophy does not seek new information; that its tasks lie elsewhere.) Or as Cavell puts it, "the extreme variation in human responses to this fact of civilized nature is not a function of any difference in our access to information; no one knows, or can literally see, essentially anything here that the others fail to know or can see."[20]

Thus, philosophy here moves squarely in the realm of what was already there before us: no new knowledge about animals, but a new way of seeing what we knew.

3.3 What We Did Not Know We Knew?

A third theme characterizing the post-Wittgensteinian philosophical practice in relation to literature is discussed by Niklas Forsberg in his book *Language Lost and Found*.[21] Here he opens up the philosophical purpose of reading literature by reference to Iris Murdoch. In an oft-quoted passage from an interview with Brian Magee, Murdoch states,

> As I said, philosophy does one thing, literature does many things and involves many different motives in the creator and the client. It makes us happy, for instance. It shows us the world, and much pleasure in art is a pleasure of recognition of what we vaguely knew was there but never saw before. Art is mimesis, and good art is, to use another Platonic term, anamnesis, "memory" of what we did not know we knew. Art "holds the mirror up to nature." Of course this reflection or "imitation" does not mean slavish or photographic copying. But it is important to hold on to the idea that art is about the world, it exists for us standing out against a background of our ordinary knowledge.[22]

Murdoch's Platonic "what we did not know we knew" works for Forsberg as a key to his own idea of the philosophical use of literature. In this view literature comes to the aid of philosophy, not by presenting, arguing for, criticizing, or illustrating philosophical ideas or positions, but by helping us discover our everyday lives, our languages, our taken-for-granted views. Reading literature for the purposes of philosophy is about uncovering what we did not see, although it was right in front of us; it is work on our vision not on our knowledge; or it is rather the work of acknowledgment.

This "anamnesis-theme," borrowed from Murdoch, works for Forsberg as a variation on a theme used by Wittgenstein and after him by philosophers like Diamond and Cavell. Murdoch may in this passage have been carried away by the poetic qualities of "anamnesis." Considering that it comes only a few lines after the claim that "literature does many things," it is at least clear that Murdoch does not intend this as a general instruction for how to recognize and read great literature. Forsberg sides with Murdoch here, not wishing to delimit the philosophical or other potentials of literature in any way. But displayed together with the idea of art as the mirror of nature, and the Wittgensteinian and post-Wittgensteinian themes I discussed before, the passage suggests a quite specific picture of what there is to be discovered in literature, for the purposes of philosophy.

Considered from this angle, literature, as a verbal art form, is a kind of ordinary language philosophy; it is about wording our world in ways that help to expose for ourselves its random minutiae. Its transformative and philosophical power lies in its capacity to reveal to us our conceptual confusions, our self-deceptions, and the ways we speak and make sense. It is the mirror, which can help us remember what we are. But it is not a place where we encounter what we did not know: or if we do, this is not of primary importance to philosophy.

These three interrelated themes—thinking for ourselves, seeing aspects, and discovering what we did not know we knew—can easily be connected to the chain of remarks by Wittgenstein, which I quoted before. There it was established that philosophy does not present a theory or hypothesis, and that philosophical problems are not empirical ones, that they are about how we see things. All of these lines of reasoning come together in post-Wittgensteinian ethical readings of literature, in a specific way of articulating what such readings are about: literary texts do not present theories or hypotheses; they do not give us facts about a matter or argue the rightness of a given normative view. Neither do they illustrate positions that are already established elsewhere. Or they can indeed do all of these, but such things are not what makes a literary text ethically or philosophically interesting. The real philosophical and ethical work of novels or short stories, in this view, has to do with our concepts, and the way things appear to us, the ways we conceptualize the things that are already known to us. They do their work as a part of "working on oneself. On one's own understanding. On the way one sees things. (And on what one demands of them.)"[23]

Adding these pieces of perspective together, we get kind of moral philosophical inquiry that has several important attractions in the context of academic philosophy of today. In this view moral philosophy is a work on our own understanding, on different ways of looking at things that are so near to us that we hardly even notice them. It is a philosophy that allows us to foreground specific cases, individual experiences, pertinent expressions, images: all of these things that give life to a text, whether it be literary or philosophical. It is both concrete, in the sense of talking about substantial cases, and relatively undogmatic, in the sense of not seeking to formulate a fixed and general truth about things moral.

Its principal charm lies in how it lets us, by means of philosophy, enter a world of situations and experiences, and seeks to make visible the weave of our lives together. We get closer to an artist's repertoire of thinking: in moods, nuances, the use of a holistic intelligence, to replace the abstract, theoretical, argumentative aims of mainstream Anglophone philosophy. We get an inquiry into moral things, which attends to our real moral world, such as we find it, and proceed from there. It acknowledges that our own world is not transparent to us, and that uncovering it may take a lot of work.

I want to emphasize that I am sympathetic to this kind of ethics: these are all perspectives that I have benefited from academically and intellectually, and they have helped me, like many others, to rediscover the subject matter of moral philosophy. But there has always been, for me, an element of discomfort in this practice as well, which has to do with the delimitation of philosophical inquiry to what is, in some sense, already ours. The philosophical question, as we saw, was supposed to be conceptual, not empirical. This has warranted studies of ethics as we talk it, of "what we did not know we knew" that is "what we already knew," it is work on "how we see things" but not an expansive work that seeks to know new things; such that are not already before us. But does the nonempirical nature of the philosophical *question* warrant the exclusion of empirical *means* in philosophy?

The standard post-Wittgensteinian procedure captures very well a certain spirit of philosophical work as work on our own horizon of understanding. This is something that Wittgenstein shares with philosophers like John Dewey, Iris Murdoch, Michel Foucault, R. G. Collingwood, Charles Taylor, and J. L. Austin. However, the Wittgensteinian and post-Wittgensteinian idea of work on our own understanding (in this respect in contrast to the work of Foucault, Taylor, or Dewey, for example) has a tendency to become unnecessarily introvert, to the point of misrepresenting what work on our own understanding may require. By severing the properly philosophical investigations from empirical ones, and more broadly, from the search for new knowledge, there is a risk that our work on our concepts and our horizon of understanding is unnecessarily inhibited, and the moral philosophy done in the tracks of Wittgenstein wanders away from potential and useful philosophical allies.

4 The Rationale for Excluding the Empirical

The tendency to reject new knowledge as a means to philosophical insight derives from Wittgenstein's methodological instructions outlined above and it seems to go well with the general idea of philosophy as transformation rather than acquisition of knowledge. In philosophy after Wittgenstein, it leads its own complex life.

In his essay "Must We Mean What We Say," Stanley Cavell insists that a native speaker does not require a linguist to tell him how his own language is properly used. He is rather the source of such knowledge, and that the philosophically interesting inquiry is the one that the native speaker conducts within the auspices of his own understanding. Philosophy, Cavell argues, is an investigation from a first-person perspective, and it is a kind of category mistake to cite empirical facts, for example, about language use, to someone engaged in philosophical elucidation.[24]

A slightly different variety of the idea (that empirical knowledge is not what we are after in philosophy) is offered by Lars Hertzberg. In the introduction to *The Limits of Experience* he observes that the papers contained in the volume "are united above all in a criticism of the notion that experience teaches us what forms of discourse we must adopt if we are to speak meaningfully about various aspects of the world in which we find ourselves."[25] His primary concern is to show the ineptness, in philosophy, of any cheerful empiricism, which neglects the complex human dimension of interpretation and sensemaking. He also talks about his view as a "rejection of the notion of some logical structure given in advance of our language."[26] His real worry, thus, is that we might try to pursue philosophy as the uncovering of such *a priori* structures, and that we labor under this mistake when consulting experience rather than looking at practices of meaning making. The consequence, however, is a reaffirmation of a dichotomy between empirical knowledge and the properly philosophical study of meaning.

Talking more specifically about moral philosophy Benjamin De Mesel observes that "in moral matters we do not have, as in empirical matters, the idea of fresh evidence and new discoveries. While the characteristic reaction to an advance in scientific knowledge is 'Goodness me, who would have thought of that!,' the characteristic response to a moral insight is 'Of course, I should have thought of that!'"[27]

There is much of philosophical and exegetic interest that could be said about these passages and their more exact relation to Wittgenstein's central methodological passages. I will not delve into this here, but only display them as evidence of the direction of the philosophical imagination that they exhibit, that steers away, for a variety of interlinked reasons, from the empirical. In § 109 Wittgenstein insisted that our *problems* are not empirical, and that they need to be addressed by attention to our language. Cavell's, Hertzberg's, and de Mesel's instructions offer a kind of goading in this direction. There is not exactly a prohibition against bringing empirical insights, new experience, new facts, historical records, etc. to the philosophical table. But there is a readiness to suspect anyone who does so has misunderstood what philosophy is properly about. Philosophical papers are not usually the place to bring up personal experience, but here it is perhaps relevant to say that I have in Wittgensteinian contexts repeatedly been chastised for bringing up considerations, which do not fit into the mold of "conceptual, not empirical." There is a mold, and scholars are urged to fit into it.

But the direction of concern in these passages exhibits a limited interest in and a limited understanding of the plurality of roles that new knowledge, empirical research, and empirical facts can have in philosophical thought and in answering distinctly philosophical questions. When people bring up empirical objections in philosophical conversations they are not necessarily enthralled by some wrongheaded conception of the all-saving power of the empirical, nor making a category mistake. They might actually be doing something that is quite congenial to Wittgenstein's conception of philosophy as a struggle to understand our own form of life and the concepts we live by. This is what we need to consider.

5 Two Thoughts in J. L. Austin's "A Plea for Excuses"

To bring out more clearly the nature of my reservations to the ousting of the empirical I will briefly turn to a philosopher quite close to Wittgenstein in his conception of philosophical method, namely J. L. Austin. In his essay "A Plea for Excuses," he investigates our ways of talking about excuses.[28] We should think of this as a way of doing moral philosophy, because, as it turns out, our ways of making excuses and referring to and relying on them reveal quite a bit about our moral views and conceptions, about appropriate blame, guilt, and amends. The paper is a model case of ordinary language philosophy in a register shared by Austin and Wittgenstein, attending to the things we do with words in situations. I will not look at how he proceeds here, but rather focus on two famous methodological injunctions that he uses to characterize his philosophical practice: the first one is the idea of philosophy as an inquiry into "what we should say when." The second one is an idea of "*field work* in philosophy." I will look at these in turn, moving toward the conclusion that the idea of fieldwork in philosophy points beyond the framework of philosophical inquiry that I have sketched out thus far, in ways that should be taken seriously by post-Wittgensteinian philosophers.

First, "what we should say when." This phrase occurs at a juncture in the text where Austin proceeds toward a brief justification of his method, which he characterizes as "to proceed from 'ordinary language,' that is, by examining *what we should say when*, and so why and what we should mean by it."[29] Like similar remarks by Wittgenstein, this gives room for the interpretation that philosophical inquiry into ordinary language will reveal for us a standard of correct use. But there is little to support such interpretation. Austin notes plainly that "we should know what we mean and what we do not" and that we need to "forearm ourselves against the traps that language sets us."[30] Such traps may be due to our own prejudices or to simplifications produced by philosophical theories that linger in our supposedly "ordinary" understanding. In fact,

> our common stock of words embodies all the distinctions men have found worth drawing, and the connections they have found worth marking, in the lifetime of many generations: these surely are likely to be more numerous, more sound, since they have stood up to the long test of the survival of the fittest, and more subtle, at least in all ordinary and reasonably practical matters than any that you or I are likely to think up in our armchairs of an afternoon—the most favoured alternative method.[31]

I'm going to bear with the oddities and internal contradictions in this brief genealogy of ordinary language: if our current concepts are those that have survived a Darwinian competition, surely they cannot embody *all* the distinctions that men have found worth making! In any case, we need to focus on Austin's essential and useful point: the greater richness of ordinary language, for ordinary purposes of life, as compared to most philosophical language. The challenge for philosophy, for Austin as for Wittgenstein, is to incorporate, rather than overlook or destroy, the complex reasoning and practices inscribed in our language use. And this is important because philosophical attention to language, for both, is always also about "the realities we use the words to talk about." Thus, simplifications in our understanding of language will produce simplifications in our understanding of the world.[32]

A good place to start this kind of work, for Austin, is a concept, or a word, that has not already been amply treated in and thus shaped by philosophy. Thus, "excuses" may be a good starting point, whereas a word like "time" is not. And in aesthetics we could be well advised to start from "the dainty and the dumpy" rather than the beautiful.[33] But of course not just any word will be philosophically interesting: the dainty and excuses get their philosophical force from being "neighboring, analogous or germane in some way to some notorious centre of philosophical trouble." With these two conditions (philosophical virginity and proximity to philosophical trouble) met, we have reason to expect that we have found what Austin calls "a good site for *field work* in philosophy."[34] To get us properly started with the inquiry on excuses, Austin, perhaps surprisingly, points us to two books, *the dictionary* and *the law*.

What should surprise us here, coming from the direction of post-Wittgensteinian philosophy, is the rather "empirical" character of Austin's recommendation. What is found in the dictionary is not already contained in the native speaker's knowledge. The dictionary provides rather the linguist's point of view: it is an evolving product of empirical study that we use to check and widen our intuitions of what is passable and possible, in our mother tongue or some other language.

The law is still something else: far from being a meditation on things that are already contained in a native speaker's repertoire, it is a reservoir of complex and quite technical thinking. Law reflects the complexities of ordinary thinking, because it relies on ordinary sensibilities for its legitimacy, and also shapes them. But diving into law is quite far removed from a study of what we already knew. Quite often, we do not know what the law says and we certainly do not figure it out by examining our native proclivities. Thus looking at the law is fieldwork in a quite substantial sense of the term, a diving into what we did not know in order to find out something new. And rightly so, because in many cases the work that we may and do bring to bear on how we see things, and what our words mean, requires going beyond what we already knew in rather substantial respects. Most importantly, this kind of figuring out can involve many tasks that qualify as, or require, empirical inquiry. It can involve research on or empirical attention to how "we" use language. Philosophers' access to their vernacular ways of speaking and thinking is often full of philosophically induced prejudice, and we can be completely oblivious of the fact that what we bring forth as our native speaker's insight is quite far from the forms that we actually employ outside the seminar room. The relevant empirical work can also involve work on how others have used language: conceptual history or sociolinguistics can, by means of contrast, provide striking insights into our own lives in language. Sometimes we also need to add to our knowledge about the things we talk about when philosophizing: settling questions of animal consciousness or equitable society from an armchair is precisely the kind of practice that gives philosophy a bad name. We may need to attend (empirically) to animals or societies.

Philosophical inquiry, as work on our own understanding, cannot be replaced by empirical studies, but it can include empirical study or archival study or insights derived from these, and such insights may be precisely what in some cases moves a distinctly philosophical inquiry forward. Philosophy is porous, open toward and answerable to what is not philosophy. Most philosophical discussions are responsive in relation to this dependency, and allow for empirical interventions: "you assume that such and such as a matter of conceptual content, but in fact empirical studies show that thus and so, which makes your 'conceptual' claim look quite problematic." Only in contexts of Wittgensteinian philosophy have I encountered a methodologically motivated rejection of empirical objections. This is not to say that this is the only place where such rejections are found, but here they are all the more striking, because one has reason to expect an intellectual, reflective, and context-sensitive discussion, instead of a theoretical one governed by strict though often implicit rules of dogmatic argumentative professionalism.

6 Beyond Conceptual and Empirical

Summing up the discussion thus far, I am in favor of the idea of philosophy as work on how we see things, and also largely sympathetic of the methodological and topical emphases of moral philosophers who work in the footsteps of Wittgenstein. My major and recurring source of concern is the derogatory treatment of empirical interventions, either tacitly assumed or explicitly bolstered by reference to the methodological passages of PI quoted above. Originally, my concerns circled around the rejection of empirical input, often finding that philosophers were starving philosophy of necessary food by reference to a dogmatically interpreted methodological reflection.

But the solution to the problem is not just to adopt a more permissive attitude to empirical input in philosophy. What we rather need is some more careful reflection on what it means to conduct an inquiry in "the realm of meaning," on "how we live our lives in language," or on "our concepts." What is it to do "fieldwork in philosophy," in Austin's sense, while taking both "fieldwork" and "philosophy" very seriously—if we maintain that philosophy is work on how we see things, how we live our lives in language, and that fieldwork is a systematic exposure to something that is not already contained in our lives?

Moving in this direction it is useful to compare the Wittgensteinians' work, not with the theoretically inclined analytic philosophers, but with other thinkers who share Wittgenstein's idea of philosophy as work on how we see things. At the beginning of his *Archeology of Knowledge* Michel Foucault memorably writes, "I am no doubt not the only one who writes in order to have no face. Do not ask who I am and do not ask me to remain the same: leave it to the bureaucrats to see that our papers are in order."[35] Philosophy, in this spirit, is a transformative activity, which does not aim at theoretical completion but at a continuous work on our conceptions.

For Foucault, the transformative philosophical work on his own understanding involved extensive historical study, and for many thinkers inspired by him, say philosopher Ian Hacking, sociologist Nikolas Rose, or anthropologist Paul Rabinow, empirical and historical materials are essential part of philosophical work. Rabinow explicitly thematizes his work as "fieldwork in philosophy" in a foreword to a new edition of his 1970s book *Reflections on Fieldwork in Morocco*.[36] Borrowing the phrase from Pierre Bourdieu's preface to the French translation of the first edition of the very same book, Rabinow is not necessarily communicating with Austin's thinking here. But the connection is not incidental. These thinkers are not exchanging philosophy for empirical study, but often rather pursuing philosophy in and through their thinking over empirical objects or cases, much like post-Wittgensteinian philosophers do in and through their thinking over literary texts or examples derived from movies, biographies, or the like.

In such cases the "empirical" stuff attended to is not "facts" or "information" but rather an intermediary object, an enabler, a catalyst, or a fermenting yeast for making sense of something larger than the object. Or, perhaps ideally, it is both approached for its own sake, its capacity to arouse the interest of the researcher, and for its promise of allowing insight into something distinctively philosophical. Supposedly, most scientific work has a kind of double aim: to learn to know the immediate object, but with a larger objective in view. That larger objective of a scientific study may be a scientific theory, generalization, or the answer to a vexing scientific question. In "fieldwork in philosophy," that larger objective is a philosophical one, and typically, here "philosophical" does not indicate theoretical generalization, but rather a kind of transformation of our conceptual propensities, our ways of "seeing as."

Thus *Reflections on Fieldwork in Morocco*, recounting in detail the erratic human interactions of Rabinow's first encounter with what anthropologists call "the field," can be seen as a philosophical reconsideration of the notion and idea of anthropological fieldwork. Hacking's *The Taming of Chance* is a philosophical study of the emergence of something we take absolutely for granted: our reliance on probability calculations.[37] Vinciane Despret's study on what animals can do is really a study of some theoretical and conceptual prejudices that form obstacles to actually studying animals.[38] Bruno Latour's and Steve Woolgar's *Laboratory Life* is a study that prompts among other things to a philosophical reconsideration of scientific knowledge acquisition.[39] Common to all of these is that they do not offer a theoretical account of fieldwork, probability, human-animal relations, or science, but invite alterations in the readers' conceptions of what the topic is and how it connects to other things.

Such studies are essentially ventures into things that were *not* already known to the author or the reader. Their transformative efforts are premised on extensive learning of new things, facts, pieces of information, history, and theoretical complexes. They involve familiarizing ourselves with complex sets of more or less widely shared presuppositions, not just our own. Are such things "hidden" in the sense indicated by Wittgenstein in PI § 126? At least they are not "open to view." The Wittgensteinian metaphoric of "hidden" and "open to view" in that passage seems inapt for talking about this kind of work, because we are not dealing here with a dynamics of visible surface phenomena that are being explained by reference to some hidden mechanism. The anatomy of this kind of work is different and calls for different metaphors. In spite of this, the idea that all we need is already before us easily travels beyond its proper context, and transforms into an intransparent methodological dogma: if it is philosophy, it is work on what is already open to view.

But why do all that archival digging? Why vacuum the literature for accounts of human-animal encounters? Why do ethnography with scientists in a laboratory? That is, surely these can all be part of honorable scientific endeavors, but why drag them into philosophy? One answer is that, in the right hands, such endeavors can do a work that is very similar to Wittgenstein's attempts to bring our ways of using language into view, or Cora Diamond's ways of using literature to bring our moral sensibilities into view. There is a deep affinity between the work of such thinkers and Wittgensteinian philosophers in the effort of making our form of life visible to ourselves, and combat persistent misunderstandings of it.

Though immersed in empirical or historical materials of different kinds they seek to bring into view our preconceptions, our taken-for-granted distinction, our concepts, and our ways of valuing. They are inquiries into our form of life, our concepts, on how we as a human collective share ways of talking, judging, knowing, and valuing. Such inquiries attend to different materials than the orthodox Wittgensteinian, but get their light, that is their purpose, from a philosophical question or problem (cf. PI § 109). Of course, not all lab ethnography, not all collections of animal stories, and not all archival work on philosophically interesting concepts are philosophy: sometimes such studies are just science or, in the case of Despret's animal stories, essayism. The difference is not always easy to tell with confidence, but the authors of such work usually know.

In fact, for some thinkers Wittgenstein has been an essential inspiration for moving out of philosophy proper, into some neighboring field seen as philosophically more resonant, more conductive to understanding our lives in language. A question of a distinctly philosophical nature can take many kinds of intermediary objects and involve many kinds of empirical or factual questions on the way. A philosopher who takes his or her cue from Wittgenstein should easily recognize such work as philosophical, and as philosophy, when it is so, and should recognize it as moral philosophy or relevant to moral philosophy, when it has distinctive implications for our moral lives.

But the idea that our studies—that is, *questions and answers*—should not be empirical obstructs this recognition and steers the interests and imagination of the philosopher unnecessarily onto the paths of what is already open to view: the details of literary moral interactions, familiar enough to be "ours." Deflections from this path are met with amused bewilderment in the case of senior scholars and friendly advice in the case of junior ones. Post-Wittgensteinian ethics becomes a neat attention to literary and similar examples, and a circulation of suitable references, while the serious spirit of a transformative, self-reflective encounter with our form of life is circumscribed and useful connections to neighboring fields of inquiry and thought are neglected.

These are of course primarily risks: all those involved in ethics after Wittgenstein can judge the extent to which they are realized, or perhaps come up with an account of why serious philosophical inquiries into our ethical form of life *must* rely on what was already open to view.

Partly the question is about what it means to be faithful to Wittgenstein when considering issues that were not on his radar. What would Wittgenstein have thought of the mentioned kinds of empirical or empirically curious studies of our concepts and our forms of life? Surely they bring along new complexities to his original picture of philosophical work, but it is very difficult to imagine that he would have quoted PI § 109 at them.

In any case, in the end, doing moral philosophy in the spirit of Wittgenstein must, as I see it, primarily be about doing moral philosophy in the light of one's own best understanding. In the process, we may need to measure the costs and benefits of hanging on to habitual interpretations of some of his methodological directives. We can perhaps take our cue from others: "Don't think, look and see" (PI § 66) is a good one to work with.

Notes

1. This publication was supported within the project of Operational Programme Research, Development and Education (OP VVV/OP RDE), "Centre for Ethics as Study in Human Value," cofinanced by the European Regional Development Fund and the state budget of the Czech Republic. The first draft of the chapter was presented in April 2016, when I was completing the manuscript of my *Descriptive Ethics: What Does Moral Philosophy Know about Morality* (New York: Palgrave Macmillan, 2016). The parallel genesis of the book and this essay is seen in references and in philosophical concerns, which are here furthered developed and specified.
2. Cf. D. Z. Phillips, *Interventions in Ethics* (Albany, NY: SUNY Press, 1992).
3. Peter Winch, *Ethics and Action* (London: Routledge and Kegan Paul, 1972), 191. This was of course the ethos of much early and mid-twentieth-century Anglophone moral philosophy. Here it is voiced as a criticism of the idea that philosophy could offer generalizing normative expert guidance: an idea that had won increasing currency in the analytic ethics of the 1960s and 1970s.
4. See Cora Diamond, *The Realistic Spirit* (Cambridge, MA: MIT Press, 1991), and Alice Crary, *Inside Ethics* (Cambridge, MA: Harvard University Press, 2016). There seems to be a certain revival of thinking about the significance of perspective in contemporary analytic moral philosophy and epistemology, but the broader implications of this are yet to be seen.
5. For discussion of this practice and the use of narrative literature in it, see Nora Hämäläinen, *Literature and Moral Theory* (New York: Bloomsbury, 2015), 64–73, and idem, *Descriptive Ethics*, 64–6.
6. Phillips insists that the purpose of such exercises is to overcome our propensity to generalize in ethics, while authors like Diamond and Crary have a more generous understanding of the moral functions of such discussions in fostering our moral understanding.
7. For example, Raimond Gaita, "Narrative, Identity and Moral Philosophy," *Philosophical Papers* 32, no. 3 (2003): 261–77.
8. Ludwig Wittgenstein, *Philosophical Investigations* (Oxford: Blackwell, 1998), 49e–50e. Hereafter abbreviated *PI*.
9. Ibid., 47e; (emphasis in original).
10. In this latter I depart from the line of, for example, Oskari Kuusela who in his books, *The Struggle against Dogmatism* (Cambridge, MA: Harvard University Press, 2008) and *Wittgenstein on Logic as the Method of Philosophy: Re-examining the Roots and Development of Analytic Philosophy* (Oxford: Oxford University Press, 2018), affirmatively considers Wittgenstein as providing a distinctive methodology for philosophy, and seeks to spell out what it is.

11 Cf. Diamond, *The Realistic Spirit*, 367–81.
12 Ibid., 373; (emphasis in original).
13 Ibid., 291–308.
14 Ibid., 367–81.
15 Cf. Peter Winch, *Trying to Make Sense* (Oxford: Basil Blackwell, 1987), 156–7.
16 See Wittgenstein, *Philosophical Investigations*, 193e–229e (IIxi).
17 Cora Diamond, "The Difficulty of Reality and the Difficulty of Philosophy," in *Philosophy and Animal Life*, ed. Stanley Cavell, Cora Diamond, John McDowell, Ian Hacking, and Cary Wolfe (New York: Columbia University Press, 2008), 43–89.
18 Stanley Cavell, "Companionable Thinking," in *Philosophy and Animal Life*, ed. Stanley Cavell, Cora Diamond, John McDowell, Ian Hacking, and Cary Wolfe (New York: Columbia University Press, 2008), 94–5.
19 Stanley Cavell, *Disowning Knowledge In Seven Plays of Shakespeare*, 2nd ed. (Cambridge: Cambridge University Press, 2008).
20 Cavell, "Companionable Thinking," 93.
21 Cf. Niklas Forsberg, *Language Lost and Found* (New York: Bloomsbury, 2013).
22 Iris Murdoch, *Existentialists and Mystics* (London: Chatto & Windus, 1997), 12.
23 Ludwig Wittgenstein, *The Big Typescript: TS 213*, ed. and trans. C. Grant Luckhardt and Maximillian A. E. Haue (Oxford: Blackwell, 2005), § 86.
24 Cf. Stanley Cavell, "Must We Mean What We Say," in idem., *Must We Mean What We Say* (Cambridge: Cambridge University Press, 1976). For a longer discussion of this, see Hämäläinen, *Descriptive Ethics*.
25 Lars Hertzberg, *The Limits of Experience* (Helsinki: Acta Philosophica Fennica, 1994), 11.
26 Ibid., 12.
27 Benjamin De Mesel, *The Later Wittgenstein and Moral Philosophy* (Dordrecht: Springer, 2018), 24.
28 John L. Austin, "A Plea for Excuses," in *Philosophical Papers*, 3rd ed. (Oxford: Oxford University Press, 1979), 175–204.
29 Ibid., 181.
30 Ibid., 181–2.
31 Ibid., 182.
32 For a useful discussion of this see Niklas Forsberg, "Where's the Disagreement? J. L. Austin and A. J. Ayer on the Significance of the Ordinary," *Language and Communication* 49 (2016): 45–55.
33 Austin, "A Plea for Excuses," 182–3.
34 Ibid., 183.
35 Michel Foucault, *The Archeology of Knowledge* (London: Routledge Classics, 2002), 19.
36 Paul Rabinow, *Reflections on Fieldwork in Morocco*, Thirteenth Anniversary Edition, with a New Preface by the Author (Oakland: University of California Press, 2007), xv–xvi.

37 Cf. Ian Hacking, *The Taming of Chance* (Cambridge: Cambridge University Press, 1990).
38 See Vincane Despret, *What Would Animals Say If We Asked the Right Questions* (Minneapolis, MN: University of Minnesota Press, 2016).
39 See Bruno Latour and Steve Woolgar, *Laboratory Life: The Construction of Scientific Facts*, 2nd ed. (Princeton: Princeton University Press), 1986.

Works Cited

Austin, John L., "A Plea for Excuses," in J. O. Urmson and G. J. Warnock (eds.), *Philosophical Papers*, 3rd ed., 175–204, Oxford: Oxford University Press, 1979.

Cavell, Stanley, "Must We Mean What We Say," in Stanley Cavell, *Must We Mean What We Say*, Cambridge: Cambridge University Press, 1976.

Cavell, Stanley, *Disowning Knowledge In Seven Plays of Shakespeare*, 2nd ed., Cambridge: Cambridge University Press, 2008.

Crary, Alice, *Inside Ethics*, Cambridge, MA: Harvard University Press, 2016.

De Mesel, Benjamin, *The Later Wittgenstein and Moral Philosophy*, Dordrecht: Springer, 2018.

Despret, Vincane, *What Would Animals Say If We Asked the Right Questions*, MinneapolisN: University of Minnesota Press, 2016.

Diamond, Cora, *The Realistic Spirit*, Cambridge, MA: MIT Press, 1991.

Diamond, Cora, "The Difficulty of Reality and the Difficulty of Philosophy," in Stanley Cavell, Cora Diamond, John McDowell, Ian Hacking, and Cary Wolfe (eds.), *Philosophy and Animal Life*, 43–89, New York: Columbia University Press, 2008.

Forsberg, Niklas, *Language Lost and Found*, New York: Bloomsbury, 2013.

Forsberg, Niklas, "Where's the Disagreement? J.L. Austin and A.J. Ayer on the Significance of the Ordinary," *Language and Communication* 49 (2016): 45–55.

Foucault, Michel, *The Archeology of Knowledge*, London: Routledge Classics, 2002.

Gaita, Raimond, "Narrative, Identity and Moral Philosophy," *Philosophical Papers* 32, no. 3 (2003): 261–77.

Hacking, Ian, *The Taming of Chance*, Cambridge: Cambridge University Press, 1990.

Hämäläinen, Nora, *Literature and Moral Theory*, New York: Bloomsbury, 2015.

Hämäläinen, Nora, *Descriptive Ethics: What Does Moral Philosophy Know about Morality*, New York: Palgrave Macmillan, 2016.

Hertzberg, Lars, *The Limits of Experience*, Helsinki: Acta Philosophica Fennica, 1994.

Kuusela, Oskari, *The Struggle against Dogmatism*, Cambridge, MA: Harvard University Press, 2008.

Kuusela, Oskari, *Wittgenstein on Logic as the Method of Philosophy: Re-examining the Roots and Development of Analytic Philosophy*, Oxford: Oxford University Press, 2018.

Latour, Bruno, and Steve Woolgar, *Laboratory Life: The Construction of Scientific Facts*, 2nd ed., Princeton, NJ: Princeton University Press, 1986.
Murdoch, Iris, *Existentialists and Mystics*, London: Chatto & Windus, 1997.
Phillips, Dewi Z., *Interventions in Ethics*, Albany, NY: SUNY Press, 1992.
Rabinow, Paul, *Reflections on Fieldwork in Morocco*, Thirteenth Anniversary Edition, with a New Preface by the Author, Oakland: University of California Press, 2007.
Winch, Peter, *Ethics and Action*, London: Routledge and Kegan Paul, 1972.
Winch, Peter, *Trying to Make Sense*, Oxford: Basil Blackwell, 1987.
Wittgenstein, Ludwig, *Philosophical Investigations*, Oxford: Blackwell, 1998.
Wittgenstein, Ludwig, *The Big Typescript: TS 213*, ed. and trans. C. Grant Luckhardt and Maximillian A. E. Haue, Oxford: Blackwell, 2005.

3

The Texture of Importance
Ethics after Cavell and Diamond

Sandra Laugier

An essential essay by Cora Diamond is called "The Importance of Being Human," and this is also the title I chose for a small collection of her writings on moral philosophy in French.[1] Stanley Cavell and Cora Diamond have refocused moral reflection or shifted it toward the question of importance, of *what matters*. The subversive force of this approach to ethics has appeared to me over the years, while I was teaching—and translating into French—Diamond's and Cavell's works. It is of course in Wittgenstein (and Austin for Cavell) that these principles are rooted, but Diamond's and Cavell's readings of these texts, what they do *after* Wittgenstein, had a deeply liberating effect, toward a redefinition of ethics, and moral life, as refocused on our ordinary lives. It has also helped me (and so many others) to explore and determine what matters to me (to them).

Understanding what importance is, and that philosophy is about the recounting of importance, helps one understand what Wittgensteinian ethics is about. What does it mean to refocus moral reflection toward the question of *what matters*? How does it matter? For me, speaking of "Ethics after Wittgenstein" means simply the new acknowledgment of importance that Cavell and Diamond achieved after Wittgenstein. My aim in this chapter is to present the transformative power of this perspective.

1 Ordinary Concepts

Let's start with Cavell. Stanley Cavell's work is—among many other things—a redefinition of ethics: it transforms our view of the way ethics and knowledge bear on our ordinary lives. Cavell's teaching on film—in the way he draws our attention to gestures, particulars, details of our ordinary lives—is the basis of such a transformation of ethics and a different approach to morals. This is an ethics of perception and sensitivity, and an ethics of importance. I will define this approach by the idea, expressed in the title of Chapter 3 of *Pursuits of Happiness*, "The Importance of Importance." The expression comes from Austin:

> What, finally, is the importance of all this about pretending? I will answer this shortly, although I am not sure importance is important: truth is.[2]

Austin is, as we all know, Cavell's first master, and also a very strong and lasting influence as appears in recent texts like "Performative and Passionate Utterances." My point here is that Austin's presence (importance) in Cavell's work is connected to this transformation of ethics and that such a transformation of ethics is a new understanding, or reinstatement, of importance.

I haven't been able to find in Cavell's Chapter 3 of *Pursuits of Happiness*, "The Importance of Importance," an explicit reference, or treatment of, Austin's idea of the importance (or nonimportance) of importance. The chapter as a whole is about importance, and Cavell reads as a crucial moment of the 1940 movie *Philadelphia Story* the declaration of the infamous publicist Sidney Kidd about the event of the wedding as being of "national importance." The whole movie, and its narrative, may be seen as an acknowledgment of what the actual importance of this wedding is: what is happening at the end (what you see on Kidd's picture, the remarriage) is what is "of national importance."

> It could mean for example that they understand their marriage as exemplifying or symbolizing their society at large, quite as of they were its royalty, and their society as itself embarked on some adventure. George is confusedly thinking something more or less like this when he declares towards the end that his and Tracy's marriage will be "of national importance."[3]

It takes a whole movie, and sometimes many years, to get a clear idea of what is important, and to find the right application of the concept: and finding the right application of the concept of importance would, then, be understanding what is important to you—what are the important turns, or moments, or movies, in your life, or what you care about. Finding the right application of the concept of importance would be understanding "the importance of importance."

"Importance" is an important word for Dexter and throughout the film.[4] It is an important word for Cavell, as is shown by the strategic reappearance of the motif of importance in *Cities of Words*. First about *The Philadelphia Story*:

> Importance is an important word for Tracy's former (and future) husband C. K. Dexter Haven, who applies it, to Tracy's chagrin, to the night she got drunk and danced naked on the roof of the house—it is her saying impatiently to him that he attached too much importance to that silly escapade that prompts him to say to her, "it was immensely important."[5]

But we shouldn't understand the chapter, and Cavell's treatment of what importance is, as a rebuttal of Austin's seemingly ironic sentence "I am not sure importance is important." The question is not: is importance or truth important? The question is to understand—and it is one of Cavell's greatest accomplishments to show—that truth and importance are one and the same, or that importance is just as important as truth, and just as demanding and precise a concept. Just as Austin says parenthetically in a passage of *Truth*, which is later quoted parenthetically by Cavell:

> To ask "Is the fact that S the true statement that S or that which it is true of?" may beget absurd answers. To take an analogy: although we may sensibly ask "do we *ride* the word 'elephant' or the animal?" and equally sensibly "Do we *write* the word and the animal?" it is nonsense to ask "Do we *define* the word or the animal?" For defining an elephant (supposing we ever do this) is a compendious description of an operation involving both word and animal (do we focus the image or the battleship?) and so speaking about "the fact that" is a compendious way of speaking about a situation involving both words and world.[6]

Cavell comments on, or at least uses, this Austinian point in *Pursuits of Happiness* about the mutual expression of words and world:

> J. L. Austin was thinking about the internality of words and world to one another when he asked, parenthetically in his essay "Truth," "do we focus the image or the battleship?"[7]

The matter of importance is a matter of focusing, and film is a means to teach us how to focus, how to see fine details, how to see what matters. Importance and truth are not separate things, but are both *important*: the two words define the way my own experience matters (to myself and to the world), or counts. The motif of counting is thus important in Cavell's work, and especially in his moral work on film (the perfectionist moment in *It Happened One night* (Frank Capra, 1934) where Clark Gable makes an account of the sum, "fully itemized,"

Claudette Colbert has cost him, which Cavell correlates to the way Thoreau gives an account of the cost of his cabin).

> In *It Happened one Night* Clark Gable is not interested in a $10 000 reward but he insists on being reimbursed in the amount of $39.60, his figure fully itemized. (. . .) The figure Gable claims is owed to him is of the same order as the figure, arrived at with similar itemization, Thoreau claimed to have spent in building his house, $28.12 ½. The purpose of these men in both cases is to distinguish themselves, with poker faces, from those who do not know what things cost, what life costs, who do not know what counts.[8]

Recounting of importance, taking up the details where it lies, is the task of philosophy, and what connects it most closely to film. But it means transforming our idea of what is important. Wittgenstein asks significantly,

> Where does our investigation get its importance from, since it seems to destroy everything great and interesting?[9]

Wittgenstein's point, explored thoroughly by Cavell in his work, is that, just as importance is about truth and vice versa, the importance of the grammatical investigation is precisely in this, that "it seems to destroy everything great and interesting," displaces our interests, focus, care. Here Cavell connects his teaching on film to his reading of *Philosophical Investigations*:

> His answer in effect is that it is precisely philosophy's business to question our interests as they stand: it is our distorted sense of what is important (call it our values) that is distorting our lives.[10]

The idea is a shift in the task of philosophy, in ideas of what is important, what we are asked to let interest us, as Cavell notes in his preface to *The Claim of Reason*.

> His consolation is to reply that "What we are destroying is nothing but structures of air. But after such consolation, what consolation?"—What feels like destruction, what expresses itself here in the idea of destruction, is really a shift in what we are asked to let interest us, in the tumbling of our ideas of the great and the important.[11]
>
> (This relocation of importance and interest is what in *The Claim of Reason*, following my reading of Wittgenstein's *Investigations* I call the recounting of importance, and assign as a guiding task of philosophy).[12]

The strength of this conception of ethics is that it takes further Wittgenstein's questioning of the classical conception of concepts as applying to experience and of particular situations as "falling" under general concepts. Such attention to particular situations is rooted in the conceptual.

> Concepts lead us to make investigations; are the expression of our interest, and direct our interest.[13]

Experience and concept still play different roles in the general economy of our relations with things. The ipseity of experience, an ingredient of the "reality" we give to "things," is not the same as the normativity of the concept, which, when it is adequately applied, gets a hold on reality, which can be evaluated and described as true or false, correct or incorrect. However, many concepts are fed by this experience.

This is to acknowledge (the meaning of) the fact that to be able to think certain things we must put ourselves in the place of certain people, have certain experiences, immerse ourselves in forms of life. And that the concrete, actual ability to think a certain thing requires a certain form of "fit" to the real that is only acquired by long practice, and itself supposes a number of factual connections with the real. And this is Cavell's topic.

> To subject these enterprises and their conjunction to our experiences of them is a conceptual as much as an experiential undertaking.[14]

As soon as we pay attention, we are struck by how specific our judgments can be, and how they call into play a web of relations that are extremely determined within the world. Or, as Wittgenstein says, what is true or false is what humans say—that is, real people, and what they actually say in real circumstances. At the same time, a determining aspect of what we call "thought" is that no matter how rooted it may be—and it is essential that it is—it can always be applied beyond the circumstances in and for which it was formed.

> By concepts, we are giving ourselves means to make reality intelligible. There is no aspect of human experience that we cannot or do not turn into thought. The task of philosophy is to untangle the logic of all this with patience and humility. Here Cora Diamond uses the image of the knots. We imagine, like Frege, that "it would be impossible for geometry to formulate precise laws if it used strings as lines and knots in the strings as points." In the same way, we believe that ethics cannot be done without the idea of a norm and of an ethical *must* that are quite separate from ordinary reality with its strings and knots, the weave of our life that Wittgenstein evokes in various places.[15]
>
> Just as logic is not, for Wittgenstein, a particular subject, with its own body of truths, but penetrates all thought, so ethics has no particular subject matter; rather, an ethical spirit, an attitude to the world and life, can penetrate any

> thought and talk. So the contrast I want is that between ethics conceived as a sphere of discourse among others in contrast with ethics tied to everything there is or can be, the world as a whole, **life**.[16]

This attitude or spirit concerns the whole of thinking: the ability to project our words and concepts in new contexts, to be ready to *lose our concepts*. It is a sensitivity to "conceptual forms of life"—the sensitive character of the moral concepts that shape and share our lives.

Ethics after Wittgenstein is both normative and descriptive. It is a description of *our life with concepts*. The question of realism is deeply transformed by attention to the particular and by the sensitivity of our concepts to experience. Such radical transformation of concepts is what I call our life with concepts: the fact that they are in this world/in or of the "ordinary world."

> What they had not realized was what they were saying, or, what they were *really* saying, and so had not known *what they meant*. To this extent, they had not known themselves, and not known the world. I mean, of course, the ordinary world. That may not be all there is, but it is important enough: morality is that world, and so are force and love; so is art and a part of knowledge (the part which is about the world); and so is religion (wherever God is).[17]

The ordinary world is the world of importance, of what matters. Ordinary concepts are in and of this world; as in, for example, what Cavell calls in his autobiography "the philosophy of the concepts of pawnbroking."

> The concepts of grace and of redeeming are only beginning suggestions of the poetry of pawn broking. Counting, especially counting up the monthly interest owed, upon redemption (I mean upon the pawner's returning with his ticket to redeem his pledge), was another of my responsibilities. Here we encounter certain opening suggestions of *the philosophy of the concepts of pawn broking*. The concept of what we count, especially count as of interest or importance to us, is a matter fundamental to how I think of a motive to philosophy, fundamental to what I want philosophy to be responsive to and to illuminate. Something like the poetry and philosophy caught intermittently in the ideas of redemption and grace and interest and importance (or mattering) was of explicit fascination to me before I stopped working in the pawn shop, the year I graduated high school. The first stories I tried writing were stabs at elaborations of such connections.[18]

Concepts are about counting: *telling* is another word for counting or recounting or giving an account.

> And Tracy had toward the beginning defended George to Dexter by claiming that he is already of national importance, in response to which Dexter winces

and says she sounds like *Spy* magazine. Yet George and Tracy may be wrong not in the concept of importance but in their application of the concept.[19]

2 The Moral Texture of Importance

To have an experience means to perceive *what is important*. What interests Cavell in film is the way our experience makes what counts emerge, what allows it to be seen. Cavell is interested in the development of a capacity to see the importance, the appearance, and the significance of things (places, people, motifs).

> The moral I draw is this: the question what becomes of objects when they are filmed and screened—like the question what becomes of particular people, and specific locales, and subjects and motifs when they are filmed by individual makers of film—has only one source of data for its answer, namely the appearance and significance of just those objects and people that are in fact to be found in the succession of films, or passages of films, that matter to us.[20]

What defines importance, circularly, is "to express their appearances, and define those significances, and articulate the nature of this mattering."[21] Understanding what importance is, and that philosophy is about the recounting of importance, helps one understand what Wittgensteinian ethics is about. It means that depicting our ordinary lives does not mean simply describing our practices, what we do. Ethics cannot be described simply by reference to our customs, and our practices cannot form a foundation for ethics, because they themselves are unknown to us. Cora Diamond follows Cavell in her central idea, that our practices are *exploratory* and not merely given, as if we had a complete view before us of what we think, say, and mean. The point is not so much to argue as to explore, to "change the way we see things." This leads us to change our notion of justification. There is, for Diamond, no subject matter specific to ethics.

> I begin by contrasting two approaches to ethics. The first is characteristic of philosophers in the English-speaking tradition. We think that one way of dividing philosophy into branches is to take there to be, for every kind of thing people talk and think about, philosophy of that subject matter. Thus we may, for example, take psychology to be an area of thought and talk, a branch of inquiry, and so to have, corresponding to it, philosophy of psychology, containing philosophical consideration of that area of discourse. We may then think that there is thought and talk that has as its subject matter what the good life is for human beings, or what principles of actions we should accept; and then

philosophical ethics will be philosophy of that area of thought and talk. But you do not have to think that; and Wittgenstein rejects that conception of ethics. Just as logic is not, for Wittgenstein, a particular subject, with its own body of truths, but penetrates all thought, so ethics has no particular subject matter; rather, an ethical spirit, an attitude to the world and life, can penetrate any thought and talk. So the contrast I want is that between ethics conceived as a sphere of discourse among others in contrast with ethics tied to everything there is or can be, the world as a whole, life.[22]

This might seem to make ethics more general. But it does just the opposite: Diamond's aim is to define an ethics of the particular, just as Wittgenstein suggests we forget our "craving for generality" and attend to the ordinary and various, *different* uses of language. This is also an ethics of what our moral life *looks like*, the face or aspect of ethics.[23] But that does not mean simply describing our practices, "what we do" as simplistic readings of Wittgenstein might suggest. Diamond criticizes them: "Our practices are exploratory, and it is indeed only through such exploration that we come to see fully what it was that we ourselves thought or wanted to say."

This leads us to change our notion of justification, and of practice. Diamond here refers again to Cavell:

> The force of what we are able to say depends on its relation to the life of the words we use, the place of those words in our lives; and we may make the words tell by argument, by image, by poetry, by Socratic redescription, by aphorism, by Humean irony, by proverbs, by all sort of old and new things. And the judgment whether we produce illumination or obfuscation by doing so, the judgment whether there is truth in our words or self-deception, is not in general something on which there will be agreement. Ethics *is not* like mathematics; the role of agreement, the kind of agreement that there is in ethical thought, is not to be laid down in advance on some general Wittgensteinian principles. We need to see—in ethics as in mathematics—what agreement *belongs to* the intelligibility of the language we use.

Cavell is then the main source, for Diamond, Nussbaum, and others, of the ethical understanding of literature, of examples, of riddles, and of stories. The use of literature is not simply as illustration, but as with all *examples* (see Wittgenstein's *Blue Book* and Cavell's *The Claim of Reason*), it helps us see something more clearly. It helps us to see what we expect from ethics, to *say what we mean* by ethics.

Following Diamond, Hilary Putnam also placed himself in the tradition that aims to vindicate this kind of approach to ethics, his reference being here not only Cavell but mainly Iris Murdoch.[24] It consists in paying attention to what we say, to the ways in which our common expressions guide us, or lead us astray. It is certainly not the same as falling back on our "practices" or conventions. What is interesting is the way Murdoch insists on disagreement, misunderstandings, and distances, instead of community and agreement. I quote here from an unpublished Putnam conversation with Jacques Bouveresse:

> So it's interesting that the second generation of Wittgensteinian, people that were very close to W and their immediate followers were strongly concerned with ethics. And one thing that is in common between Deweyan ethics and Wittgensteinian ethics is a dissatisfaction with the way ethics has become identified with a very cut and dry debate in philosophy departments. (. . .) Our ethical lives cannot be captured with a half a dozen words like "ought," "right," "duty," "responsibility," "fairness," "justice" and the like, and the ethical problems that concern us cannot be identified with the debates between these very abstract metaphysical propositions of the natural laws, utilitarian, common sense etc. schools, we have to break out of the ethics in these overly restrictive, not only overly restrictive but also overly metaphysical ways.[25]

Diamond critiques a fascination in ethics comparable to that of Frege and Russell in logic, a fascination with an ideal of rationality that can "ground all moral arguments." But not everything in ethics happens by way of arguments. We believe that ethics cannot be done without the idea of a norm and of an ethical *must* that are quite separate from ordinary reality with its strings and knots, the weave of our life that Wittgenstein evokes in various places.[26] A focus on the latter is the *realistic spirit*: seeing that what matters, what needs attending to, is the knots and strings, the weave of our ordinary lives. We find here an image shared by Henry James and by Wittgenstein, that of a tapestry, which evokes the weaving together of the conceptual and the empirical.

This is exactly what Cavell describes, in maybe his most quoted and still underestimated passage, as the "whirl" of our ordinary lives:

> We learn and teach words in certain contexts, and then we are expected and expect others to project them into further contexts. Nothing insures that this projection will take place (in particular, not the grasping of universals nor the grasping of books of rules). It is a vision as simple as it is difficult, and as difficult as it is (and because it is) terrifying.[27]

Turmoil and details define what has to come to our attention. Wittgenstein uses his idea of family resemblance to dispute the idea of ethical concepts and of moral philosophy. Above all this is an exploration of the way our ethical preoccupations are embedded in our language and our life, in an ensemble of words that extends beyond our ethical vocabulary itself, and their complex connections with a variety of institutions and practices. In order to describe ethical understanding we would have to describe *all* of this, all these particular uses of words, of which a general definition cannot be given.

Our ethical lives, Putnam said, cannot be captured with half a dozen words like "ought," "right," "duty," "responsibility," "fairness," "justice," and the like: our ordinary language, as Austin has shown in his "Plea for excuses," is much more refined and "sharp-eyed": better at drawing differences (cf. Laugier 2013a). What matters is not so much moral judgment or understanding as perception, synoptic vision: an *ordinary* perception.[28] Wittgenstein suggests a *Gestalt* approach in ethics, by bringing out the necessity of recourse to a narrative *background* and to define our vision: our particular moral views emerge from a background. Here is how Diamond defines this background:

> Our particular moral views emerge from a more general background of thought and response. We differ in how we let (or do not let) moral concepts order our life and our relations to others, in how our concepts structure the stories we tell of what we have done or gone through.[29]

3 Ethics and Perception of What Matters

Wittgenstein pointed this out in his 1933 course about our uses of the words "game," "beautiful," and "good." The elements of the moral vocabulary have no sense except in the context of our customs and of a form of life. Better, they come to life against the background (the *praxis*) that "gives our words their sense"—a moral sense that is never fixed, and is always particular. "Only in the practice of a language can a word have meaning." Sense is determined not only by use, or "context" (as many analyses of language have recognized, whatever you might call it), but it is embedded and perceptible only against the background of the practice of language, which changes through what we do in it.

One might thus be tempted to take ethics in the direction of a particularist ontology—one that puts abstract particulars (derived, for example, from perception) at the center of a theory of values or a realism of particulars. But that would be again to miss the import of the idea of family resemblance, which is precisely the negation of all ontology. Wittgenstein criticizes the craving for generality.

Iris Murdoch, in "Vision and Choice in Morality," evokes in this connection the importance of attention in ethics (care: to pay attention, to be attentive, caring). Murdoch describes differences in ethics as differences of *Gestalt*:

> Here moral differences look less like differences of choice, given the same facts, and more like differences of vision. In other words, a moral concept seems less like a movable and extensible ring laid down to cover a certain area of fact, and more like a total difference of *Gestalt*.[30]

There are no univocal moral concepts that can simply be applied to reality to pick out a set of objects; rather, our concepts depend, for their very application, on the *vision* of the "area," on the narration or description we give of it, on our personal interest and our desire to explore: on what is important for us. Here, in the idea of importance, we have another formulation of care: what is important (what matters) to us, what counts.

Now activities of this kind certainly constitute an important part of what, in their ordinary life, a person "is like." When we apprehend and assess other people we do not consider only their solutions to specifiable practical problems; we consider something more elusive, which may be called their total vision of life, as shown in their mode of speech or silence, their assessments of others, their conception of their own lives, what they think attractive or praiseworthy, what they think funny: in short, the configurations of their thought which show continually in their reactions and conversation. These things, which may be overtly and comprehensibly displayed or inwardly elaborated and guessed at, constitute what, making different points in the two metaphors, one may call the texture of one's being or the nature of one's personal vision.

Moral expressiveness is at the core of Diamond's moral realism: not the right/wrong dualism or matters of choice and decision but how a person is "like." Cavell pursues exactly this line, about film and the movies that matter to us:

> The moral I draw is this: the question what becomes of objects when they are filmed and screened—like the question what becomes of particular people, and specific locales and subjects and motifs when they are filmed by individual makers of film—has only one source of data for its answer, namely the appearance and significance of just these objects and people that are in fact to be found in the succession of films, or passages of films, that matter to us. To express their appearances, and define those significances, and articulate the nature of this mattering, are acts that help to constitute what we might call film criticism.[31]

The importance of film lies in its power to make what is important, what matters, emerge: "to magnify the sensation and meaning of a moment." Attention to particulars is this specific attention to the invisible importance of things and moments, the covering over of importance in our ordinary life. To redefine ethics by starting from what is important, and its connection with the vulnerability of our experience, might be the starting point for an ethics of the *particular*. We can look to a whole cluster of terms, a language-game of the particular: attention, care, importance, what matters. Our capacity for attention is the result of the development of a perceptive capacity: to see a detached detail, or gesture, against its background. Here importance lies in details.

> We do continually have to make choices—but why should we blot out as irrelevant the different backgrounds of these choices, whether they are made confidently on the basis of a clear specification of the situation, or tentatively, with no confidence of having sufficiently explored the details? Why should *attention to detail*, or belief in its inexhaustibility, necessarily bring paralysis, rather than, say, inducing humility and being an expression of love?[32]

Moral philosophy must change its field of study, from the examination of general concepts and norms to the examination of particular visions, of individuals' "configurations" of thought: attention to detail, to the seemingly unimportant. The task of ethics is to perceive "the texture of a human's being or the nature of his/her personal vision." It is in the use of language ("choice" of expressions, style of conversation) that a person's moral vision shows overtly or develops intimately. For Murdoch this vision is not a theory but a vision of a texture of being (the texture might be visual, aural, or tactile). This texture is not a matter of moral choices, but of "what matters," of what makes and expresses the differences between individuals. See again Diamond:

> But we cannot see the moral interest of literature unless we recognize gestures, manners, habits, turns of speech, turns of thought, styles of face as morally expressive—of an individual, or of a people. The intelligent description of such things is part of the intelligent, the sharp-eyed, description of life, of what matters, makes differences, in human lives.[33]

What matters is what makes a difference. These are the differences that must be the object of a "sharpened, intelligent description of life." This notion of *human life* is connected to Wittgenstein's idea of a form of life, which also defines a texture. We might also think of the "open texture" that Waismann spoke of in *Verifiability* referring to the dependence of our words and our claims on their uses. "Texture" thus refers to an unstable reality that cannot be fixed by concepts, or by determinate particular objects, but only by the recognition of gestures, manners, and styles. A form of life, from the point of view of ethics, can be grasped only in a perception—attention to textures or moral patterns. These patterns are perceived as "morally expressive." What is perceived is not, therefore, objects or a "moral reality" but moral expression, which is not possible or recognizable in the absence of the background provided by a form of life.

In her extraordinary essay "Moral Differences and Distances," Diamond finds an example of this in the life of Hobart Wilson as told in an article in the *Washington Post*. Or consider literary characters as Henry James describes them, in teaching us to see them correctly. In his preface to *What Maisie Knew*, James explains how he wants to actually describe and depict, to really *see*. The whole novel is a critique of perception, connected to the ability to really see, judge, appreciate what Maisie is.

But film is the best approach to what it is to *get* to see something properly.

The background of a form of life is neither causal nor stuck like a décor, but living and mobile. One can speak here of forms of *life* (*life-forms*, as Cavell says, instead of *forms of life*): the forms that our life takes under an attentive gaze, the "whirl" (*Gewimmel*) or turmoil of life in language.

4 Missing the Adventure

> It is what human beings say that is true or false, and they agree in the language that they use. That is not agreement in opinions but *in form of life*.[34]
>
> How could human behavior be described? Surely only by showing the actions of a variety of humans as they are all mixed up together. Not what *one* man is doing *now*, but the whole hurly-burly, is the background against which we see an action.[35]

Here two representations of ethics and two approaches to moral perception are opposed: that of the background (cf. Searle, for whom institutions constitute the fixed background that allows us to interpret language, to perceive, and to follow social rules) and that of the perceptual texture of life. The term "background" appears in Wittgenstein in order to designate a background of description that makes the nature of actions appear, and not, as Searle suggests, in order to *explain* anything. The background cannot have a causal role, for it is language itself in all its instability and its dependence on practice:

> Our *particular* moral views emerge from a more general background of thought and response. We differ in how we let (or do not let) moral concepts order our life and relations to others, in how concepts structure the stories we tell of what we have done or gone through.[36]

We perceive action, but taken in the midst of a bustle, the whirl of the form of life in which it emerges and which gives it its meaning and importance. It is not the same thing to say that the application of a rule is causally determined by a background and to say that it is describable against a background of human actions and connections. The background does not determine ethical meaning (for there is no such thing). Rather it allows us to perceive what is important and meaningful for us (the important moment). The meaning of an action is given by the way it is perceived against the background of a form of life. The "accepted," given background does not "cause" our actions or expressions but it allows us to *see* them clearly. Here the conceptual adventure intervenes as part of moral perception. There is adventure in every situation that mixes uncertainty, instability, and "the sharpened sense of life." Diamond shows how Henry James defines this adventurousness that belongs to the *form* of moral thought:

> A human, a personal "adventure" is no a priori, no positive and absolute and inelastic thing, but just a matter of relation and appreciation—a name we conveniently give, after the fact, to any passage, to any situation, that has added the sharp taste of uncertainty to a quickened sense of life. Therefore the thing is, all beautifully, a matter of interpretation and of the particular conditions; without a view of which latter some of the most prodigious adventures, as one has often had occasion to say, may vulgarly show for nothing.[37]

This taste of adventure is what Cavell is constantly referring to in *Pursuits of Happiness* about the "Green world" and the adventurousness of the couples in the films, especially about *The Philadelphia Story* and its sense of society being embarked in an adventure. Perception, defined as care, is activity, mobility, and improvisation. What is important is to *have* an experience (not to derive something *from* experience). Dewey and Emerson both make the point. To *have* an experience means to perceive what *matters*.

Experience itself, if one trusts it, becomes an adventure itself. Failure of attention to experience, failure to perceive what is important, makes one miss the adventure. Thus one can see experience as an adventure at once of intellect and of sensibility (one opens oneself to experience). There can be no separation, in experience, of thought (spontaneity) from receptivity (vulnerability to reality). This is what, according to James, *constitutes experience.*

Ordinary concepts must be sensitive to this experience and may be understood more like clusters and textures than as a delimited ring. Ordinary ethics is an ethics of perception, of what our moral life is *like*. "I had attempted," Diamond adds, to "describe features of what moral life *is* like, without saying anything at all about what it must be like."[38]

Diamond writes that our practices are *exploratory*, and not given. They have to provide us with a vision of what we think, say, or mean. It is a matter of exploring more than arguing, a matter of "changing the ways we look at things."[39]

5 Life-Forms and Differences

This approach to expression, which makes it possible to respond, is a product of attention and of care. It is the result of an education of sensibility. Here we recall the Cavellian theme of "an education for grownups": in recognizing that education does not end with childhood, and that we still need, once grown-up, an appropriate education, we see that education is not just a matter of knowledge. This is the point of Wittgenstein's insistence on the idea of learning a language. Learning a language consists in learning an ensemble of practices that could not be "founded" in a language or causally determined by a social and natural basis but are learned at the same time as language itself, and that are the changing texture of our life.

> Pain occupies *this* place in our life, it has *these* connections.[40]

The question of education, on Cavell's reading of Wittgenstein (by contrast with Lovibond's or McDowell's), is infused by skepticism: learning does not offer me a guarantee for the validity of what I do, only the approval of my elders or of the community can do that, and that approval is not something merely given or obvious. Nothing, in sum, founds our practice of language, except this practice itself—"this whirl of organism that Wittgenstein calls *forms of life*." Here we can return to the way Austin defines the method of ordinary language philosophy, and the critique mounted by Wittgenstein against the "craving for generality" characteristic of philosophy. The attention to the ordinary that Wittgenstein advocates goes against our tendency, in science as in philosophy, to theorize the world, and our tendency to look for general meanings in our words independently from the context of expression and from our agreement on/in use.

> If we reach this agreement, we shall have some data ("experimental" data, in fact) which we can then go on to explain. Here, the explanation will be an account of the meanings of these expressions, which we shall hope to reach by using such methods as those of "Agreement" and "Difference."[41]

Our ordinary language is the best tool of perception, in drawing and discovering differences in reality:

> Part of the effort of any philosopher will consist in showing up differences, and one of Austin's must furious perceptions is of the slovenliness, the grotesque crudity and fatuousness, of the usual distinctions philosophers have traditionally thrown up. Consequently, one form his investigations take is that of repudiating the distinctions lying around philosophy—dispossessing them, as it were, by showing better ones. And better not merely because finer, but because more solid, having, so to speak, a greater natural weight; appearing normal, even inevitable when the others are luridly arbitrary; useful when the other seem twisted; real where the others are academic.[42]

Attention to our ordinary uses of language is then the way to access, touch reality. As Austin says, "we are using a sharpened awareness of words to sharpen our perception of the phenomena." The realism of ordinary language philosophy turns out to me its perception and articulation of importance.

> When we examine what we should say when, what words we should use in what situations, we are looking again not *merely* at words but also at the realities we use the words to talk about: we are using a sharpened awareness of words to sharpen our perception of, though not as the final arbiter of, the phenomena. For this reason I think it might be better to use, for this way of doing philosophy, some less misleading name than those given above—for instance, "linguistic phenomenology," only that is rather a mouthful.[43]

To pay attention to language, to *care* for/about what others say and what we say, and mean, is not only an ethical principle but also a cognitive one. And this takes us back to the ethics of perception and attention.[44]

> To subject these enterprises and their conjunction to our experiences of them is a conceptual as much as an experiential undertaking; it is our commitment to being guided by our experience but not dictated by it. I think of this as checking one's experience. I mean the rubric to . . . capture the sense of consulting one's experience [. . .] and turning your experience away from its expected, habitual

track, to find itself its own track: coming to attention. [. . .] I think of this authority as the right to take an interest in your own experience.[45]

Perception, or more precisely misperception, misappreciation, is what can lead us to "miss the adventure": what Austin calls "thoughtlessness, inconsiderateness." Knowledge is not enough. In order to get importance, we need to properly *appreciate* situations, as Austin explains,

> It happens to us, in military life, to be in receipt of excellent intelligence, to be also in self-conscious possession of excellent principles (the five golden rules for winning victories), and yet to hit upon a plan of action which leads to disaster. One way in which this can happen is through failure at the stage of appreciation of the situation, that is at the stage where we are required to cast our excellent intelligence into such a form, under such heads and with such weights attached, that our equally excellent principles can be brought to bear on it properly, in a way to yield the right answer. So too in real, or rather civilian, life, in moral or practical affairs, we can know the facts and yet look at them mistakenly or perversely, or not fully realize or appreciate something, or even be under a total misconception.[46]

Ethics after Wittgenstein, then, has to take into account this vulnerability in our use of language and in our ordinary lives. Ethics becomes, as Austin suggests, a matter of appreciation—involving both accurateness and attention. In her powerful comment of Cavell's work, Diamond comes to explaining the significance of this attention.

What I have meant to suggest . . . is that the hardness there, in philosophical argumentation, is not the hardness of appreciating or trying to appreciate a difficulty of reality. In the latter case, the difficulty lies in the apparent resistance by reality to one's ordinary mode of life, including one's ordinary modes of thinking: to appreciate the difficulty is to feel oneself being shouldered out of how one thinks, how one is apparently supposed to think, or to have a sense of the inability of thought to encompass what it is attempting to reach.[47]

Failure of perception, or more precisely misperception, misappreciation, is what can lead us to miss our own adventure: what Austin called "thoughtlessness, inconsiderateness"—an inability to think.

6 Thoughtlessness

Austin concludes,

> Even thoughtlessness, inconsiderateness, lack of imagination, are perhaps less matters of failure in intelligence or planning than might be supposed, and more

matters of failure to appreciate the situation. A course of E. M. Forster and we see things differently: yet perhaps we know no more and are no cleverer.[48]

Cavell's autobiography, *Little Did I Know*, acknowledges importance by pursuing the experience and reading of film in autobiographical writing. The "source of data" is still

> The appearance and significance of just these objects and people that are in fact to be found in the succession of films, or passages of films, that matter to us.[49]

The importance of film lies in its power to make what matters emerge: "to magnify the sensation and meaning of a moment." Film cultivates in us a specific ability to see the too often invisible importance of things and moments and emphasizes the covering over of importance in ordinary life. For importance is essentially what can be *missed*, remains unseen until later, or possibly, forever. The pedagogy of film is that while it amplifies the significance of moments, it also reveals the "inherent concealment of significance."

What interests Cavell most, in film, is the way our experience there makes (visually) emerge, makes visible what is important, what matters. It is the development of a capacity *to see what is important* that allows us to redefine experience—experience *is* not only of the appearance and meaning of things (places, persons, patterns) but also of the hiddenness of significance.

> It is part of the grain of film to magnify the feeling and meaning of a moment, it is equally part of it to counter this tendency, and instead to acknowledge the fateful fact of a human life that the significance of its moments is ordinarily not given with the moments as they are lived so that to determine the significant crossroads of a life may be the work of a lifetime. It is as if an inherent concealment of significance, as much as its revelation, were part of the governing force of what we mean by film acting and film directing and film viewing.[50]

What Cavell describes is something else than attention or inattentiveness—it is "an inherent concealement of significance, as much as its revelation." Experience reveals itself as defined by our quasi-cinephiliac capacity for seeing detail, reading expressions. The structure of expression articulates the concealment *and* the revelation of importance, and such is the texture of life (our life form). This is the difficulty that Cavell describes when he speaks of the temptation of inexpressiveness and of isolation and shows the essential vulnerability of human experience (another name for skepticism). We experience "the appearance and significance" of things (places, faces, patterns, words), but only afterward, after words. *Little did I know.*

Failure to pay attention to importance, it turns out, is as much a moral failure as it is (in Austin's words) a cognitive one. Yet we discover importance not only through accurate and refined perception but also through our suffering and misperception, in other words, through our failures to perceive. Because "missing the evanescence of the subject" is constitutive of our ordinary lives, it is also at the core of writing an autobiography—as well as being the ultimate truth of skepticism.

Cavell gives us in his autobiography, *Little Did I Know*, an unexpected take on the evanescence of film, and reverses the brilliant move of the opening of *The World Viewed*. He finds the words, in telling and detailing scenes and accurate details from his life in the context of his present life, to break the curse film is the name of, and to express the hidden importance of moments of his life, past and present. The "unspeakable importance" is put before our eyes. To tell the unspeakable and guess the unseen becomes an everyday, ongoing task.

> We involve the movies in us. They become further fragments of what happens to me, further cards in the shuffle of my memory, with no telling what place in the future. Like childhood memories whose treasure no one else appreciates, whose content is nothing compared to their unspeakable importance for me.[51]

This redefinition of the task of philosophy through the search of importance (what is important to me, what is important to us) and the recognition of our failures to acknowledge importance, to "guess the unseen from the seen," may be the main teaching of Cavell's and Diamond's philosophy. We discover importance not only through accurate perception but also through accepting our inabilities and misperceptions, our being unable to see, our failure to perceive, our persistently "missing the subject." This is reminiscent of "the relocation of interest and importance, the recounting of importance" that Cavell assigned as a guiding task of philosophy:[52] but now a further relocation is needed, because importance is to be defined through our essential failure to see the importance of things.

> Take as an example Martha Nussbaum's argument that *The Golden Bowl* elicits from us as readers an acknowledgement of our own imperfection. We are repeatedly struck, while reading it, by the inadequacies of our own attention and thus learn something about ourselves.[53]

Importance may be concealed *as* it is revealed to us. This is something Diamond tells us about "missing the adventure" by studying a different kind of blindness: blindness to what is actually going on in a novel, because we are precisely caught in moral issues and, for example, care so much for a character that we are blind to what is happening to her.

In *The Portrait of a Lady*, we like Isabel so much that we are blind to her "power of appreciation" and to other readings of the situation. Our very *care* blinds us.

> We readers of *The Portrait of a Lady* may find ourselves reading the novel with the question: Should Isabel or should she not go back to Osmond? (. . .) The moral issue *what she should do* so interests us, we like her so much, we hate so much her having to go back or thinking she must go back to this horrible man, that we do not actually see *her* fully; do not see her as the great maker of something out of what happens to her, we do not see the relevance of her genius for appreciation. We may miss the sense of what she does, miss her adventure, impoverish our own, through our very concern for her.[54]

What remains, then, to be explored after Wittgenstein is the mode of appearance of this hidden importance of things, the way we are essentially blind to it—that is, *meant* to be blind to it, in order to share the adventures of the characters we are *interested* in.

Could importance of some kind be essentially, eternally dissimulated from us? To overcome skepticism is to overcome our inability or refusal to see what matters to us: "to fail to guess the unseen from the seen, to fail to trace the implications of things—that is to fail the perception that that there *is* something to be guessed and traced, right or wrong." This question remains at the core of ordinary ethics.

Notes

1 C. Diamond, *L'importance d'etre humain et autres essais de philosophie morale*, tans. S. Laugier and E. Halais (Paris: Presses Universitaires de France, 2011).
2 J. L. Austin, *Philosophical Papers* (Oxford: Clarendon Press, 1994), 271.
3 Stanley Cavell, *Pursuits of Happiness* (Cambridge, MA: Harvard University Press, 1981), 147.
4 Ibid., 148.
5 Stanley Cavell, *Cities of Words* (Cambridge, MA: Harvard University Press, 2005), 40.
6 Austin, *Philosophical Papers*, 124.
7 Cavell, *Pursuits of Happiness*, 204.
8 Ibid., 5–6.

9   Ludwig Wittgenstein, *Philosophical Investigations* (Oxford: Blackwell, 1953), § 118.
10 Cavell, *Cities of Words*, 40.
11 Stanley Cavell, *The Claim of Reason* (New York: Cambridge University Press, 1979), xxi.
12 Cavell, *Cities of Words*, 262.
13 Wittgenstein, *PI* § 570.
14 Cavell, *Pursuits of Happiness*, 11.
15 Ludwig Wittgenstein, *Remarks on the Philosophy of Psychology II*, ed. G. H. von Wright and H. Nyman, trans. C. G. Luckhardt and A. E. Aue (Chicago: University of Chicago Press, 1980), § 862.
16 Cora Diamond, "Ethics, Imagination, and the Method of Wittgenstein's *Tractatus*," in *The New Wittgenstein*, ed. A. Crary and R. Read (New York: Routledge, 2000), 153.
17 Stanley Cavell, *Must We Mean What We Say?* (Cambridge: Cambridge University Press, 1969), 40.
18 Stanley Cavell, *Little Did I Know: Excerpts of Memory* (Stanford, CA: Stanford University Press, 2010), 115–16.
19 Cavell, *Pursuits of Happiness*, 147.
20 Stanley Cavell, *Themes Out of School* (San Francisco, CA: North Point Press, 1984), 182–3.
21 Ibid., 183.
22 Diamond, "Ethics, Imagination, and the Method of Wittgenstein's *Tractatus*," 153.
23 See my "The Will to See: Ethics and Moral Perception of Sense," trans. J. Chalier. *Graduate Faculty Philosophy Journal* 34, no. 2 (2013): 263–81.
24 See, for example, Hilary Putnam, *Words and Life*, ed. J. Conant (Cambridge, MA: Harvard University Press, 1994).
25 Hilary Putnam, unpublished interview with J. Bouveresse.
26 See, for example, Wittgenstein, *RPP* II § 862.
27 Cavell, *Must We Mean What We Say?* 52.
28 Laugier, "The Will to See: Ethics and Moral Perception of Sense."
29 Cora Diamond, "Moral Differences and Distances," in *Commonality and Particularity in Ethics*, ed. L. Alanen et al. (Houndmills: MacMillan, 1997), 220. See Laugier, "The Will to See: Ethics and Moral Perception of Sense."
30 Iris Murdoch, "Vision and Choice in Morality," in *Existentialists and Mystics: Writings on Philosophy and Literature*, ed. Iris Murdoch and Peter J. Conradi (London: Chatto and Windus, 1997), 82.
31 Cavell, *Themes Out of School*, 183.
32 Murdoch, "Vision and Choice in Morality," 88.
33 Cora Diamond, *The Realistic Spirit, Wittgenstein, Philosophy, and the Mind* (Cambridge, MA: MIT Press, 1991), 375.

34 Wittgenstein, *PI* §241. See my "Voice as Form of Life and Life Form," *Nordic Wittgenstein Review* 4 (2015): 3–82 and "Ordinary Language as Lifeform," in *Language, Forms of life, and Logic*, ed. C. Martin (Berlin: De Gruyter, 2018).
35 Wittgenstein, *RPP* II, § 629.
36 Cora Diamond, "Henry James, Moral Philosophy, Moralism," *The Henry James Review* 18, no. 3 (1997): 251.
37 Henry James, *The Art of the Novel*, quoted in Diamond, *The Realistic Spirit*, 314.
38 Diamond, *The Realistic Spirit*, 27.
39 Ibid.
40 Ludwig Wittgenstein, *Zettel*, ed. G. E. M. Anscombe and G. H. von Wright (Berkeley: University of California Press, 1967), § 532–3; emphasis in original.
41 Austin, *Philosophical Papers*, 274.
42 Cavell, *Must We Mean What We Say?* 102–3.
43 Austin, *Philosophical Papers*, 182.
44 See my "The Will to See: Ethics and Moral Perception of Sense," 263–81.
45 Cavell, *Pursuits of Happiness*, 11–12.
46 Austin, *Philosophical Papers*, 194.
47 Cora Diamond, "The Difficulty of Reality," in *Philosophy and Animal Life* (New York: Columbia University Press, 2008), 58.
48 Austin, *Philosophical Papers*, 194.
49 Stanley Cavell, "What Becomes of Things on Film?" in *Cavell on Film*, ed. William Rothman (Albany: State University of New York Press, 2005), 9.
50 Cavell, "The Thought of Movies," *Themes out of School*, 11.
51 Stanley Cavell, *The World Viewed* (Cambridge, MA: Harvard University Press, 1971), 154.
52 Cavell, *Cities of Words*, 262.
53 Diamond, *The Realistic Spirit*, 377.
54 Ibid., 316.

Works Cited

Austin, J. L., *Philosophical Papers*, Oxford: Clarendon Press, 1962.
Cavell, Stanley, *Must We Mean What We Say?* Cambridge: Cambridge University Press, 1969.
Cavell, Stanley, *The World Viewed*, Cambridge, MA: Harvard University Press, 1971.
Cavell, Stanley, *The Claim of Reason*, Cambridge: Cambridge University Press, 1979.
Cavell, Stanley, *Pursuits of Happiness*, Cambridge, MA: Harvard University Press, 1981.
Cavell, Stanley, *Themes Out of School*, San Francisco, NC: North Point Press, 1984.
Cavell, Stanley, *Cities of Words*, Cambridge, MA: Harvard University Press, 2005.

Cavell, Stanley, "What Becomes of Things on Film?," in William Rothman (ed.), *Cavell on Film*, 1–10, Albany: State University of New York Press, 2005.

Cavell, Stanley, *Little Did I Know: Excerpts of Memory*, Stanford, CA: Stanford University Press, 2010.

Diamond, Cora, *The Realistic Spirit, Wittgenstein, Philosophy, and the Mind*, Cambridge, MA: MIT Press, 1991.

Diamond, Cora, "Henry James, Moral Philosophy, Moralism," *The Henry James Review* 18, no. 3 (1997): 243–57.

Diamond, Cora, "Moral Differences and Distances," in L. Alanen et al. (eds.), *Commonality and Particularity in Ethics*, 197–234, Houndsmills: MacMillan, 1997.

Diamond, Cora, "Ethics, Imagination, and the Method of Wittgenstein's *Tractatus*," in A. Crary and R. Read (eds.), *The New Wittgenstein*, New York: Routledge, 2000.

Diamond, Cora, "The Difficulty of Reality," in Stanley Cavell, Cora Diamond, John McDowell, Ian Hacking, and Cary Wolfe, *Philosophy and Animal Life*, 43–90, New York: Columbia University Press, 2008.

Diamond, Cora, *L'importance d'etre humain et autres essais de philosophie morale*, trans. S. Laugier and E. Halais, Paris: Presses Universitaires de France, 2011.

Laugier, Sandra, *Why We Need Ordinary Language Philosophy*, Chicago: Chicago University Press, 2013a.

Laugier, Sandra, "The Will to See: Ethics and Moral Perception of Sense," J. Chalier, trans. *Graduate Faculty Philosophy Journal* 34, no. 2 (2013b): 263–81.

Laugier, Sandra, "Voice as Form of Life and Life Form," *Nordic Wittgenstein Review* 4 (2015): 63–82.

Laugier, Sandra, "Ordinary Language as Lifeform," in C. Martin (ed.), *Language, Forms of Life, and Logic*, 277–304, Berlin: De Gruyter, 2018.

Murdoch, Iris, "Vision and Choice in Morality," in Iris Murdoch and Peter J. Conradi (eds.), *Existentialists and Mystics: Writings on Philosophy and Literature*, 76–98, London: Chatto and Windus, 1997.

Putnam, Hilary, *Words and Life*, ed. J. Conant, Cambridge, MA: Harvard University Press, 1994.

Putnam, Hilary Interview with J. Bouveresse (2000, unpublished).

Wittgenstein, Ludwig, *Philosophical Investigations*, ed. G. E. M. Anscombe, G. H. von Wright, and R. Rhees, Oxford: Blackwell, 1953, second edition 1958.

Wittgenstein, Ludwig, *Remarks on the Philosophy of Psychology II*, ed. G. H. von Wright and H. Nyman, trans. C. G. Luckhardt and A. E. Aue, Chicago: University of Chicago Press, 1980.

Wittgenstein, Ludwig, *Zettel*, ed. G. E. M. Anscombe and G. H. von Wright, Berkeley: University of California Press, 1967.

Part Two

Wittgenstein, Ethics, and Metaethics

4

Three Wittgensteinian Interventions in Current Metaethical Debates

Julia Hermann

1 Introduction

Current metaethical debates are at various points open to a Wittgensteinian critique. Benjamin De Mesel, for instance, has criticized the common assumption that moral language is semantically uniform.[1] This assumption is presupposed by the distinction between cognitivist and noncognitivist views. Both cognitivists and noncognitivists tend to assume that it is either the case that all moral statements express beliefs or that none of them does. As De Mesel argues, this is not something that can be taken for granted, that is, it is in need of justification, and there are good reasons to question it. He refers to Wittgenstein's concept of family resemblances and encourages metaethicists to be open to the possibility that moral judgments fulfill different functions in different contexts and to look not for a common feature that they all share but for the kind of likenesses that can be found among the members of a family.[2]

In this chapter, I make three "Wittgensteinian interventions" in current metaethical debates. They concern moral objectivity, the "ideally coherent Caligula," and moral error theory. All three interventions are characterized by a reference to the unavailability of a view from nowhere and the central place of morality in human life. My aim is to provide the reader with a general idea of what a Wittgensteinian perspective can contribute to current debates in analytic metaethics.

I begin by distinguishing the Wittgensteinian perspective taken up in this chapter from other Wittgensteinian approaches to moral philosophy (section 2). I then turn to my first intervention, which concerns the issue of moral objectivity and the claim of moral realists that there are mind-independent moral facts (section 3.1). I criticize a Platonist conception of moral objectivity and argue that objectivity in ethics is not weaker than objectivity in science, but different. A Wittgensteinian conception of objectivity is deflationary and more faithful to the actual uses of the concept. The second intervention is directed at discussions of the ideally coherent Caligula and other ideally coherent eccentrics (section 3.2). Discussions in which philosophers refer to an ideally coherent Caligula contain at least four flaws. First, they are based on a wrong dichotomy, which reveals an implausibly individualistic account of what it is to constitute a normative reason for action. Second, the participants in these debates fail to see that the moral wrongness of torturing people for fun has the status of a moral certainty. Third, the question "Should Caligula be moral?" is misguided. Fourth, arguments that involve references to the ideally coherent Caligula put too much weight on our intuitions about "far-fetched, imaginary cases."[3] The third intervention targets moral error theory (section 3.3). I formulate two Wittgensteinian objections to that theory: error theorists implicitly deny the central functions that morality fulfills in human societies, and they falsely believe that prudence could fulfill these functions.

2 Different Wittgensteinian Perspectives

There is not *one* Wittgensteinian perspective on ethics or metaethics. Rather, there are different Wittgensteinian perspectives or approaches, which show family resemblances.[4] Philosophers taking such a perspective share a general form of dissatisfaction with mainstream approaches in ethics and metaethics. The differences between their perspectives stem from how they interpret Wittgenstein and how they think his philosophical thought is related to ethics. Regarding the issue of interpretation, a central difference lies between those authors who endorse an "intrinsically-ethical reading"[5] of Wittgenstein and those who reject such a reading. The first group interprets Wittgenstein's entire work has having an ethical point. According to Stephen Mulhall, for instance, Wittgenstein's view of language has "a pervasive moral dimension—an ethical or spiritual aspect that is not retractable even in principle to certain kinds of words, or certain kinds of uses of words."[6] According to the second group, which includes myself, there is "no distinctively moral viewpoint [...] in Wittgenstein's later philosophy," but this philosophy, and *On Certainty* in particular, "can be of help in our thinking about ethics and ethical issues."[7] Regarding the relationship between Wittgenstein's thought and ethics, we have to distinguish between philosophers who seek to interpret the few things that Wittgenstein actually said or is reported to have said on ethical matters and those who are concerned with the ethical and metaethical implications of his remarks about meaning, rule-following, justification, and so forth.[8] I belong to the latter group.

My Wittgensteinian perspective has three central elements, which are closely related. First, I conceive of morality as a set of overlapping practices or language-games.[9] Examples of moral language-games include morally praising and blaming, reminding someone of a promise she has made, trying to convince someone of a moral position, and asking for moral reasons. By comparing the use of language with the playing of a game like chess, Wittgenstein seeks to emphasize that speaking a language is part of an activity.[10] Just like playing, it involves "*acting* in accordance with certain rules."[11] The game analogy also highlights the multifaceted functions that language can have in our life, the "diversity of ways we make sense."[12] Describing the world we live in is only one function out of many.

Second, I hold that the use of language for "moral purposes" is interwoven with nonverbal action. Think, for instance, of a situation in which somebody accuses somebody else of having broken a promise. Her use of certain words is accompanied by certain gestures and a certain tone of voice, and followed by certain behavior, for example, treating the other person differently or trying to avoid her company.

Third, I believe that moral language-games are not only *interwoven with* nonverbal action but also *grounded in* action ("primacy of practice").[13] By this, I mean that more sophisticated moral practices rest on simpler moral practices and ultimately on primitive actions and reactions. Examples of more sophisticated moral practices are deliberating about moral issues and justifying moral beliefs. Less sophisticated practices include helping a friend in need and morally blaming someone. Nonverbal reactions to pain or signs of distress provide examples of primitive reactions that ground moral language-games. Wittgenstein holds that "more complicated forms [of the language-game; J.H.]" develop from the "primitive form of a language-game," which "is a reaction."[14] He gives the following example of the prelinguistic behavior on which a language-game is based: "to tend, to treat, the part that hurts when someone else is in pain; and not merely when oneself is—and so to pay attention to other people's pain behaviour."[15] Another example of a primitive reaction is the behavior toward someone with toothache: "In its most primitive form it is a reaction to somebody's cries and gestures, a reaction of sympathy or something of the form. We comfort him, try to help him."[16]

A metaethics inspired by Wittgenstein accepts the *Priority of Moral Practice Thesis*: good metaethical inquiry either starts from moral practice or is at least heavily constrained by it.[17] Let me now turn to my first Wittgensteinian intervention.

3 Three Wittgensteinian Interventions

3.1 A Wittgensteinian Conception of Moral Objectivity

Moral realists hold that moral statements are true or false independently of what human beings think about them.[18] They believe that moral facts or truths are mind-independent and that moral belief aims at representing those facts correctly.[19] In addition, they claim that the existence of mind-independent moral facts is necessary for securing a robust notion of ethical objectivity.[20] Anti-realists deny that mind-independent moral facts exist, and some of them, Sharon Street for instance, hold that we therefore have to live without such a robust notion of moral objectivity. They thus agree with their opponents that the possibility of "strong" objectivity in ethics depends on the existence of mind-independent moral facts.[21]

From a Wittgensteinian perspective, both parties in this debate make at least two problematic assumptions: the assumption that "objective" means the same in all contexts and the assumption that the paradigm context is that of science. Anti-realists take their notion of moral objectivity to be weaker than the realist notion. Both realists and anti-realists believe that no moral judgment is as objective as a judgment in physics. This reveals a commitment to a conception of objectivity that links the possibility of (strong) objectivity to "the possibility of a view from nowhere."[22] But since in ethics we cannot transcend our personal standpoint, a view from nowhere is an illusion.[23] In the natural sciences, it probably is so, too.[24] The robust realist's "Platonist objectivism"[25] is untenable. The Wittgensteinian moral philosopher[26] asks analytic metaethicists to be open to the possibility that "objective" means different things in different contexts: something else in science than in ethics and something else in one ethical context than in another.

Recently, Jeroen Hopster has argued that the "folk" conception of moral objectivity is graded—some moral judgments are regarded as more objective than others, depending on their subject matter.[27] He refers to findings in experimental philosophy and argues that they can be accounted for by anti-realists, who can secure moral objectivity, albeit objectivity in a weaker sense.[28] Like the other participants in this debate, he believes that only moral realism can secure a strong notion of moral objectivity—one modeled on the scientific notion of objectivity. Hopster argues that in light of the experimental findings, his anti-realist notion of objectivity has just the right degree of strength. The notion he proposes links objectivity to "standpoint-invariance": "if a moral judgment purports to be objective, it purports to withstand scrutiny from a diverse set of evaluative standpoints."[29] An evaluative standpoint is defined as "the full set of normative judgments that an agent makes."[30]

While Hopster's anti-realist conception of moral objectivity acknowledges that truth in ethics is not standpoint-independent, his claim that this notion of objectivity is weaker than the Platonist notion leaves the Platonist ideal in place.[31] By calling the Platonist notion of objectivity "strong," Hopster, albeit involuntarily, conveys that it is superior—an ideal that cannot be reached in ethics. Within a Wittgensteinian framework, by contrast, the view-from-nowhere conception of moral objectivity is not an unreachable ideal, but an illusion. Objectivity in ethics—and in other domains—does not require a "Platonist view-from-nowhere."[32] The Wittgensteinian suggestion is to conceive of objectivity in ethics not as weaker than objectivity in science but as different. Distinguishing between stronger and weaker forms of objectivity requires a neutral standard, which is not available.[33] Realists and anti-realists take the scientific standard and make it look as if it was neutral.

While Hopster seems to implicitly endorse the second of the problematic assumptions mentioned above (the assumption that the paradigm case is that of science), he does not endorse the first assumption, that is, he does not hold that "objective" means the same in all contexts. By contrast, he submits that there are different senses of objectivity and that a conception of objectivity may be suitable for one domain but not for another.[34] Consequently, he should at least qualify his talk about stronger and weaker forms of objectivity.

A philosopher who explicitly denies the first assumption and has proposed a different conception of objectivity is Arthur Ripstein. He holds that objectivity always requires some sort of independence. What sort of independence it requires depends on "the nature of the inquiry."[35] In the natural sciences, the required independence is causal, but in other areas of inquiry, such as moral inquiry, causal independence is of no interest.[36] In order for beliefs to be causally independent, they must "be caused by objects that exist apart from believers."[37] Ripstein formulates the general independence condition, of which causal independence is a species, thus, "in order for [a belief; J.H.] to be objective, my thinking it must not make it so."[38] According to Ripstein, "[w]e can only make sense of the notion of objectivity by contrasting it with some sort of bias."[39] Its contrast with a particular account of bias also "pretty much exhaust[s]" the notion of objectivity.[40] Since Ripstein's independence condition is metaphysically innocent, his conception of objectivity is deflationary.[41]

What is the right standard for moral judgment, if it is not causal independence, as Ripstein argues?[42] According to Ripstein, in moral discourse, as in other normative discourses, objectivity requires "endorsement independence": if I am to suppose that my belief about the wrongness of factory farming is objective, "I must at least suppose it to hold independently of the fact that I happen to endorse it."[43] I must suppose that "the fact of acceptance does not provide the grounds for acceptance."[44] Unlike in the case of causal independence, I need not suppose my belief "to be caused by objects that exist apart from believers."[45] Any appeal to mind-independent moral facts is unnecessary. Because what matters in moral discourse is the authority of norms; endorsement independence is the appropriate sort of independence here, according to Ripstein. The claim of moral norms "must not be exhausted by the fact that one happens to care about them."[46]

Ripstein emphasizes that objectivity is not a property.[47] Apart from a claim to "the general sort of independence appropriate to the domain of inquiry," every claim to objectivity carries with it a claim to another sort of independence: independence from something particular.[48] In every case, there are specific sorts of biases that one seeks to avoid. In moral discourse, this can be, for instance, the distorting influence of a certain religious upbringing, a racist or sexist attitude, or a peculiar personal preference.[49]

Unlike Hopster, who proposes to conceive of moral objectivity in terms of standpoint-invariance instead of mind-independence, Ripstein sticks to an understanding of objectivity in terms of independence, but rejects the equation of objectivity with *causal* independence. What kind of independence is required for a claim to be objective varies between domains of inquiry. Although Ripstein does not mention Wittgenstein, his account of objectivity is Wittgensteinian in spirit. As De Mesel points out, a "deflationary conception of objectivity without metaphysical depth" is plausible in the light of the philosophy of the later Wittgenstein.[50] He also refers to such a conception as a "Wittgensteinian conception of objectivity."[51] A deflationary account of objectivity is more "faithful to the contexts in which we use the concept" than a Platonist conception.[52]

Hopster's account qualifies as a deflationary account as well and can be called Wittgensteinian in spirit to some degree. His criterion for the objectivity of moral judgments—standpoint-invariance—is more demanding and more elaborate than Ripstein's criterion of endorsement independence. It reflects the perception of moral objectivity as graded: "the *degree* of objectivity of a moral judgment is a function of the diversity of evaluative standpoints under which its truth or falsity holds fixed. The more diverse these standpoints are [...] the more objective the resultant judgment."[53]

What I find slightly problematic about Hopster's proposal is his use of the notion of ideal coherence. On his anti-realist view, the standard of correctness suitable for moral judgments involves reference to that notion, and so does his criterion of standpoint-invariance. In order to know what follows from an agent's evaluative standpoint, we have to answer the following question: "what judgment would this agent make if she were ideally coherent, imaginative and informed about the relevant non-normative facts?" [54] That question is unanswerable, and therefore, it is impossible to establish the correctness of a moral judgment. Consequently, establishing its objectivity is impossible, too. We cannot answer the question because, as Hopster sometimes admits, human beings are never ideally coherent and imaginative, because we have no clear idea of what being ideally coherent and imaginative amounts to, and because we can never say with certainty what the relevant nonnormative facts are. The question amounts to the question as to what judgment some kind of perfect being would make, a being as much unlike humans as aliens are. How on earth can we know this?

3.2 Wittgensteinian Concerns about the "Ideally Coherent Caligula"

My second example of a Wittgensteinian intervention into current metaethical discussions concerns the "strange characters" that "inhabit the world of metaethics," as Sharon Street puts it, thereby referring to the purely hypothetical characters that she calls "ideally coherent eccentrics."[55] Prominent examples of such strange figures include Derek Parfit's "man with Future Tuesday Indifference"[56] and two queer characters invented by Allan Gibbard: the "ideally coherent anorexic"[57] and the "ideally coherent Caligula." [58] Here I focus on the last character, which differs from the other two by endorsing a value that is not merely utterly curious but also morally repugnant. The ideally coherent Caligula "aims solely to maximize the suffering of others."[59]

In current debates between normative realists and normative anti-realists, realists like to refer to intuitions about ideally coherent eccentrics in support of their position.[60] Realists find the following implication of an attitude-dependent account of normative reasons intuitively implausible: "The ideally coherent Caligula has most normative reason to torture people for fun."[61] They take this implication to show that attitude-dependent accounts must be false.[62] According to attitude-dependent accounts of normative reasons, a person's normative reasons depend on her evaluative attitudes.[63] Street, who endorses such an account, argues that the implication is intuitively plausible. Seeing this requires imagining carefully what the ideally coherent Caligula is like, thereby noting just how much he differs from real human beings. As Street describes him, the ideally coherent Caligula "judges that he has most normative reason to torture others for fun, and this conclusion (it is stipulated) follows perfectly from within his own practical standpoint: he is utterly consistent in holding that he has this reason, and he is making no mistakes about matters of non-normative fact."[64] Normative realists hold that Caligula is mistaken about his reasons.[65] He in fact has a reason not to torture others for fun, one that is independent of his evaluative attitudes. That reason is grounded in a mind-independent moral fact. According to Street's "Humean antirealism" or "Humean constructivism," "characters like an ideally coherent Caligula are entirely possible, and were such a person ever to exist in real life, he would indeed have most normative reason to torture others for fun."[66] Of course, there will never be an ideally coherent Caligula in real life. The only place where we can encounter ideally coherent eccentrics is our imagination.[67]

From a Wittgensteinian perspective, there are several problems with the example of the ideally coherent Caligula and the way it is used in current debates. I now address four such problems.

3.2.1 A False Dichotomy

The disagreeing parties in this debate assume that there are only two options: either a person's normative reasons depend on her evaluative attitudes ("attitude-dependent conception of normative reasons"[68]) or they are grounded in mind-independent facts ("attitude-independent conception of normative reasons"[69]).[70] Normative realists think that we must be able to refer to attitude-independent normative reasons, since otherwise we lack the resources to deny that the ideally coherent Caligula has most normative reason to do something as immoral as torturing people for fun. In the absence of attitude-independent normative reasons, moral norms would not be binding for everyone and thus not be objective in the strong sense of the term. Here the Platonist conception of objectivity discussed in section 3.1 of this chapter is at work. In addition to rejecting the identification of objectivity with causal independence, the Wittgensteinian criticizes the highly individualistic conception of what constitutes one's normative reasons to act. Normative standards are shared standards. They are shared by the participants in a practice. So there is a third option, which is much more plausible than the other two: what people have normative reason to do does not solely depend on any individual's evaluative attitudes but also on shared normative standards. In virtue of being a (competent) participant in normative practices, a person has reason to follow the rules of those practices. The shared standards of a practice constitute reasons for action for competent participants in the practice. If he were a (competent) participant in moral practices, the ideally coherent Caligula could not be correctly described as having most normative reason to torture people for fun. However, as Street rightly notes, this hypothetical character looks much like an alien.[71] He appears to lack any moral feeling whatsoever, which moves him beyond the addressees of moral arguments. As Jeroen Hopster points out, "creatures like Caligula may not be regarded as *moral* agents."[72] The task of trying to provide a philosophical theory that establishes the objectivity of moral norms in the sense that these norms would provide even an ideally coherent Caligula with overriding reasons for action is misguided. The addressees of such a theory are moral agents, not amoral aliens.

As a reaction to this objection, proponents of an attitude-independent conception might slightly modify the example: instead of imagining just an individual ideally coherent Caligula, they now ask us to imagine an entire society of ideally coherent Caligulas. If reasons are socially constituted, an individual ideally coherent Caligula who is part of a society of ideally coherent Caligulas has most normative reason to torture people for fun, or so they claim.[73] To this move the Wittgensteinian responds that such a society would not be a society of moral agents. There are limits to what shape a society's moral norms can take. These limits are set by the functions that morality fulfills in human societies, by certain facts about the world we live in, such as scarcity of resources, and by human nature.[74] Not only would a society of ideally coherent Caligulas not be a society of moral agents, it would also not be a human society. The advocate of an attitude-independent conception of normative reasons is asking us to imagine a society of aliens.

3.2.2 *The Moral Wrongness of Torturing People for Fun Constitutes a Moral Certainty*

At a fundamental level, the participants of normative practices do not follow the rules of those practices for a reason. They follow them "*blindly*."[75] Meredith

Williams speaks about "bedrock practices."[76] A particular feature of the ideally coherent Caligula is that he judges and acts in a way that is diametrically opposed to how competent moral agents judge and act at bedrock. A morally competent agent does not need any reasons for not torturing others for fun. Our shared moral practices reveal that torturing others for fun is a paradigmatic case of moral wrongness. It could be regarded as a "moral certainty," that is, as something that competent moral agents cannot reasonably doubt.[77] People debate about whether there are situations in which torture can be morally justified, but it is generally taken for granted that torturing others (just) for fun is beyond the moral pale. Regimes that torture inmates defend their torturing practice by reference to its alleged conduciveness to finding out the truth, or by reference to its deterring effects. That it is beyond doubt for morally competent agents that torturing others for fun is wrong is shown by how they talk, think, feel, and act. Such agents simply do not torture others for fun. To borrow a formulation from Wittgenstein: "This is simply what I do."[78] Realists and anti-realists alike falsely assume that it makes sense to say that someone has most normative reason not to torture people for fun.

3.2.3 *The Question "Should Caligula Be Moral?" Is Misguided*

Street does not deny the moral wrongness of torturing people for fun.[79] The question that is of interest to her is whether the ideally coherent Caligula *should* be moral, that is, "whether Caligula has most normative reason *full stop* to do what he has most 'moral reason' to do."[80] The Wittgensteinian is sympathetic to Street's claim that in many cases, "an accurately imagined ICE will look more like an interesting visitor from another planet than a human being."[81] Street calls this the "'alien visitor' analogy"[82] and notes that it is particularly important to keep in mind when considering ideally coherent eccentrics that are amoral, such as the ideally coherent Caligula. However, if Caligula were a human being, the question Street is interested in would not make sense, because a human being that has moral reasons for action is a morally competent agent, and such an agent cares about being moral. The question as to whether she should be moral requires a view from nowhere, which, as we already saw, is an illusion. The question can be compared to the question "Should she be a human being as opposed to a tree?"[83]

When the question "Why be moral?" arises in (nonphilosophical) practice, it is motivated by the experience that moral obligations conflict with nonmoral interests.[84] Let me give an example. I promised my father that I would help him paint his walls on Sunday, but when I wake up on Sunday morning, the weather is beautiful and I would much prefer a day trip to the seaside with my friends. Such harmless examples add up, and we encounter situations in which doing what morality requires is very inconvenient for us. When we ask ourselves in a particular situation whether we actually have to do what morality requires and cannot simply disregard moral claims, we are not reflecting from an extramoral standpoint, or a view from nowhere. Yet that is what the philosophical why be moral question requires. The question "Should Caligula be moral?" looks meaningful because it superficially resembles questions such as "Should I keep my promise and help my father instead of going to the beach?"[85]

Directed at an alien visitor, the question does not make sense either. The formulation "whether Caligula has most normative reason *full stop* to do what he has most 'moral reason' to do" implies that Caligula has most moral reason to not torture people for fun. Yet he does not. Since he clearly does not qualify as a moral agent, the norms of human moral practices will not constitute reasons for him. Therefore, if Caligula is not a morally competent agent, he does not have any moral reasons, and if he were such an agent, Street's question would not make sense because there is no standpoint available from which it can be meaningfully asked.

3.2.4 We Cannot Imagine What It Would be Like to Be an Ideally Coherent Caligula

Street and others who refer to ideally coherent eccentrics in their arguments draw on our intuitions about "far-fetched, imaginary cases."[86] These cases remind me of some equally exotic scenarios contemplated by Wittgenstein, such as the example of the wood sellers who determine the price of wood by surface area and not by volume.[87] I interpret Wittgenstein as saying that the language-game that those people are playing is so utterly different from ours that we cannot imagine what it would be like to act like them. Following him, I would claim that we do not (and cannot) have reliable intuitions about ideally coherent eccentrics, since they are too far removed from normal human beings. Our intuitions about such cases amount to wild guesses. While Street acknowledges this remoteness by comparing these eccentrics to aliens, she nevertheless thinks that people's intuitions about such cases can be used to support her favorite metaethical theory.

To sum up, from a Wittgensteinian perspective, metaethical discussions about the ideally coherent Caligula contain several flaws. I discussed four of them. First, they are based on a false dichotomy. That dichotomy reveals a rather implausible individualistic picture of what constitutes a normative reason to act. Second, the participants fail to see that the moral wrongness of torturing people for fun constitutes a moral certainty. They assume that there have to be reasons for people to refrain from grossly immoral actions, and that it makes sense to say that someone has most normative reason not to torture people for fun. Third, the question "Should Caligula be moral?" is misguided. Fourth, arguments that involve references to the ideally coherent Caligula put too much weight on our intuitions about "far-fetched, imaginary cases."[88]

3.3 Wittgensteinian Objections to Moral Error Theory

My third and final Wittgensteinian intervention is directed at moral error theory (hereafter, sometimes simply "error theory"). Error theory is a radical view that unsurprisingly does not have a whole lot of advocates, but it seems that most metaethicists take its truth to be a coherent possibility. In his introduction to metaethics, Simon Kirchin calls the challenge posed by error theory "revolutionary."[89]

According to error theory, moral discourse is irredeemably flawed. We partake in it in order to communicate true propositions, but we never succeed in doing so. Error theorists accept three main theses.[90] The first two are semantic: (1) moral judgments express truth-apt beliefs and (2) they express truth-apt beliefs about moral facts. The third thesis is substantial or metaphysical: (3) there are no moral facts.[91] According to error theorists, when we make moral judgments, we refer to objective moral properties, which do not exist. Therefore, the claim "Killing is wrong" is untrue, and so is its negation. Error theorists claim that there is no such thing as moral normativity. Against the objection that their position is highly implausible, error theorists have argued that getting rid of moral normativity would not change much, since there would still be prudential normativity, which would suffice to keep people from acting "immorally," at least most of the time. In what follows, I present two "Wittgensteinian" objections to error theory.[92]

3.3.1 *Moral Practices Are Central to the Human Form of Life*

By claiming that moral reasons do not exist and that there is no such thing as moral normativity, error theorists seem to refuse to participate in moral practices. However, these practices are a central part of human life, and human beings have no genuine alternative to participating in them. Barry Stroud says with regard to the practices of calculation and inference that "[t]o ask whether our human practices or forms of life themselves are 'correct' or 'justified' is to ask whether we are 'correct' or 'justified' in being the sorts of things we are."[93] Our engagement in moral practices is no less central to the human form of life than are calculating and inferring. Also for making moral evaluations it holds that we do not decide to engage in this practice "any more than we decide to be human beings as opposed to trees."[94] Moral discourse is among the human practices with regard to which it does not make sense to question their justification.

Peter Strawson makes a similar argument.[95] According to him, to ask whether our reactive attitudes are justified is "to overintellectualize the facts."[96] While we can meaningfully ask for justification within the framework of reactive attitudes ("Is this particular attitude towards this particular person justified?") ("internal justification"), the question as to whether that framework of attitudes as a whole is justified does not make sense: "The existence of the general framework of attitudes itself is something we are given with the fact of human society. As a whole, it neither calls for, nor permits, an external 'rational' justification."[97] Strawson compares the question "Is our framework of reactive attitudes as a whole justified?" with the question as to whether our practice of inductive reasoning is justified.[98]

The view that moral practices have this central status is supported by anthropological findings and evolutionary accounts of morality.[99] Relativists and universalists disagree about whether any moral norms are universally valid, but no one in the debate denies that all human societies have moral norms.[100] It can reasonably be assumed that moral norms have developed in response to the demands of group living. These norms and the capacity to be guided by them enable humans to live together in bigger groups and to engage in larger cooperative endeavors (as compared to our ancestors), and to act altruistically toward nonkin.[101] Error theory implicitly denies the central functions that moral norms and practices have in human societies and assumes that morality is something that we could simply decide to get rid of.

The Wittgensteinian denies that there is an extramoral standpoint from which we could ask whether our moral practices are as a whole correct. Such a standpoint would be the view from nowhere that realists think is required by objectivity. As Mario Brandhorst puts it, "there is no view from nowhere in fundamental ethical orientation."[102] Brandhorst ascribes to Wittgenstein the view that we can distinguish between true and false moral outlooks, but only "given our ethical outlook, in the light of our attitudes and our commitments."[103] An ethical outlook is the result of a process of moral upbringing, in which we have developed certain capacities (e.g., empathy and moral judgment) and dispositions (e.g., the disposition to react to certain behavior with moral emotions such as outrage or condemnation). The error theorist ignores that stepping outside of morality would not "merely" require us to abandon all our moral beliefs but also to get rid of numerous dispositions and capacities. I can stop playing chess without having to unlearn it, but stepping outside of morality would require losing moral competence. Unlike chess, morality is deeply engrained in human life. We are moral beings all the way down. The error theorist underestimates how deep we have to dig if we want to eradicate morality.

3.3.2 *Getting Rid of Moral Reasons Would Change Everything*

The second objection to moral error theory is closely related to the first. Against the objection that their position is utterly implausible, error theorists have come up with the argument that since there exist numerous prudential reasons to refrain from actions that we falsely call "immoral," we do not need moral norms for keeping people from carrying out such actions. There are no moral reasons, but the prudential reasons that the vast majority of people have oblige them to refrain from killing, cheating, torturing, and so on.

This move of the error theorist in defense of her position does not succeed. First of all, acting morally *means* restricting your own pursuit of the good life for the sake of the well-being of others.[104] The entire concept of morality would be useless if respect for the well-being of others did not require moral normativity. Second, the error theorist takes people's prudential reasons to refrain from "immoral behavior" to rest on an individual desire, the desire to live a happy life, while moral prohibitions are anchored in shared moral practices, which children master in the course of moral upbringing. Moral norms are shared norms. That people usually regard arbitrarily shooting at strangers as wrong and refrain from it is due to their moral upbringing, and to certain facts, such as the social nature of human beings and the requirements of group living. The Wittgensteinian asks the error theorist to think about how the authority of moral norms is grounded in human practices and how radically different a world without morality would be.[105]

The claim that prudence alone would suffice to ensure that humans do not steal, cheat, etc. on a large scale has little plausibility. The error theorist's denial of the existence of moral normativity seems to entail that we should get rid of moral upbringing. Let us for a moment assume—as implausible as it is—that it would be possible to free ourselves from that. What would the consequences be? Without moral upbringing, people would not acquire or develop any of the following: moral beliefs, dispositions to have feelings of guilt, shame, remorse, and indignation in certain situations, and empathy. A society in which such dispositions and capacities were lacking would not seem to be a human society anymore. The practical consequences of abandoning moral education seem terrifying. The error theorist is plainly wrong in thinking that prudence can fulfill the functions of morality even approximately. Fear of punishment such as being imprisoned, for instance, is not sufficient for ensuring that "moral" norms are upheld. The view that the authority of moral norms is grounded in sanctions has been widely criticized.[106] If moral action was motivated by the aim to avoid "external sanctions" such as punishment, contempt, and exclusion from the moral community, people would lack the motivation to act morally in situations in which these negative consequences are very unlikely, for instance because it is very unlikely that anyone will find out that they violated a moral norm.[107] While a philosopher who is not an error theorist can try to solve this problem by resorting to the role of "inner sanctions" such as feelings of guilt and loss of self-respect, this option is unavailable to the error theorist, since if we were to abandon morality, and with it moral upbringing, such inner sanctions would not exist. Neither would many of the external sanctions usually referred to, such as contempt and exclusion. The error theorist is left with legal sanctions such as legal punishment, which makes the argument less convincing, since the class of actions that are unlikely to lead to legal sanctions is significantly bigger than the class of actions that are unlikely to lead either to legal or to moral sanctions. Finally, it has been shown that not even children justify their moral judgments by reference to punishment.[108] Small children say that the moral wrongness of actions such as pulling somebody's hair is independent of negative consequences such as punishment.[109]

4 Conclusion

I picked out three topics in current analytic metaethics and commented on them from a Wittgensteinian perspective. The first topic was moral objectivity. I criticized a Platonist conception of objectivity and argued that objectivity in ethics is not weaker than objectivity in science, but different. A Wittgensteinian conception of objectivity is deflationary and more faithful to the actual uses of the concept.

The second Wittgensteinian intervention was directed at the ideally coherent Caligula. Discussions of this curious character contain several flaws, of which I discussed four. First, they are based on a false dichotomy. That dichotomy reveals a rather implausible individualistic picture of what constitutes a normative reason to act. Second, the participants fail to see that the moral wrongness of torturing people for fun constitutes a moral certainty. They assume that there have to be reasons for people to refrain from grossly immoral actions, and that it makes sense to say that someone has the most normative reason not to, for instance, torture people for fun. Third, the question "Should Caligula be moral?" is misguided. Fourth, the arguments put forward by realists and anti-realists draw on our intuitions about "far-fetched, imaginary cases."[110] It is impossible for us to have clear intuitions about such cases, since ideally coherent eccentrics are just too remote from actual human beings.

Finally, I addressed moral error theory. Advocates of that theory implicitly deny the central functions that moral norms and practices have in human societies, and they assume that morality is something that we could simply decide to get rid of. They underestimate how deep we have to dig if we want to eradicate morality. Humans—with the exception of psychopaths—are moral beings all the way down. That in the absence of moral reasons, there would still be prudential reasons is cold comfort, given that prudence cannot fulfill the functions morality has in human societies.

All three interventions emphasized that morality is deeply anchored in human life and that the view from nowhere is an illusion. All of them were moreover corrective in nature. It would be interesting to explore the more positive contributions that a Wittgensteinian metaethicist can make. This I leave for another chapter.[111]

Notes

1 See Benjamin De Mesel, "Are Moral Judgments Semantically Uniform? A Wittgensteinian Approach to the Cognitivism – Non-Cognitivism Debate," in *Ethics in the Wake of Wittgenstein*, ed. Oskari Kuusela and Benjamin De Mesel (London: Routledge, 2019), 126–48.

2 Cf. Ludwig Wittgenstein, *Philosophical Investigations*, trans. G. E. M. Anscombe, 3rd ed. (Oxford: Basil Blackwell, 1968), § 66. Wittgenstein nicely illustrates his concept of family resemblances by means of the similarities of different games. They exhibit "a complex web of similarities that are overlapping and criss-crossing" (Ibid.; my transl.).

3 Sharon Street, "In Defense of Future Tuesday Indifference: Ideally Coherent Eccentrics and the Contingency of What Matters," *Philosophical Issues* 19 (2009): 273–98, 279.
4 See the other contributions to this volume. See also, for example, Benjamin De Mesel, *The Later Wittgenstein and Moral Philosophy* (Dordrecht et al.: Springer, 2018); Cora Diamond, "Truth in Ethics: Williams and Wiggins," in *Ethics in the Wake of Wittgenstein*, ed. Benjamin De Mesel and Oskari Kuusela (London: Routledge, 2019); Yaniv Iczkovits, *Wittgenstein's Ethical Thought* (Basingstoke: Palgrave Macmillan, 2012); Paul Johnston, *Wittgenstein and Moral Philosophy* (London: Routledge and Kegan Paul, 1989).
5 Nigel Pleasants, "Wittgenstein, Ethics and Basic Moral Certainty," *Inquiry* 51, no. 3 (2008): 241–67, 242.
6 Stephen Mulhall, "Ethics in the Light of Wittgenstein," *Philosophical Papers* 31, no. 3 (2002): 293–321, 315. This interpretation can also be ascribed to Crary, Diamond, Iczkovits, and Johnston.
7 Pleasants, "Wittgenstein, Ethics and Basic Moral Certainty," 242. See also Judith Lichtenberg, "Moral Certainty," *Philosophy* 69, no. 268 (1994): 181–204, 184; Julia Hermann, *On Moral Certainty, Justification and Practice: A Wittgensteinian Perspective* (Basingstoke: Palgrave Macmillan, 2015), 6–8.
8 An example of the former approach is Mario Brandhorst, "Correspondence to Reality in Ethics," *Philosophical Investigations* 38, no. 3 (2015): 227–50.
9 See Hermann, *On Moral Certainty*, 30–2. I use "practice" and "language-game" interchangeably.
10 See Wittgenstein, *Philosophical Investigations*, § 23.
11 Ludwig Wittgenstein, *Remarks on the Foundations of Mathematics*, trans. G. E. M. Anscombe, ed. G.H. von Wright et al., third, revised and reset ed. (Oxford: Basil Blackwell, 1978), part V, 1; emphasis in original.
12 Russell B. Goodman, "Wittgenstein and Ethics," *Metaphilosophy* 13, no. 2 (1982): 138–48, 141.
13 For this view see also Hermann, *On Moral Certainty*, 111–13. For Wittgenstein's view that *epistemic* language-games are grounded in action see ibid., 58–66.
14 Ludwig Wittgenstein, "Cause and Effect: Intuitive Awareness," in *Philosophical Occasions 1912-1951*, ed. James C. Klagge and Alfred Nordmann (Indianapolis and Cambridge: Hackett Publishing Company, 1993), 370–426, 395.
15 Ludwig Wittgenstein, *Zettel*, trans. G. E. M. Anscombe and G. H. von Wright, ed. G. E. M. Anscombe and Georg Henrik von Wright, 2nd ed. (Oxford: Blackwell, 1981), 540.
16 Wittgenstein, "Cause and Effect," 381.
17 I owe this thesis to Wouter Kalf.
18 Melis Erdur, "Moral Realism and the Incompletability of Morality," *Journal of Value Inquiry* 52, no. 2 (2018): 227–37, 227.

19 See, for example, David Enoch, *Taking Morality Seriously: A Defense of Robust Realism* (Oxford: Oxford University Press, 2011); Russ Shafer-Landau, *Moral Realism: A Defence* (New York: Oxford University Press, 2003). On a broader understanding of "moral realism," moral realists do not necessarily have to claim that moral facts are mind-independent. The group of moral realists who endorse mind-independence is sometimes called "robust realists." See Enoch, *Taking Morality Seriously*.
20 See Jeroen Hopster, "Two Accounts of Moral Objectivity: From Attitude-Independence to Standpoint-Invariance," *Ethical Theory and Moral Practice* 20 (2017): 763–80, 764.
21 See ibid., 765–6. Street said this explicitly during a discussion at the conference "Objectivity in Ethics" at Utrecht University in 2016.
22 Benjamin De Mesel, "Wittgenstein and Objectivity in Ethics: A Reply to Brandhorst," *Philosophical Investigations* 40, no. 1 (2017): 40–63, 52.
23 See ibid. In section 3.3, I explain why we cannot transcend our personal standpoint.
24 See Arthur Ripstein, "Questionable Objectivity," *Noûs* 27, no. 3 (1993): 355–72, 359 and 363.
25 De Mesel, "Wittgenstein and Objectivity in Ethics," fn. 74.
26 Throughout the chapter, I refer to "the Wittgensteinian moral philosopher" or "the Wittgensteinian," although as explained earlier there are different Wittgensteinian perspectives and consequently different kinds of Wittgensteinian moral philosophers, a particular one of which is speaking here.
27 Hopster, "Two Accounts of Moral Objectivity," 769.
28 He refers, for instance, to Geoffrey P. Goodwin and John M. Darley, "Why Are Some Moral Beliefs Perceived to be More Objective than Others?" *Journal of Experimental Social Psychology* 48 (2012): 250–6.
29 Hopster, "Two Accounts of Moral Objectivity," 765 and 773.
30 Ibid., 770.
31 Hopster himself does not call the realist notion "Platonist."
32 De Mesel, "Wittgenstein and Objectivity in Ethics," 52.
33 I thank Benjamin De Mesel for drawing my attention to this point.
34 Hopster, "Two Accounts of Moral Objectivity," 778.
35 Ripstein, "Questionable Objectivity," 358.
36 Cf. ibid., 357 and 361.
37 Ibid., 358.
38 Ibid.
39 Ibid., 367.
40 Ibid., 361.
41 Cf. De Mesel, "Wittgenstein and Objectivity in Ethics," 48.

42 See Ripstein, "Questionable Objectivity," 362.
43 Ibid., 358.
44 Ibid.
45 Ibid.
46 Ibid., 359.
47 Cf. ibid., 360.
48 Ibid.
49 See ibid., 359.
50 De Mesel, "Wittgenstein and Objectivity in Ethics," 49.
51 Ibid. Another example of a "Wittgensteinian" conception of moral objectivity is Alice Crary, *Beyond Moral Judgment* (Cambridge, MA: Harvard University Press, 2007).
52 De Mesel, "Wittgenstein and Objectivity in Ethics," 52. See also Ripstein, "Questionable Objectivity," 356.
53 Hopster, "Two Accounts of Moral Objectivity," 773; emphasis in original.
54 Ibid., 771.
55 Street, "In Defense of Future Tuesday Indifference," 273.
56 Derek Parfit, *Reasons and Persons* (Oxford: Oxford University Press, 1984), 124.
57 Allan Gibbard, *Wise Choices, Apt Feelings* (Cambridge, MA: Harvard University Press, 1990), 171.
58 Allan Gibbard, "Morality as Consistency in Living: Korsgaard's Kantian Lectures," *Ethics* 110 (1999): 140–64, 145.
59 Street, "In Defense of Future Tuesday Indifference," 273.
60 Normative realism is a broader category than moral realism.
61 Ibid., 275.
62 Proponents of an attitude-independent conception include Ronald Dworkin, "Objectivity and Truth: You'd Better Believe It," *Philosophy & Public Affairs* 25 (1996): 87–139; David Enoch, "An Outline of an Argument for Robust Metanormative Realism," in *Oxford Studies in Metaethics*, vol. 2, ed. Russ Shafer-Landau (Oxford: Clarendon Press, 2007), 21–50. See Street, "In Defense of Future Tuesday Indifference," fn. 9.
63 By the term "evaluative attitudes," Street refers to "an agent's values, desires, states of approval and disapproval, unreflective evaluative tendencies, and consciously and unconsciously held normative judgments" (Street, "In Defense of Future Tuesday Indifference," fn. 8).
64 Sharon Street, "Objectivity and Truth: You'd Better Rethink It," in *Oxford Studies in Metaethics*, vol. 11, ed. Russ Shafer-Landau (Oxford: Clarendon Press, 2016), 293–334, 296.
65 In the older one of the two papers by Street to which I am referring in this section, Street uses the attitude-independent/attitude-dependent terminology and not the

realism/anti-realism terminology because the debate she is interested in "may be viewed as a substantive normative debate in which expressivists such as Blackburn and Gibbard endorse an attitude-independent view" (Street, "In Defense of Future Tuesday Indifference," fn. 9).

66 Street, "Objectivity and Truth," 296. Kantian anti-realists deny the possibility of such a character, but for reasons of space I shall leave that position aside here.
67 See ibid., 294.
68 Street, "In Defense of Future Tuesday Indifference," 274.
69 Ibid.
70 Very recently, some metaethicists have developed more nuanced views. See the recent literature on metaethical grounding, for example, Enoch, "How Principles Ground," in *Oxford Studies in Metaethics*, vol. 14, ed. Russ Shafer-Landau (Oxford: Clarendon Press, 2019). These metaethicists do not accept the strong dichotomy. I thank Jeroen Hopster for pointing this out to me.
71 Ibid., 281.
72 Hopster, "Two Accounts of Moral Objectivity," 775; emphasis in original.
73 I owe this possible response to Benjamin De Mesel.
74 See Hermann, *On Moral Certainty*, 184.
75 Wittgenstein, *Philosophical Investigations*, § 219; emphasis in original.
76 Meredith Williams, *Wittgenstein, Mind and Meaning* (London: Routledge, 1999), 198.
77 See Hermann, *On Moral Certainty*, and idem, "Moral Certainty," in *International Encyclopedia of Ethics* (Oxford: Wiley-Blackwell, 2018). See also Pleasants, "Wittgenstein, Ethics and Basic Moral Certainty," and idem, "Wittgenstein and Basic Moral Certainty," *Philosophia* 37, no. 4 (2009): 669–79.
78 Wittgenstein, *Philosophical Investigations*, § 217.
79 Street, "In Defense of Future Tuesday Indifference," 292.
80 Ibid.; emphasis in original.
81 Ibid., 281. ICE does not stand for the German high-speed train, but for "ideally coherent eccentrics."
82 Ibid.
83 See Barry Stroud, "Wittgenstein and Logical Necessity," *The Philosophical Review* 74, no. 4 (1965): 504–18, 518.
84 See Charles Larmore, *The Autonomy of Morality* (Cambridge and New York: Cambridge University Press, 2008), 88.
85 For a critique of the question "Why be moral?" see also Hermann, *On Moral Certainty*, 157–60.
86 Ibid., 279.
87 Wittgenstein, *Remarks on the Foundations of Mathematics*, part I, § 150.
88 Street, "In Defense of Future Tuesday Indifference," 279.

89 Simon Kirchin, *Metaethics* (Basingstoke: Palgrave Macmillan, 2012), 181.
90 See, for example, Richard Joyce, *The Evolution of Morality* (Cambridge, MA: MIT Press, 2006), 5; Wouter Kalf, *Moral Error Theory* (Basingstoke: Palgrave Macmillan, 2018); John Mackie, *Ethics* (Harmondsworth: Penguin, 1977). The most famous moral error theorist is John Mackie.
91 I owe the formulation of the three premises to Wouter Kalf.
92 I developed these objections in a dialogue with Wouter Kalf.
93 Stroud, "Wittgenstein and Logical Necessity," 504–18, 518.
94 Ibid.
95 I am grateful to Benjamin De Mesel for drawing my attention to the similarities between the arguments of Strawson and Stroud.
96 Peter F. Strawson, "Freedom and Resentment," in *Free Will*, ed. Gary Watson, 2nd ed. (Oxford and New York: Oxford University Press, 2003), 72–93.
97 Ibid., 91.
98 Ibid., fn. 7.
99 See, for example, William Fitzpatrick, "Why There Is No Darwinian Dilemma for Ethical Naturalism," in *Challenges to Moral and Religious Belief: Disagreement and Evolution*, ed. Michael Bergmann and Patrick Kain (Oxford: Oxford University Press, 2014), 237–55; Philip Kitcher, *The Ethical Project* (Cambridge, MA and London: Harvard University Press, 2011).
100 See, for example, John Ladd (ed.), *Ethical Relativism* (Belmont, CA: Wadsworth Publishing Company, 1973).
101 See Allen Buchanan and Russell Powell, "The Limits of Evolutionary Explanations of Morality and their Implications for Moral Progress," *Ethics* 126, no. 1 (2015): 37–67; idem, "Toward a Naturalistic Theory of Moral Progress," *Ethics* 126, no. 4 (2016): 983–1014; Kitcher, *The Ethical Project*; Michael Tomasello, *A Natural History of Human Morality* (Cambridge, MA: Harvard University Press, 2016).
102 Brandhorst, "Correspondence to Reality in Ethics," 231.
103 Ibid. As clarified above, unlike Brandhorst, I am not in the business of figuring out what the later Wittgenstein's actual view on these matters was, but what view would fit into his philosophy.
104 Cf. Ursula Wolf, "Vom moralischen Sollen," in *Moral und Sanktion. Eine Kontroverse über die Autorität moralischer Normen*, ed. Eva Buddeberg and Achim Vesper (Frankfurt and New York: Campus, 2013), 35–49, 43–4.
105 See Julia Hermann, "Die Praxis als Quelle moralischer Normativität," in *Moral und Sanktion: Eine Kontroverse über die Autorität moralischer Normen*, ed. Eva Buddeberg and Achim Vesper (Frankfurt and New York: Campus, 2013), 137–66.
106 See Eva Buddeberg and Achim Vesper (eds.), *Moral und Sanktion: Eine Kontroverse über die Autorität moralischer Normen* (Frankfurt and New York: Campus, 2013). An example of such a view is Peter Stemmer, *Handeln zugunsten anderer. Eine*

moralphilosophische Untersuchung (Berlin and New York: De Gruyter, 2000). Stemmer takes the moral "must" (with which he replaces the moral ought) to be constituted solely by sanctions (Ibid., 101).

107 For the distinction between external and internal sanctions, see John Stuart Mill, "*Utilitarianism*," in *Collected Works of John Stuart Mill*, 33 vols., ed. John M. Robson (Toronto: University of Toronto Press, 1965–91), vol. X, Chapter 3.

108 See Elliot Turiel, *The Development of Social Knowledge: Morality and Convention* (Cambridge and New York: Cambridge University Press, 1983).

109 See ibid.

110 Ibid., 279.

111 I am indebted to Benjamin De Mesel and Jeroen Hopster for their helpful comments on an earlier version of this chapter. I also thank the participants of the conference *Doing Ethics after Wittgenstein* (University of Zürich and Collegium Helveticum, 2016) and the participants of the *Practical Philosophy Colloquium* at Utrecht University for their critical comments and questions. Finally, I gratefully acknowledge financial support from the Netherlands Organisation for Scientific Research.

Work Cited

Brandhorst, Mario, "Correspondence to Reality in Ethics," *Philosophical Investigations* 38, no. 3 (2015): 227–50.

Buchanan, Allen, and Rusell Powell, "The Limits of Evolutionary Explanations of Morality and their Implications for Moral Progress," *Ethics* 126, no. 1 (2015): 37–67.

Buchanan, Allen, and Rusell Powell, "Toward a Naturalistic Theory of Moral Progress," *Ethics* 126, no. 4 (2016): 983–1014.

Buddeberg, Eva, and A. Vesper (eds.), *Moral und Sanktion: Eine Kontroverse über die Autorität moralischer Normen*, Frankfurt and New York: Campus, 2013.

Crary, Alice, *Beyond Moral Judgment*, Cambridge, MA: Harvard University Press, 2007.

De Mesel, Benjamin, "Wittgenstein and Objectivity in Ethics: A Reply to Brandhorst," *Philosophical Investigations* 40, no. 1 (2017): 40–63.

De Mesel, Benjamin, "Are Moral Judgments Semantically Uniform? A Wittgensteinian Approach to the Cognitivism – Non-Cognitivism Debate," in Oskari Kuusela and Benjamin De Mesel (eds.), *Ethics in the Wake of Wittgenstein*, 126–48, London: Routledge, 2019.

Diamond, Cora, "Truth in Ethics: Williams and Wiggins," in Oskari Kuusela and Benjamin De Mesel (eds.), *Ethics in the Wake of Wittgenstein*, London: Routledge, 2019.

Dworkin, Ronald, "Objectivity and Truth: You'd Better Believe It," *Philosophy & Public Affairs* 25 (1996): 87–139.

Enoch, David, "An Outline of an Argument for Robust Metanormative Realism," in Russ Shafer-Landau (ed.), *Oxford Studies in Metaethics*, vol. 2, 21–50, Oxford: Clarendon Press, 2007.

Enoch, David, *Taking Morality Seriously: A Defense of Robust Realism*, Oxford: Oxford University Press, 2011.

Enoch, David, "How Principles Ground," in Russ Shafer-Landau (ed.), *Oxford Studies in Metaethics*, vol. 14, Oxford: Clarendon Press, 2019.

Erdur, Melis, "Moral Realism and the Incompletability of Morality," *Journal of Value Inquiry* 52, no. 2 (2018): 227–37.

Fitzpatrick, William, "Why There Is No Darwinian Dilemma for Ethical Naturalism," in Michael Bergmann and Patrick Kain (eds.), *Challenges to Moral and Religious Belief: Disagreement and Evolution*, 237–55, Oxford: Oxford University Press, 2014.

Gibbard, Allan, *Wise Choices, Apt Feelings*, Cambridge, MA: Harvard University Press, 1990.

Gibbard, Allan, "Morality as Consistency in Living: Korsgaard's Kantian Lectures," *Ethics* 110 (1999): 140–64.

Goodman, Russell B., "Wittgenstein and Ethics," *Metaphilosophy* 13, no. 2 (1982): 138–48.

Goodwin, Geoffrey P., and John M. Darley, "Why Are Some Moral Beliefs Perceived to be More Objective than Others?," *Journal of Experimental Social Psychology* 48 (2012): 250–6.

Hermann, Julia, "Die Praxis als Quelle moralischer Normativität," in Eva Buddeberg and Achim Vesper (eds.), *Moral und Sanktion. Eine Kontroverse über die Autorität moralischer Normen*, 137–66, Frankfurt and New York: Campus, 2013.

Hermann, Julia, *On Moral Certainty, Justification and Practice: A Wittgensteinian Perspective*, Basingstoke: Palgrave Macmillan, 2015.

Hermann, Julia, "Moral Certainty," in Hugh LaFollette (ed.), *International Encyclopedia of Ethics*, Oxford: Wiley-Blackwell, 2018.

Hopster, Jeroen, "Two Accounts of Moral Objectivity: From Attitude-Independence to Standpoint-Invariance," *Ethical Theory and Moral Practice* 20 (2017): 763–80.

Iczkovits, Yaniv, *Wittgenstein's Ethical Thought*, Basingstoke: Palgrave Macmillan, 2012.

Johnston, Paul, *Wittgenstein and Moral Philosophy*, London: Routledge and Kegan Paul, 1989.

Joyce, Richard, *The Evolution of Morality*, Cambridge, MA and London: MIT Press, 2006.

Kalf, Wouter, *Moral Error Theory*, Basingstoke: Palgrave Macmillan, 2018.

Kirchin, Simon, *Metaethics*, Basingstoke: Palgrave Macmillan, 2012.

Kitcher, Philip, *The Ethical Project*, Cambridge, MA and London: Harvard University Press, 2011.

Ladd, John (ed.), *Ethical Relativism*, Belmont, CA: Wadsworth Publishing Company, 1973.

Larmore, Charles, *The Autonomy of Morality*, Cambridge and New York: Cambridge University Press, 2008.

Lichtenberg, Judith, "Moral Certainty," *Philosophy* 69, no. 268 (1994): 181–204.
Mackie, John L., *Ethics: Inventing Right and Wrong*, Harmondsworth: Penguin 1977.
Mill, John Stuart, "*Utilitarianism*," in John Robson (ed.), *Collected Works of John Stuart Mill*, 33 vols., vol. X, Toronto: University of Toronto Press, 1965–91.
Mulhall, Stephen, "Ethics in the Light of Wittgenstein," *Philosophical Papers* 31, no. 3 (2002): 293–321.
Parfit, Derek, *Reasons and Persons*, Oxford: Oxford University Press, 1984.
Pleasants, Nigel, "Wittgenstein, Ethics and Basic Moral Certainty," *Inquiry* 51, no. 3 (2008): 241–67.
Pleasants, Nigel, "Wittgenstein and Basic Moral Certainty," *Philosophia* 37 (2009): 669–79.
Ripstein, Arthur, "Questionable Objectivity," *Noûs* 27, no. 3 (1993): 355–72.
Shafer-Landau, Russ, *Moral Realism: A Defense*, Oxford: Oxford University Press, 2003.
Stemmer, Peter, *Handeln zugunsten anderer. Eine moralphilosophische Untersuchung*, Berlin and New York: de Gruyter, 2000.
Strawson, Peter F., "Freedom and Resentment," in Gary Watson (ed.), *Free Will*, 2nd ed., 72–93, Oxford and New York: Oxford University Press, 2003.
Street, Sharon, "In Defense of Future Tuesday Indifference: Ideally Coherent Eccentrics and the Contingency of What Matters," *Philosophical Issues* 19 (2009): 273–98.
Street, Sharon, "Objectivity and Truth: You'd Better Rethink It," in Russ Shafer-Landau (ed.), *Oxford Studies in Metaethics*, vol. 11, 293–334, Oxford: Clarendon Press, 2016.
Stroud, Barry, "Wittgenstein and Logical Necessity," *The Philosophical Review* 74, no. 4 (1965): 504–18.
Tomasello, Michael, *A Natural History of Human Morality*, Cambridge, MA: Harvard University Press, 2016.
Turiel, Elliot, *The Development of Social Knowledge: Morality and Convention*, Cambridge and New York: Cambridge University Press, 1983.
Williams, Meredith, *Wittgenstein, Mind and Meaning*, London: Routledge, 1999.
Wittgenstein, Ludwig, *Philosophical Investigations*, trans. Gertrude E. M. Anscombe, 3rd ed., Oxford: Basil Blackwell, 1968.
Wittgenstein, Ludwig, *Remarks on the Foundations of Mathematics*, trans. Gertrude E. M. Anscombe, ed. Georg H. von Wright et al., 3rd revised and reset ed., Oxford: Blackwell, 1978.
Wittgenstein, Ludwig, *Zettel*, trans. Gertrude E. M. Anscombe and Georg H. von Wright, ed. G. E. M. Anscombe and G. H. von Wright, 2nd ed., Oxford: Blackwell, 1981.
Wittgenstein, Ludwig, "Cause and Effect: Intuitive Awareness," in James C. Klagge and Alfred Nordmann (eds.), *Philosophical Occasions 1912–1951*, 370–426, Indianapolis and Cambridge: Hackett Publishing Company, 1993.
Wolf, Ursula, "Vom moralischen Sollen," in Eva Buddeberg and Achim Vesper (eds.), *Moral und Sanktion. Eine Kontroverse über die Autorität moralischer Normen*, 35–49, Frankfurt and New York: Campus, 2013.

5

Wittgensteinian Anti-Anti-Realism
One "Anti" Too Many?

Hans-Johann Glock

Ethics occupies a peculiar role in Wittgenstein's thinking. He attached overarching personal importance to questions of moral value. Furthermore, he sought to infuse his own life, that of his friends, and, occasionally, of society as a whole with spiritual value, making it better both morally and aesthetically. Yet his written and recorded discussions of ethics are relatively brief and often obscure. Nevertheless, they have had a considerable influence both on Wittgenstein scholarship and Wittgensteinian philosophy.

Wittgenstein's personal moral outlook was contemplative and egocentric. In both respects it was shaped by Schopenhauer and by Weininger's *Sex and Character*, which proclaimed that "logic and ethics are fundamentally the same, they are no more than duty to oneself."[1] Striving for logical clarity is a moral obligation, but one owed to oneself rather than to others. In memoirs, some of his friends report that Wittgenstein was often oblivious to the effect that his actions—including those ostensibly directed against himself, such as his famous confessions—might have on those around him.[2] Throughout his life, Wittgenstein struggled against the temptations of philosophical solipsism, a position which Schopenhauer referred to as "theoretical egoism." By the same token, it is only mild hyperbole to characterize Wittgenstein's personal attitude to others as *practical solipsism*—a tendency to ignore the perspective of others in one's interactions with them. As we turn from Wittgenstein's personal character to his (first-order) moral and political convictions, what is on offer constitutes a mixed blessing. During the 1920s and 1930s, he expressed anti-Semitic views; and throughout his life he was prone to misogynist sentiments. Wittgenstein was rightly sceptical of certain aspects of the twentieth-century belief in progress. Unfortunately, his political opinions were marred by a predilection for dogmatic-*cum*-authoritarian ideologies—Bolshevism, Catholicism—which place individual liberty and well-being below the pursuit of "higher" goals.[3] To be fair, many of these objectionable remarks were made in conversation, and none of them were intended for publication. One moral remains nonetheless. As a philosophical dialectician, Wittgenstein was a genius. But as a moral mentor and cultural critic he was a loose cannon.[4]

Some of the specific moral and political views propounded by Aristotle, Kant, Nietzsche, and Marx—to mention just a few—were profoundly problematic, even by the standards of their times. Nevertheless these thinkers made substantive contributions to our understanding of morality and politics. Something similar may hold for Wittgenstein. By contrast to his ethical, cultural, and political convictions, his reflections on language and the nature of philosophy have had a strong, albeit intermittent, influence on analytic moral philosophy, in particular on meta-ethics. However, this influence is not just diffuse, it points in opposite directions. In two respects, at least, he inspired views that seem to be irreconcilable. The first is the meta-philosophical question of what contribution philosophy can make to moral thought. The second is the meta-ethical question of what semantic and epistemic status moral concepts, judgements, and statements have. My article explores both of these interconnected legacies historically, exegetically, and substantively. It starts out by explaining how Wittgenstein came to play a role both in the reduction of moral philosophy to meta-ethics on the one hand, the revival of normative ethics on the other. In the sequel it deals at much greater length with the fact that he has been claimed both by anti-realist-*cum*-non-cognitivist and by realist-*cum*-cognitivist positions. Here the main focus will be on so-called "anti-anti-realism" (AAR). This position was conceived by John McDowell and Sabina Lovibond in the 1980s and criticized by Simon Blackburn. It is well worth revisiting, however. First, it is the most explicit and radical version of Wittgensteinian realism concerning ethics. Secondly, it raises issues central to the current revival of pragmatism and anti-representationalism. AAR challenges the contrast drawn by "local" expressivists[5] between propositions that are in the business of representing reality and capturing *bona fide* facts—notably those of science—and propositions that are not, ethical propositions constituting a paradigmatic case. To that extent, AAR is aligned with "global" expressivists,[6] the important difference being that AAR regards all propositions as primarily descriptive or factual. Finally, while AAR fails both exegetically and philosophically, its insights and errors provide crucial lessons for any attempt to use Wittgenstein's ideas in striking the delicate balance between realism and anti-realism concerning ethics.

1 Wittgenstein's Conception of Philosophy and the Rise and Fall of Meta-Ethics

Both the early and the later Wittgenstein deny that philosophy has the task of describing or explaining reality. It does not furnish metaphysical insights into a special kind of reality or *de re* essences—as traditional philosophy and contemporary essentialism maintain. Nor does it add to our empirical knowledge about reality, reducing to a part or continuation of natural science, as Quinean naturalism has it. Legitimate philosophy, according to Wittgenstein, is a *second-order* enterprise. It reflects on the logical or conceptual structures embodied in language.

For the early Wittgenstein, legitimate philosophy boils down to logic. Unlike science, it does not itself represent any kind of reality. Instead, it reflects on the (quasi-transcendental) preconditions of representing reality. Philosophy is the "logical clarification of thought." It investigates the nature and limits of *thought*, because it is in thought that we represent reality. Echoing Kant, the *Tractatus* aims to draw the bounds between legitimate discourse, which represents reality, and illegitimate speculation—notably metaphysics (4.11ff.).[7] At the same time, it gives a linguistic twist to the Kantian tale. Language is not just a secondary manifestation of something non-linguistic. For thoughts are neither mental processes nor abstract entities, but themselves propositions (*Sätze*), sentential signs which have been projected onto reality (3.5f.).[8] Thoughts can be completely expressed in language, and philosophy can establish the limits and preconditions of thought by establishing the limits and preconditions of the *linguistic expression of thought*. Indeed, these limits *must* be drawn in language. They cannot be drawn by propositions talking about both sides of the limit. By definition, such propositions would have to be about things that cannot be thought about and thereby transcend the bounds of sense. The limits of thought can only be drawn *from the inside*, namely by delineating the "rules of logical grammar" or "logical syntax" (Preface, 3.32–3.325). These rules determine whether a combination of signs is meaningful, that is, capable of representing reality either truly or falsely. What lies beyond these limits is not unknowable things in themselves, as in Kant, but only nonsensical combinations of signs. Proper philosophy is the "critique of language." It cannot be a doctrine, since there are no philosophical propositions. It is an *activity*, namely of *logical analysis*. Without propounding any propositions of its own, philosophy clarifies the logical form of the meaningful propositions of science by translating them into an ideal notation. This positive task is complemented by the negative task of demonstrating that the propositions of metaphysics violate the rules of logical syntax since they resist such translation.

The *Tractatus*, as well as conversations with Wittgenstein during his so-called transition period, profoundly influenced the logical positivists of the Vienna Circle. They adopted a verificationist "criterion of meaningfulness": only those propositions are "cognitively meaningful" which are capable of being verified or falsified. On the basis of this criterion, they condemned metaphysics as meaningless, because it is neither *a posteriori*—like empirical science—nor analytic—like logic and mathematics. Metaphysical pronouncements are vacuous: they neither make statements of fact that can ultimately be verified by sensory experience; nor do they explicate the meaning of words or propositions. Legitimate philosophy boils down to what Rudolf Carnap called "the logic of science."[9] Its sole task is the logico-linguistic analysis of those propositions which alone are strictly speaking meaningful, namely those of science.

Wittgenstein himself resented the way in which the logical positivists invoked his *Tractatus* in support of their "scientific world view."[10] Their scientism extolled (natural) science as the epitome of rationality. By contrast, he was firmly convinced of the superiority of the artistic spirit and religious point of view. As regards treating metaphysics as nonsensical, however, he sold the ticket on which they travelled. The main difference is the saying/showing distinction, which the logical positivists ignored. Wittgenstein had maintained that there are metaphysical truths about the logical structure which language and the world must share. At the same time, these truths cannot be expressed in meaningful propositions; they show themselves in non-metaphysical, empirical propositions properly analyzed.

While the logical positivists assimilated the *Tractatus* by way of understanding and misunderstanding, Wittgenstein had substantially modified his views of language and philosophy. The latter retains its status as a critique of language, now under the label "grammatical investigations."[11] Unlike science, philosophy is concerned not with truth, or matters of fact, but with concepts or meaning. Philosophical problems are conceptual confusions which arise out of the distortion or misapprehension of words with which we are perfectly familiar outside philosophy. These problems should not be answered by constructing theories: instead, they need to be dissolved through describing the established non-philosophical use of the words concerned and contrasting it with their deviant use in philosophical theories. In abandoning the picture theory of the *Tractatus*, Wittgenstein recognized that meaningful language is not restricted to description, the representation of possible states of affairs. By the same token, unlike Carnap's logic of science, Wittgenstein's grammatical investigations are not confined to investigating the empirical propositions of science; they extends to *all forms of discourse*, including value judgements or statements of a moral and aesthetic kind.

Partly under Wittgenstein's influence, other analytic philosophers took a linguistic turn, while relaxing the restriction of logico-linguistic and conceptual analysis to scientific discourse. Both logical positivists like Ayer and conceptual analysts like Stevenson and Hare confined moral philosophy to "meta-ethics"—a second-order discipline which does not issue any moral claims but instead analyses moral concepts, judgements, and argument. "Ethics, as I conceive it, is the logical study of the language of morals."[12] H. L. A. Hart provided a comparable stimulus to legal and political theory.[13] He treated the philosophy of law as the analysis of legal discourse. In particular, he tried to avoid futile metaphysical disputes about the nature of obligations and rights through the analysis of legal concepts. And he was emphatic in tracing this method to Wittgenstein. What is common to these otherwise disparate theories is the conviction that practical philosophy remains *neutral* with respect to first-order, axiological or normative questions concerning moral or political values and obligations.

The idea that practical philosophy reduces to the analysis of value concepts and statements increasingly fell out of favour from the 1950s onwards. The reasons for this demotion of meta-ethics were highly diverse.[14] Curiously, Wittgenstein played a part not just in the exaltation of meta-ethics, but also in this demotion. In recent years, he has been invoked in support of the radical view that meta-ethics as standardly conceived is impossible, since ethics lacks a subject matter to begin with.[15] While I shall not discuss this proposal here, I have criticized some exegetical and meta-philosophical views on which it is based elsewhere.[16]

More distant and subliminal, yet also more important, is Wittgenstein's part in the *rehabilitation of normative ethics*. It has largely gone unnoticed that several trailblazers of this development in the 1950s and 1960s were directly or indirectly associated with Wittgenstein. These included G. H. von Wright on the one hand, the Oxford trio G. E. M Anscombe, Iris Murdoch, and Philippa Foot on the other.[17] Whereas the import of Wittgenstein's meta-philosophical outlook for the ascendancy of meta-ethics is easy to appreciate, this contrary influence is more difficult to fathom. This holds all the more since the aforementioned authors drew much more explicitly on other (in turn highly diverse) normative ethical outlooks, such as Aristotelianism, Thomism, or utilitarianism. Nevertheless, it stands to reason that Wittgenstein played a role. Part of the explanation lies in the fact that some of his explorations of *non-ethical concepts*—notably those concerning action, will, reason, and normativity—stimulated the kind of *moral psychology* on which the aforementioned authors drew in advocating normative views.[18]

A second part of the explanation is this. The later Wittgenstein adopted an anthropological approach to language, one which considers philosophically problematic terms and language-games within the wider context of human activity. This positively invites an anthropological perspective on ethics, in particular of a broadly Aristotelian kind. Wittgenstein did not go down that road himself. As we shall see, he was personally committed to a non-cognitivist and loosely speaking existentialist conception of morality. But it opened avenues for others, especially von Wright and Foot.

A final part of the explanation, I submit, concerns philosophical style and personality. Whatever its meta-philosophical merits, the reduction of moral philosophy to meta-ethics exuded an air of anodyne professionalism and detachment. This runs counter to the spirit that Wittgenstein bequeathed to his pupils, a spirit that he also projected through his work. Although his remarks appear officially inimical to philosophy issuing moral pronouncements, throughout his life he was driven by ethical and aesthetic attitudes and sentiments, and obsessed with the moral propriety of conduct—especially his own.[19] In order to translate this intense ethical passion into an explicit advocacy of moral values, all it took was casting doubt on the feasibility of drawing a hard and fast distinction between descriptive and non-descriptive uses of language, or, to put it in a more traditional fashion, on the time-honoured Humean distinction between is and ought, fact and value. It is at this juncture that the Janus-faced legacy of Wittgenstein to the *meta-philosophical* debate about the nature and scope of moral philosophy carries over into his equally ambivalent legacy for the *meta-ethical* debate about the status and role of moral concepts and statements.

2 Terminological-*cum*-Conceptual Prolegomena

Descriptivist conceptions of a form of discourse hold that the relevant statements aim at or have the function of describing some aspect of reality, that they are *truth-apt*, i.e. capable of being true or false. *Realist* conceptions of a form of discourse hold that these statements are indeed responsible to some type of objective reality or fact. *Cognitivist* conceptions hold that they are capable of embodying a type of knowledge, i.e. that we can know at least in principle whether these statements are true or false. The three positions are closely connected, without coinciding. One can be a descriptivist and realist without being a cognitivist. Thus one might hold that statements of a certain type are objectively true or false, while doubting our capacity to know which. One can also be a cognitivist without being a descriptivist and realist. Thus one might also hold that there are types of knowledge that do not concern matters of fact, e.g. because they are of a *sui generis* practical kind.

As regards (meta-)ethics, anti-descriptivism, anti-realism, and non-cognitivism often coincide. But one can be a moral sceptic. Furthermore, the Kantian vision of a special type of "practical" reason implies cognitivism without descriptivism and realism: moral statements are not strictly speaking descriptive or factual, yet can nonetheless be rational and an object of knowledge. Conversely, according to Mackie's "error theory,"[20] moral concepts and judgements are indeed descriptive or factual. The trouble, he avers, is that nothing corresponds to moral concepts in reality, which is purely physical. From this he draws the disconcerting conclusion that our moral judgements are all and sundry mistaken. According to Mackie, they fail to be true, because they presuppose the existence of an array of moral properties and facts.[21] But there simply is no such moral (aspect of) reality for moral statements to capture.

In meta-ethics and beyond, "cognitivism" often serves as a category which encompasses the metaphysical and the semantic positions that I have called, respectively, "realism" and "descriptivism." It is preferable in principle to reserve that term for a distinct epistemological stance, in line with its literal meaning. For better or worse, however, the authors I am concerned with do not distinguish systematically between descriptivism, realism, and cognitivism, under any heading. They tend to label their targets indiscriminately as anti-realism, non-cognitivism, projectivism, and subjectivism. For this reason, I shall for the most part follow the terminology with which these positions are commonly associated, drawing further distinctions only when necessary.

3 Wittgensteinian Anti-Realism

At first sight, Wittgenstein's remarks on ethics, such as they are, are totally at odds with realist and cognitivist accounts. His early discussions converge emphatically on at least one point: ethics and matters of value more generally *transcend linguistic expression*. Attempts to formulate ethical convictions do not just fail to capture facts or embody knowledge, they are downright *nonsensical*. According to the picture theory of the *Tractatus*, only the empirical propositions of science are meaningful, since they depict contingent states of affairs (truly or falsely). What Wittgenstein calls the "higher" (6.42, 6.432), all areas of *value*, share with the logical structures of language the fate of being *ineffable*; they cannot be said but only be shown. While everything factual is "accidental," ethics, aesthetics, and logic are linked by virtue of trying to express what could not be otherwise, the "preconditions of the world" (6.13, 6.421).[22] Whereas the logical structure of language is displayed by empirical propositions—provided that they have been properly analyzed—ethical value is *not even shown* by any empirical propositions, although it may be shown in actions, attitudes, or works of art.[23] Ethics is not just "transcendental" but "transcendent." Values "cannot lie *within* the world," which "itself is neither good nor evil"; their "bearer" is a Schopenhauerian metaphysical *Will* outside the world (6.41–3).[24]

Wittgenstein's most sustained treatment of moral philosophy is "A Lecture on Ethics" of 1929, which elaborates the idea that ethics is ineffable. It expands Moore's definition of ethics as the enquiry into what is good, to accommodate everything that has value and concerns the meaning of life, including aesthetics.[25] Again following Moore, Wittgenstein distinguishes a trivial or *relative*, from an ethical or *absolute* sense of terms of appreciation. The relative sense simply implies satisfaction of certain standards, as in "You play tennis well." By contrast, the absolute sense is elusive, since no factual statement can ever be or imply an absolute judgement of value such as "You ought to behave decently" or "Torture is always wrong."

Wittgenstein radicalizes Moore's claim that "good" is indefinable: ethics is deep precisely because it inevitably transgresses the limits of language. Fortunately, this is quite wrong. While judgements of absolute value like "One ought to keep promises" may not be factual, they are neither nonsensical nor mystifying in the way Wittgenstein envisages. They have a perfectly intelligible and indeed humdrum use, notably in educating children and enforcing codes of conduct that human societies depend on. Indeed, far from being based on scrutinizing the role of ethics in human life, Wittgenstein's insistence on the ineffable nature of ethics is explicitly stipulative: "I would reject any significant description (of ethics) *ab initio*, on the ground of its significance." Behind this stipulation lies the conviction that "words will only express facts," which restricts significance to factual description.[26]

This credo—a consequence of the picture theory—is later abandoned. It may be "impossible" to describe what ethical (and aesthetic) appreciation consists in. The reason is not the ineffability of anything other than empirical facts, however. Instead, the obstacles are two-fold. First, many ethical notions are family resemblance concepts which defy definition in terms of necessary and sufficient conditions. Secondly, they are dependent on a wider *context*: we must focus not on the appearance of ethical terms and statements, which resembles that of other words, but on their specific role within our whole culture.[27] The ethical *shows* itself no longer in the attitudes of a lonely self, but in social patterns of action. As a result, sibylline pronouncements on the indefinability of ethical terms and the illegitimacy of ethical judgements give way to (underdeveloped) investigations into their use.[28]

The early Wittgenstein's contrast between factual statements and the allegedly futile attempts to express ethical views, along with his "middle" verificationist ideas, stimulated the emotivism of the logical positivists.[29] Ethical statements are neither synthetic statements of fact nor analytic. Like metaphysical statements, therefore, they lack cognitive or factual meaning. Instead they express the speaker's sentiments of approval or disapproval.

Originally, Wittgenstein's scattered remarks about ethics were familiar only to a select group of disciples and friends. They came to the attention of a wider philosophical public only from the 1960s onwards. As a result, they had little direct impact on the rise of non-cognitivist positions in meta-ethics. At the same time, the general stress that the later Wittgenstein placed on non-descriptive uses of language was one among several sources of that development, another being Austin's attack on the "descriptive fallacy."[30] This holds especially of Stevenson, who was a student of Wittgenstein's in 1933. According to his emotivism,[31] ethical statements do not just express (dis-)approval of an action, but also serve to engender it in others. It also holds, to a lesser extent, of Hare's universal prescriptivism, according to which ethical statements are normative rather than descriptive or expressive, in that they issue prescriptions that the speaker regards as universalisable. The lesson they extracted was that not all uses of language are descriptive or fact-stating. More recently, Wittgenstein's views on language and human practice have influenced the "quasi-realism" of Simon Blackburn.[32] The additional lesson he extracted, following his conversion to pragmatism, was that successful discursive practices, including morality, are "alright," even if they are not fact-stating.

4 Wittgensteinian Realism

The lesson of Wittgenstein's meta-ethical reflections appears to be very much in line with the general gist of non-cognitivism and anti-realism (see section 7).

Nonetheless he has also inspired some forms of cognitivism and realism. His method of describing the use of philosophically troublesome expressions in a wider context was the major influence on the lose movement of conceptual analysis that dominated British philosophy in the 1950s and 1960s.[33] In applying this type of conceptual analysis to moral notions and statements, many of its practitioners formed a picture of moral discourse that differed significantly from that of Stevenson and Hare.

Many of the early critics of non-cognitivism were conceptual analysts more or less strongly indebted to Wittgenstein, at least as for the methodological advice of paying attention not just to isolated employment of moral terms but to their overall use in our discourse. On such grounds Peter Geach argued that non-cognitivism cannot do justice to the occurrence of moral statements in inferences, because the latter requires propositions that are *truth-apt*.[34] Foot and Warnock maintained that the sharp distinction between descriptive and prescriptive uses of language is untenable. Among the most pervasive moral concepts are "thick concepts" such as rudeness, concepts which include *both* descriptive *and* evaluative-*cum*-prescriptive elements. John Searle argued that by appeal to institutional facts it is after all possible to derive prescriptive from descriptive statements, an "ought" from an "is."[35] More recently, "moral particularism" has insisted that while there are no general moral principles, moral judgements concerning specific cases can be factual and evince knowledge. And this proposal has been backed by appeal to Wittgenstein's discussion of family resemblance and rule-following, among other things.[36]

Wittgenstein has also had an impact on the wider revival of intuitionism (especially in Britain), of which particularism is but a very particular manifestation. Intuitionism about morality was initiated by Moore's claim that good is a non-natural simple property, to which we have access by a kind of rational intuition (1903). It was subsequently developed by Prichard and Ross, who elaborated on the analogy between moral judgements on the one hand, perceptual judgements and the allegedly quasi-perceptual intuitions involved in mathematics on the other. By this token, moral judgements state the presence or absence of such non-natural properties and are based on something akin to perceptions. Taking up this idea, contemporary neo-intuitionists like McDowell and Wiggins explored similarities between moral and perceptual judgements and analogies between values and secondary qualities like colours. On that basis they urged a rethink of the non-cognitivist dichotomy of the subjective (expression, prescription) and the objective (description).[37]

5 Anti-Anti-Realism

AAR constitutes a branch of neo-intuitionism, but stands out by drawing most explicitly and extensively on Wittgenstein. It also stands out from many other realist positions inspired by Wittgenstein in that it invokes Wittgenstein's claims on particular topics—notably truth—rather than his method.

In the 1970s and 1980s Oxford philosophers like McDowell and Lovibond invoked Wittgenstein's philosophy of language against the still prevailing non-cognitivist / anti-realist mainstream. Although McDowell rarely appeals to the original intuitionists, his position squarely fits the bill. Moral requirements are "the virtuous person's distinctive way of viewing particular situations."[38] He combines this idea with the view that, from a Wittgensteinian perspective, all indicative sentences, including moral ones, make claims to truth.

McDowell grants that his position might be characterized as moral realism. Yet he prefers the cumbersome label "anti-anti-realism." His own rationale is that it brings out that his position is "more negative than positive" (ibid., viii). But it has the additional advantage of highlighting the fact that anti-anti-realism places moral value somewhere *between* the subjective and the objective. Moral values, according to McDowell, do not "belong, mysteriously, in a reality that is wholly independent of our subjectivity and set over against it" (ibid., 159). He tries to steer a middle course between what he takes to be the Scylla of anti-realism (subjectivism, projectivism) about value and the Charybdis of a blunt realism that presupposes a dubious ontology of moral facts.

Under the influence of McDowell and Wiggins, Lovibond developed this idea at greater length in her wide-ranging and stimulating *Realism and Imagination in Ethics*. She propounded a "moral realism derived from the later philosophy of Wittgenstein."[39] But at the time her position was also known as "anti-non-cognitivism." The reasons for this terminology are two-fold. First, Lovibond's position revolves around a critique of non-cognitivism (or anti-realism), especially as promulgated by Hare and Mackie. Secondly, important parts of her book are devoted to defending intuitionism and neo-intuitionism against non-cognitivist objections.

There are interesting differences regarding intellectual background, style, and argument between McDowell and Lovibond.[40] At the same time, both concur on the following claims, which I take to be definitive of anti-anti-realism.

1. Ethical judgements and statements can be true or false.
2. Objective reality is not confined to what is captured by (natural) science.

3. Instead, it includes moral facts, i.e. ethical properties exist and are objective.
4. We have non-inferential knowledge of moral facts, which should be conceived on the model of perception.
5. Even features that are defined at least partly by reference to our understanding of them can be part of the fabric of the world.
6. The world contains features the appreciation of which has motivational force.

6 Moral Statements, Truth, and Assertion

Let us first consider the central tenet, around which the others revolve. (1.) maintains that moral statements, at least those in the *indicative mood* are truth-apt; and it extends this characterization to the moral beliefs or convictions which are expressed by moral statements. AAR backs (1.) by two further contentions, one concerning the ordinary use of "true" (OUT), the other concerning the grammar and logic of assertions (GLA).

(OUT): We *ordinarily call* moral judgements and statements true or false.
(GLA): Moral discourse displays the full *grammar and logic* of assertions.

In this context, Lovibond invokes a deflationary interpretation of Tarski's theory of truth. At the time, such an interpretation became increasingly popular, mainly in the wake of Davidson.[41] Furthermore, this form of deflationism had already been pressed into the service of moral realism by Mark Platts.[42] But in support of (1.), Lovibond also appeals at greater length to Wittgenstein. According to her, he confirms our "pre-reflective habit" of treating as "descriptive," or fact-stating all sentences which qualify by grammatical standards as propositions—i.e. all *sentences in the indicative mood*.

Now, OUT and GLA do indeed chime with Wittgenstein's general perspective on truth. Throughout his career, this perspective had a deflationary touch.[43] According to traditional views like the correspondence, coherence, consensus, or utilitarian theories, truth is a relation between a truth-bearer (judgement, proposition, belief) and a truth-maker. This relation could be one of correspondence to objects, reality, or facts; of coherence with other truth-bearers; of according with the consensus of an ideal community; or of promoting the achievements of our goals. Deflationism rejects the underlying idea that being true is a matter of standing in a relationship to a truth-maker. Instead, the essential features of truth are captured by truistic schemas like "It is true that p iff p."

The early Wittgenstein is standardly credited with a correspondence theory. Yet the official account of the *Tractatus* is an *obtainment theory of truth*. "If an elementary proposition is true, the state of affairs [it depicts] obtains (*besteht*): if an elementary proposition is false, the state of affairs does not obtain" (4.25; see 4.21). This account can be extended from the simple, elementary propositions postulated by the *Tractatus*, since all propositions with a sense are supposed to be constructed out of elementary propositions through truth-functional operations. The emerging obtainment theory of truth can be summarized as follows:

(OT) A proposition p is true iff the state of affairs it depicts obtains

OT divides the explanation of truth into two parts. One is a semantic explanation of what gives sense to (elementary) propositions, i.e. makes them truth-apt, namely a depicting relation to reality. For an elementary proposition to depict, no fact need correspond to it as a whole. But two things are required. First, something must correspond to its ultimate, atomic elements. There must be a one-to-one correlation between these elements—its constituent "names"—and the atomic elements of the situation it depicts—the "objects." Second, it must be determined what relationships between the names depict what relationship between things. "In a proposition a situation is, as it were, assembled by way of experiment" (4.031; see 2.1–2.15, 4.01–4.1).

The other part of the explanation is a *deflationary* account of the *agreement* between what a sentence says or depicts—that p and what is the case iff it is true—that p. "A proposition is true if things are as we say they are by using it" (4.062; see *Notebooks 1914–16*, 9, 113).

Unlike the early Wittgenstein, the later Wittgenstein is widely associated with deflationism. Rightly so. For he is committed to the disquotational equivalence

(DE) "'p' is true = p."

"For what does it mean, a sentence 'is true'? 'p' is true = p. (This is the answer)."[44]

But this later deflationism arose naturally out of the earlier OT. All it took were two steps:

- dropping the picture theory of sense and its attendant metaphysics of logical atomism;
- explicitly deflating the idea of agreement.

Both steps are nicely epitomized by a passage Wittgenstein dictated to Waismann in the 1930s.

> The question "What is truth?" always has a certain nimbus in logic. One imagines that the answer to it must give us information about the relation of thought to reality. One then says: Truth is the agreement of the thought with its object. To the question what the term "agreement" here means, one answers: Well, that means that the sentence p is true if the state of affairs it signifies obtains. But one sees how little is achieved by this as soon as one expresses oneself a bit more precisely. Suppose I say that it will rain tomorrow. What is the state of affairs signified by this sentence? That it will rain tomorrow. That is, in reply we get the sentence itself or some synonymous transformation of the sentence. Hence this rule holds: The expression "the state of affairs signified by p" can be replaced by p. If the words "true" and "state of affairs" are eliminated from the explanation of the former, it reads: p if p. In reality I have through this explanation made a contribution to the grammar of the word "true."[45]

Wittgenstein's later deflationism calls for three comments.

i. DE ascribes truth to interpreted sentences, i.e. to symbols rather than mere signs in the terminology of the *Tractatus*.
ii. DE purports to provide a *complete* explanation of the notion of truth.
iii. "'p' is true" and " p" are supposed to have the *same sense*.

The last two features are sticky. (ii) ignores that "true" has a distinctive use in confirming what has been said. And (iii) is mistaken because understanding "'p' is true" requires grasp of additional concepts, notably that of a truth-bearer. Although both involve the same sentence in the indicative, there is a difference between saying what is so—*p*—and saying what is true, namely (the proposition) that *p*.[46]

7 Wittgenstein's Deflationism and AAR

Such flaws notwithstanding, DIS appears to lend succour to OUT and GLA, and thereby to AAR. For it applies indistinctively to *all indicative sentences*. For instance, (DE) yields not just "'Grass is green' is true = Grass is green," but equally "'Torture is wrong' is true = Torture is wrong." It thereby prevents the anti-realist from using the notion of truth as a peg on which to hang her special treatment of moral statements. If truth is not a matter of correspondence to reality but captured by this trivial scheme, then qualms about the reference and truth-aptness of moral statements may seem to evaporate.

But this is not the end of the story. Ramsey picked up his well-known version of deflationism from the early Wittgenstein. As he acutely noted, according to deflationism there is no separate problem "as to the nature of truth and falsehood." At the same time, however, there remains a hairy problem "as to the nature of judgement or assertion."[47] Rephrased in terms more congenial to the later Wittgenstein: while deflationism does away with problems concerning "true" and its cognates, it does not answer the question of what kind of meaning or role different types of truth-apt speech-acts or statements possess. More specifically, it does not settle the issue of whether "Torture is wrong" *and thereby* "'Torture is wrong' is true" incur semantic or ontological commitments that go beyond or are distinct from those incurred by "Grass is green" and "'Grass is green' is true."

This has decisive implications. AAR notwithstanding, deflationism is *not* committed to the conclusion that all propositions that can be called "true" or "false" have *the same semantic status*. It is compatible with insisting that there are "grammatical" differences between moral assertions or judgements on the one hand, factual assertions or judgements on the other. Indeed, the later Wittgenstein insists on just such differences, as part of what one might call his *anti-formalism*. It is a mantra of his that similarity in linguistic form often disguises logical or "grammatical" differences. We must not rest content with the "surface grammar"; instead, it behoves philosophers to elucidate the "depth grammar" of expressions, the network of their conceptual connections and their overall functions within discourse (PI §§ 464, 340).

Adopting an anti-formalist perspective on our linguistic practice in turn leads to *anti-descriptivist* conclusions. First, even among *bona fide* descriptions, there are significant differences (§§ 24, 291). Secondly, it is an unwarranted prejudice that all sentences are descriptive or serve the purpose of stating facts. Contrary to the "Augustinian picture," it is not the case that the sole function of language is to *represent* reality—i.e. that all words refer to objects and all sentences describe reality. Instead, there is an irreducible "multiplicity" and "prodigious diversity of language-games" (§§ 21–7, p. 224). Nor is describing the highest common denominator of these various linguistic activities. According to Wittgenstein, first-person, present-tense psychological statements like "I am in pain now" are typically *avowals*, manifestations rather than descriptions of the mental. *Mutatis mutandis* for mathematical propositions, as well as for Wittgenstein's own grammatical remarks. To both he ascribed a *normative* rather than a descriptive status.

For all three types of sentences, Wittgenstein prevaricated over the question of whether they are truth-apt. In his more enlightened moods he acknowledged that they are, for instance in that they are subject to propositional operators and can feature in inferences. This means that they satisfy the rather demanding standards for counting as a proposition—*Satz*—canvassed in *Investigations* § 136. Other passages (§§ 22, 33, 49) condone a wider notion, according to which a proposition is any expression the utterance of which constitutes a complete move in the language-game; this obviously accommodates sentences which are not truth-apt, such as questions and imperatives. Such complications, notwithstanding, however, Wittgenstein remains adamant on one point. Even in the case of truth-apt propositions (indicative sentences), their overall "grammar," i.e. their function or role within our language and hence their semantic status, need not be that of descriptions of reality; they may well be expressive or prescriptive.[48]

Lovibond denies that there is such a fundamental divergence in function between different kinds of truth-apt propositions. She appeals to the idea that all of them *refer* to an objective reality. According to her, "the only sense of reality is that of something being talked about." "Reference to an objective reality is not a target that some propositions can fail to meet." Instead, "the only way in which an indicative statement can fail to describe reality is by *not being true*—i.e. by virtue of reality not being as the statement declares it to be."[49] Furthermore, she maintains that Wittgenstein is on her side, on account of § 402 of *Philosophical Investigations*.

> Here we are tempted to say that our way of speaking does not describe the facts as they really are. As if, for example the proposition "he has pains" could be false in some other way than by that man's not having pains. As if the form of expression were saying something false even when the proposition *faute de mieux* asserted something true. For this is what disputes between idealists, solipsists and realists look like. The one party attack the normal form of expression as if they ware attacking a statement; the others defend it, as if they ware stating facts recognized by every reasonable human being.

Lovibond's case is ingenious, but only *prima facie* compelling. In keeping with the spirit of the later Wittgenstein, we need to be wary of the assumption that *tertium non datur*.

A "way of speaking" or form of expression cannot be at fault, at least not in the sense of saying something false. It is only *statements* made within a form of expression that can say something false. That much Wittgenstein maintains, and that much is correct. Lovibond is also right in so far as Wittgenstein accepts that there is no other way for a proposition being *false* than by things not being as the proposition states them to be—in line with his deflationist account of truth. But this does *not* commit him to the stronger claim that there is no other way in which a proposition or speech-act can *fail to describe reality*. One such way consists precisely in the proposition or speech-act not describing or purporting to describe reality at all, truly or falsely.

Lovibond derives from Wittgenstein a "homogeneous or 'seamless' conception of language [. . .] free from invidious comparisons between different regions of discourse"; "all language-games" are "of equal value."[50] This is problematic, *if* seamlessness is meant to imply that there are no significant semantic differences between distinct forms of discourse or language-games. According to Lovibond, Wittgenstein continued to subscribe to a version of the *Tractatus* idea that "all propositions are of equal value" (6.4). She might also have alluded to the claim that "all facts" and "all propositions stand on the same level" in "A Lecture on Ethics."[51] But she fails to note the crucial point. By the lights of the early Wittgenstein, all propositions are on a par with respect to expressing moral value, since *all of them are factual* and hence *incapable of expressing moral value at all*. Once he recognized that the restriction of propositions to factual propositions is mistaken, he *also* recognized that propositions can serve *very different purposes*.

At the same time, Lovibond's idea of seamlessness correctly captures an important aspect of Wittgenstein's later conception of language. It is notorious that Wittgenstein rejected the idea that different language-games / forms of discourse can reflect the true nature of reality to varying degrees. This is part and parcel of his claim that language is "autonomous" and grammar "arbitrary." That is to say, our conceptual scheme, embodied in our various language-games, is not answerable to a purported essence of reality.[52]

By this token, it is not just confused to think that a language-game, form of discourse, or conceptual scheme can be *true or false*; it is also confused to think that it can be *more or less faithful to reality*, in the sense of capturing more or less accurately those features that reality objectively possesses. It follows in turn that there is no *metaphysical* perspective from which one form of discourse could be disqualified as *less realistic* than another. It does not follow, however, that scientific and moral statements have the same role or function to begin with. Because of anti-formalism, it does not even follow that all statements that we call true or false have the same role or function. For Wittgenstein, at any rate, there is a *semantic* ("grammatical") perspective from which one form of discourse can be described as *less descriptive* than another.

8 The Non-Cognitivism of the Later Wittgenstein

Wittgenstein did not just reject descriptivism as a general prejudice. He also adopted a non-descriptivist account of several forms of discourse, as indicated above. Far from constituting an exception, moral discourse is a paradigm case! This is undeniable for the transition period. As documented in section 3, in "A Lecture on Ethics" the implausible insistence that moral statements are misguided because moral value defies linguistic expression was motivated by the assumption that "words will only express [i.e., represent] facts." This prejudice restricted linguistic significance to descriptive statements. It leads to the proscription of moral statements in conjunction with Wittgenstein's abiding conviction that moral statements *cannot be factual*.[53]

Anti-descriptivism about morality is also a feature of Wittgenstein's mature thought. Crucial to ethics is its *contrast* with factual propositions and scientific theories. In spite of professing the inexplicable nature of ethics, "A Lecture on Ethics" *does* explain that contrast at least partially, namely by reference to the *action-guiding* nature of ethical judgements. While there is a logical gap between factual judgements and decisions to act, ethical judgements express directly the grounds or attitudes on which we act. This is the intrinsic motivational force that, according to claim (6.) of AAR, can be sustained by objective features of the world.

By contrast, there is no such suggestion in the later Wittgenstein. Instead, he ties this motivational force to two other features.[54] First, ethical terms replace and extend natural reactions (gestures, facial expressions) of approval and disapproval. Secondly, their "grammar" is determined not only by the object they modify, but also by the reasons individual speakers offer for applying them. For instance, calling a person or action virtuous or wicked means something different coming from a consequentialist than it does coming from a proponent of absolute values or obligations. While AAR might be able to accommodate the second claim, the first one is clearly anti-descriptivist. Indeed, it ties ethics to the aforementioned case of first-person, present-tense psychological statements. For Wittgenstein links their status as avowals to what he regards as their origin, namely in natural reactions to pain (e.g., PI §§ 244–5).

Another phenomenon that Wittgenstein regarded as closely related to ethics is religion. Both religious beliefs and moral convictions, he held, are *toto caelo* different from factual beliefs in general and scientific theories in particular. Both, he felt, concern the ultimate ends and the overall patterns of each individual person's life.[55] If one combines Wittgenstein's remarks on ethics with his reflections on religion, one arrives at what may count as his later "meta-ethics." This position revolves around the following ideas:

a. We must focus not on the appearance of ethical terms, which resemble that of other words, but on their specific role within our whole culture.
b. The ethical *shows* itself no longer in mystical attitudes of a solipsistic self, but in social patterns of action.
c. Ethical terms replace and extend natural reactions (gestures, facial expressions) of approval and disapproval.
d. Their "grammar" is determined not only by the object they modify, but also by the reasons a person offers for applying them.

Ultimately, Wittgenstein's later thought points in the direction of a *communitarian variant of expressivism*. Ethical statements express or avow a certain attitude to or perspective on human behaviour, on life and its meaning. But it tends to be the intersubjective attitudes or perspectives of a whole community or social form of life, rather than the subjective ones of individuals. A moral framework expresses the stance not so much of a person but of a community toward the question of how to act and how to lead and conceive of one's life. Furthermore, such a framework is *both* expressive of such a stance *and* prescriptive in introducing or enforcing a certain pattern of action. On the assumption that this interpretation captures the trajectory of Wittgenstein's later meta-ethics, one can venture the following explanation of what the *truth* of an *ethical* as opposed to a factual proposition *consists in*. An ethical proposition is true in so far as it accurately expresses the stance of the speaker's community and/ prescribes a course of action condoned by that stance.

It seems clear that from Wittgenstein's perspective some ethical statements, notably ethical principles of a general kind such as "It is evil to inflict harm without due cause" are grammatical propositions—i.e. *constitutive* of our moral concepts.[56] It seems equally clear that from this perspective other ethical statements, notably those concerning particular cases, *apply* these concepts. Alas, it is unclear where he would have drawn the line, and where those following in his footsteps should draw the line. It is even unclear how hard and fast such a line could be. Looking on the bright side, we may hope for some illumination of these issues from recent investigations which apply his ideas concerning paradigm cases and hinge propositions[57] to moral discourse.[58] Instead of ploughing that furrow, however, I shall end by considering another burning question, one which ties in directly with Wittgensteinian AAR.

9 Truth and "What Human Beings Say"

It is the seamless conception of language—to use Lovibond's striking phrase—that gives license to a central claim of AAR, namely that there can be no semantic or meta-ethic difference between moral discourse on the one hand, descriptive discourse on the other. But even if one leaves aside the qualifications and objections raised in the previous section, the idea of such a homogeneity faces a serious challenge. The kind of consensus one can achieve in scientific discourse, however fallible, far outstrips the kind of consensus we appear to be capable of attaining concerning matters moral. McDowell has relatively little to say concerning this challenge. By contrast, Lovibond explicitly acknowledges that there is a difference between moral discourse on the one hand, the formal and natural sciences on the other: the latter are capable of achieving a more dependable consensus than the former.[59] Entering into debates about the extent of moral consensus, its anthropological sources and its implications for topics such as moral relativism is beyond the scope of this article. It is important, however, to look at the role that *consensus* plays for the *notion of truth* according to the later Wittgenstein, and to consider possible meta-ethical implications.

In the later work we find some suggestive and tantalizing passages on the connection between consensus and truth.

> So you are saying that human agreement decides what is true and what is false? It is what human beings say that is true and false; and they agree in the language they use. (PI § 241)

> Correct or incorrect exist only in thinking, and hence in the expression of thoughts. (*The Big Typescript*, MS 124, 212–3)

> The colour words are taught as follows: "This is red," e.g. Admittedly, our language-game only comes about if there is a certain consensus. But this consensus does not enter into the language-game. Does the consensus of human beings decide what is red? Is this decided by appeal to the majority? Is this how we learnt to determine the colour?[60]

The message of such passages is multifaceted, yet reasonably clear, especially given Wittgenstein's abiding allegiance to a deflationary explanation of truth. Although Wittgenstein connects truth and consensus, this is not by way of a consensus or pragmatist theory of truth. Without consensus in the application of predicates, we would (could) not employ them, but this is *not part of their meaning*. Whether (it is true that) an object satisfies a predicate does not depend on human consensus. The bearers of both truth-values are things people say and think, or could say and think. This is a conceptual connection between truth and human thought or speech, yet without forming part of the definition of truth.[61]

Wittgenstein deals with truth the way in which AAR proposes to deal with value. Truth is not a matter of consensus; yet what it amounts to can only be explained by reference to what people (could) think, say, or do. This constitutes an important kernel of truth in the AAR reading of Wittgenstein. On the other hand, it also introduces a complication concerning the AAR's comparison of moral and secondary qualities.

For AAR moral and aesthetic values resemble secondary qualities. People and their actions really are virtuous or wicked, and objects really are beautiful or ugly. But for something to have value it must be internally related to the exercise of human moral and aesthetic understanding. The parallel treatment is evident from the following summaries.

> (SQ) An object having secondary quality Q is its being such as to appear Q to competent and well-placed observers.
>
> (MV) An object having moral value V is its being recognized as having V by competent members of a speech-community.

This is where trouble lurks. By contrast to the indirect role that consensus plays in Wittgenstein's approach to truth, SQ and MV do not just invoke notions that make sense only by reference to human thought, speech, or behaviour. That account insists that the bearers of truth and falsehood are things people can say or think. By analogy, an account of secondary qualities would insist that their bearers are *perceptibilia*, things sentient creatures can perceive. And an account of moral qualities would insist that their bearers are what one might call *practicabilia*, i.e. things people do intentionally or for a reason.

SQ and MV do not confine themselves to this kind of claim, however. Instead, they go further and *define* their respective analysanda by reference to human reactions. In the end, therefore, even AAR may lose one of its "anti-"s. In this respect, at least, it ultimately appears to be much closer to Blackburn-style anti-realism or projectivism than its adherents would be prepared to concede. But it has to be admitted that steering the kind of middle course between the Scylla of such anti-realist reductionism and the Charybdis of a realist disregard for the role of human thought and practice is fiendishly difficult in the case of truth. And, alas, there is little reason to hope that it will prove easier in the case of moral value. Nevertheless, this is the course that a further elaboration and defence of a Wittgensteinian meta-ethics needs to map out. Such a project presupposes a sound understanding of the location of Wittgenstein's own thinking on the nature of ethics, as well as that of his followers, in the complex spectrum of realism and anti-realism. And it has much to learn both from the insights and from the errors of AAR. That at any rate is the moral of this article.[62]

Notes

1. Otto Weininger, *Sex and Character* (London: Heineman, 1906), 159; German edition 1903.
2. See Fania Pascal, "Wittgenstein: A Personal Memoir," in *Recollections of Wittgenstein*, ed. Rush Rhees (Oxford: Oxford University Press, 1984), 26–62; Norman Malcolm, *Wittgenstein – A Memoir* (Oxford: Oxford University Press, 1984).
3. Cf. Ray Monk, *Wittgenstein: The Duty of Genius* (London: Cape, 1990); James Klagge, *Wittgenstein: Biography and Philosophy* (Cambridge: Cambridge University Press, 2001).
4. For more charitable assessments see William DeAngelis, *Ludwig Wittgenstein – A Cultural Point of View* (Aldershot: Ashgate, 2007); Béla Szabados, *Ludwig Wittgenstein on Race, Gender, and Cultural Identity: Philosophy as a Personal Endeavour* (Lewiston, NY: Edwin Mellen Press, 2010); James Klagge, *Wittgenstein as an Exile* (Cambridge, MA: MIT Press, 2011); Yuval Lurie, *Wittgenstein on the Human Spirit* (Amsterdam: Rodopi, 2012).
5. See Simon Blackburn, *Essays in Quasi-Realism* (Oxford: Oxford University Press, 1993); idem, *Practical Tortoise Raising and Other Essays* (Oxford: Oxford University Press, 2010).
6. Cf. Huw Price, *Naturalism without Mirrors* (Oxford: Oxford University Press, 2011).
7. All numbered references in parenthesis without date are to Wittgenstein, *Tractatus Logico-Philosophicus* (London: Routledge & Kegan Paul, 1961). All paragraph references in parenthesis without date are to Wittgenstein, *Philosophical Investigations* (Oxford: Blackwell, 1967); hereafter *PI*. Wherever possible, I have stated references in a manner that covers different editions.
8. To avoid unnecessary complications, this article does not systematically distinguish between sentences, propositions, and statements, or between beliefs, judgements, and convictions, even though these distinctions are important in other contexts.
9. Rudolf Carnap, *The Logical Syntax of Language* (London: Routledge & Kegan Paul, 1937), 279.
10. See Hans-Johann Glock, "Wittgenstein and Reason," in *Wittgenstein: Biography and Philosophy*, ed. James Klagge (New York, NY: Cambridge University Press, 2001), 195–220.

11 See Ludwig Wittgenstein, *PI* §§ 89–133; idem, *The Big Typescript: TS 213*, ed. and trans. C. Grant Luckhardt and Maximilian A. E. Aue (Oxford: Wiley-Blackwell, 2005), 406–35.
12 Richard M. Hare, *The Language of Morals* (Oxford: Oxford University Press, 1952), v.
13 Cf. Herbert L. A. Hart, *The Concept of Law* (Oxford: Oxford University Press, 1962).
14 On this Hans-Johann Glock, "Doing Good by Splitting Hairs? Analytic Philosophy and Applied Ethics," *Journal of Applied Philosophy* 28 (2011): 225–40.
15 Cf. Cora Diamond, "Wittgenstein, Mathematics, and Ethics. Resisting the Attractions of Realism," in *The Cambridge Companion to Wittgenstein*, ed. Hans Sluga and David Stern (Cambridge: Cambridge University Press, 1996), 226–60; Lars Hertzberg, "Moral Escapism and Applied Ethics," *Philosophical Papers* 31, no. 3 (2002): 251–70; Stephen Mulhall, "Ethics in the Light of Wittgenstein," ibid., 293–321.
16 See Hans-Johann Glock, "All Kinds of Nonsense," in *Wittgenstein at Work*, ed. Erich Ammereller and Eugen Fischer (London: Routledge, 2004), 221–45.
17 On the latter see David Edmonds, *Would You Kill the Fat Man?* (Princeton, NJ: Princeton University Press, 2013), and on Wittgenstein's influence on Foot see James Klagge, "Review of *Virtues and Reasons: Philippa Foot on Moral Theory*, ed. R. Hursthouse, G. Lawrence, and W. Quinn," *Ethics* 107, no. 4 (1997): 743–6.
18 See Mary Warnock, *Ethics Since 1900* (Oxford: Oxford University Press, 1966), 84, 111–14.
19 See above and Hans Oberdiek, "Wittgenstein's Ethics: Boundaries and Boundary Crossings," in *Wittgenstein and Analytic Philosophy: Essays in Honour of Peter Hacker*, ed. Hans-Johann Glock and John Hyman (Oxford: Oxford University Press, 2009), 175–202, 175–9.
20 Cf. John Leslie Mackie, *Ethics: Inventing Right and Wrong* (Harmondsworth: Penguin, 1977).
21 See ibid., 40, 48–9, 105–7.
22 See also Ludwig Wittgenstein, *Notebooks 1914–16* [German-English parallel text], ed. Gertrude E. M. Anscombe and Georg Henrik von Wright, trans. G. E. M. Anscombe, rev. ed. (Oxford: Blackwell, 1979), quoted according to date: 24.7.16; English translation in Paul Engelmann, *Letters from Ludwig Wittgenstein: With a Memoir*, ed. Brian F. McGuinness (Oxford: Blackwell, 1967).
23 See Ludwig Wittgenstein, "Letters to Engelmann," in *Briefe*, ed. Brian F. McGuinness and Georg Henrik von Wright. In German, with original version of Wittgenstein's own letters (when in English), in an appendix; German translations Joachim Schulte (Frankfurt: Suhrkamp, 1980), 9.4.17.—One referee pointed out that according to the letter to Engelmann the unutterable, is "contained in what has been uttered" in a poem by Ludwig Uhland. Since the sentences of the poem have a sense, the referee concludes that for Wittgenstein the ethical is on a par with the

logical: though itself unsayable, it is shown by propositions with a sense. But while that conclusion is licensed by the letter, it is at odds with *Tractatus* 6.53. The latter restricts "what can be said" to the "propositions of natural science," which definitely excludes poetry. My formulation is intended to circumvent these complications.

24 Cf. also Wittgenstein, *Notebooks 1914–16*, 2.8.16.
25 See George Edward Moore, *Principia Ethica* (Cambridge: Cambridge University Press, 1903).
26 Ludwig Wittgenstein, "A Lecture on Ethics," *Philosophical Review* 74 (1965): 3–12, esp. 7–9, 11–12; idem, *Wittgenstein and the Vienna Circle [1929–32]*. Shorthand notes recorded by Friedrich Waismann. Ed. Brian F. McGuinness (Oxford: Blackwell, 1979), 68–9.
27 Cf. *Lectures and Conversations on Aesthetics, Psychology and Religious Belief* (1938–46), ed. Cyril Barrett (Oxford: Blackwell, 1966), 2, 7–8.
28 See *Remarks on the Philosophy of Psychology* (1945–7, German-English parallel text), vol. I, ed. Gertrude E. M. Anscombe (Oxford: Blackwell, 1980), § 160; *Wittgenstein's Lectures, Cambridge 1932–35*. From the notes of Alice Ambrose and Margaret MacDonald, ed. Alice Ambrose (Oxford: Blackwell, 1979), 31–6.
29 See Alfred Ayer, *Language, Truth and Logic* (Harmondsworth: Penguin, 1971), ch. 6.
30 See Warnock, *Ethics Since 1900*, 81–3; Robert Arrington, "Wittgenstein on Ethics," in *The Blackwell Companion to Wittgenstein*, ed. Hans-Johann Glock and John Hyman (Oxford: Wiley-Blackwell, 2015).
31 Cf. Leslie Stevenson, "The Emotive Meaning of Ethical Terms," *Mind* 46, no. 181 (1937): 14–31; idem, *Ethics and Language* (New Haven, CT: Yale University Press, 1943).
32 See Simon Blackburn, *Essays in Quasi-Realism* (Oxford: Oxford University Press, 1993).
33 Cf. Hans-Johann Glock, "Analytic Philosophy: Wittgenstein and After," in *A Companion to Twentieth-Century Philosophy*, ed. Dermot Moran (London: Routledge), 76–117.
34 See Peter Geach, *Logic Matters* (Oxford: Basil Blackwell, 1972), ch. 8.2.
35 Cf. John Searle, *Speech Acts* (Cambridge: Cambridge University Press, 1969), ch. 8.
36 Cf. Jonathan Dancy, *Ethics without Principles* (Oxford: Oxford University Press, 2004), ch. 11.2.
37 See John McDowell, *Mind, Value and Reality* (Cambridge, MA: Harvard University Press, 1998); David Wiggins, *Needs, Values, Truth* (Oxford: Blackwell, 1991).
38 McDowell, *Mind, Value and Reality*, 71.
39 Sabina Lovibond, *Realism and Imagination in Ethics* (Oxford: Blackwell, 1983), 25.
40 At the same time, there are parallels between some of their ideas after their explicit championing of AAR, notably between McDowell's notion of "second

nature" (*Mind and World* [Cambridge, MA: Harvard University Press, 1996]) and Lovibond's discussions of ethical formation (*Ethical Formation* [Cambridge, MA: Harvard University Press, 2002]). Unfortunately, scrutinizing these would take us too far afield.

41 See Mark Platts, *Reference, Truth and Reality* (London: Routledge & Kegan Paul, 1980).
42 Cf. his *Ways of Meaning* (London: Routledge & Kegan Paul, 1979), ch. X.
43 Cf. Hans-Johann Glock, "Wittgenstein on Truth," in *Knowledge and Belief*, ed. Wilfried Löffler and Peter Weingartner (Vienna: Hölder-Pichler-Tempsky, 2004), 328-46.
44 See Ludwig Wittgenstein, *Remarks on the Foundations of Mathematics* [1937-44], ed. Georg Henrik von Wright, Rush Rhees, and Gertrude E. M. Anscombe, trans. G. E. M. Anscombe, rev. ed. (Oxford: Blackwell, 1978), 117; see *PI* § 136.
45 Ludwig Wittgenstein, *The Voices of Wittgenstein – The Vienna Circle, Ludwig Wittgenstein and Friedrich Waismann*, ed. Gordon Park Baker, trans. idem et al. (London: Routledge, 2003), 490-2.
46 See Wolfgang Künne, *Conceptions of Truth* (Oxford: Clarendon Press, 2003), ch. 2.
47 Frank Ramsey, "Facts and Propositions" (1927), reprinted in *Philosophical Papers*, ed. D. H. Mellor (Cambridge: Cambridge University Press, 1990), 34-51, 38-9.
48 See Hans-Johann Glock, *A Wittgenstein Dictionary* (Oxford: Blackwell, 1996), 50-4, 107-11, 129-35, 231-6, 320-3; Blackburn, *Practical Tortoise Raising and Other Essays*, ch. 11; Cora Diamond, "Wittgenstein, Mathematics, and Ethics. Resisting the Attractions of Realism," in *The Cambridge Companion to Wittgenstein*, ed. Hans Sluga and David Stern (Cambridge: Cambridge University Press, 1996), 226-60, 229-36.
49 Lovibond, *Realism and Imagination in Ethics*, 25-6.
50 Ibid., 25.
51 See "A Lecture on Ethics," 34.
52 Cf. Michael Forster, *Wittgenstein on the Arbitrariness of Grammar* (Princeton, NJ: Princeton University Press, 2004).
53 See Wittgenstein, "A Lecture on Ethics," 7-9, 11-2; idem, *Wittgenstein and the Vienna Circle*, 68-9.
54 Cf. *Lectures and Conversations on Aesthetics, Psychology and Religious Belief*, 2; *Wittgenstein's Lectures, Cambridge 1932-35*, 35.
55 See Glock, *A Wittgenstein Dictionary*, 320-3.
56 Cf. Robert Arrington, *Rationalism, Realism and Relativism* (Ithaca: Cornell University Press, 1989).
57 See Ludwig Wittgenstein, *On Certainty*, ed. Gertrude E. M. Anscombe and Georg Henrik von Wright, trans. Danis Paul and G. E. M. Anscombe (Oxford: Blackwell, 1975).

58 See Julia Hermann, *Moral Competence and the Limits of Reasonable Doubt: Perspectives from Wittgenstein* (Basingstoke: Palgrave, 2014); Nigel Pleasants, "Wittgenstein, Ethics and Basic Moral Certainty," *Inquiry* 51, no. 3 (2009): 241–67.
59 Cf. Lovibond, *Realism and Imagination in Ethics*, 40–50.
60 Ludwig Wittgenstein, *Zettel* (1945–8, German-English parallel text), ed. Gertrude E. M. Anscombe and Georg Henrik von Wright, trans. G. E. M. Anscombe (Oxford: Blackwell, 1967), §§ 430–1.
61 See Glock, "Wittgenstein on Truth."
62 I am grateful to two anonymous referees, as well as to the participants of the conference "Wittgensteinian Approaches to Moral Philosophy" at KU Leuven (20.-21.09.13). I should also like to thank Halvard Lillehammer, whose presentation at the British Academy conference on "Pragmatism in the Long Twentieth Century" (02.10.14) alerted me to the contrast between local and global expressivism, and to Javier Kalhat for valuable comments and editorial help. I owe more longstanding debs to Peter Hacker and Ernst-Michael Langue, for intermittent yet illuminating discussions of Wittgenstein's view of morality from the eighties onwards. Finally, I should like to thank Sabina Lovibond. Her writings and lectures (1983–84) aroused my initial interest in the meta-ethical implications of Wittgensteinian thought.

Works Cited

Arrington, Robert, *Rationalism, Realism and Relativism*, Ithaca: Cornell University Press, 1989.

Arrington, Robert, "Wittgenstein on Ethics," in Hans-Johann Glock and John Hyman (eds.), *The Blackwell Companion to Wittgenstein*, 217–32, Oxford: Wiley-Blackwell, 2015.

Ayer, Alfred, *Language, Truth and Logic*, Harmondsworth: Penguin, 1971.

Blackburn, Simon, *Essays in Quasi-Realism*, Oxford: Oxford University Press, 1993.

Blackburn, Simon, *Practical Tortoise Raising and Other Essays*, Oxford: Oxford University Press, 2010.

Carnap, Rudolf, *The Logical Syntax of Language*, London: Routledge & Kegan Paul, 1937.

Dancy, Jonathan, *Ethics without Principles*, Oxford: Oxford University Press, 2004.

DeAngelis, William, *Ludwig Wittgenstein – A Cultural Point of View*, Aldershot: Ashgate, 2007.

Diamond, Cora, "Wittgenstein, Mathematics, and Ethics: Resisting the Attractions of Realism," in Hans Sluga and David Stern (eds.), *The Cambridge Companion to Wittgenstein*, 226–60, Cambridge: Cambridge University Press, 1996.

Edmonds, David, *Would you Kill the Fat Man?* Princeton, NJ: Princeton University Press, 2013.

Engelmann, Paul, *Letters from Ludwig Wittgenstein: With a Memoir*, ed. Brian F. McGuinness, Oxford: Blackwell, 1967.

Forster, Michael, *Wittgenstein on the Arbitrariness of Grammar*, Princeton, NJ: Princeton University Press, 2004.
Geach, Peter, *Logic Matters*, Oxford: Basil Blackwell, 1972.
Glock, Hans-Johann, *A Wittgenstein Dictionary*, Oxford: Blackwell, 1996.
Glock, Hans-Johann, "Wittgenstein and Reason," in James Klagge (ed.), *Wittgenstein: Biography and Philosophy*, 195–220, New York: Cambridge University Press, 2001.
Glock, Hans-Johann, "All Kinds of Nonsense," in Erich Ammereller and Eugen Fischer (eds.), *Wittgenstein at Work*, 221–45, London: Routledge, 2004.
Glock, Hans-Johann, "Wittgenstein on Truth," in Wilfried Löffler and Peter Weingartner (eds.), *Knowledge and Belief*, 328–46, Vienna: Hölder-Pichler-Tempsky, 2004.
Glock, Hans-Johann, "Analytic Philosophy: Wittgenstein and After," in Dermot Moran (ed.), *A Companion to Twentieth-Century Philosophy*, 76–117, London: Routledge, 2008.
Glock, Hans-Johann, "Doing Good by Splitting Hairs? Analytic Philosophy and Applied Ethics," *Journal of Applied Philosophy* 28 (2011): 225–40.
Hare, Richard M., *The Language of Morals*, Oxford: Oxford University Press, 1956.
Hart, Herbert L. A., *The Concept of Law*, Oxford: Oxford University Press, 1962.
Hermann, Julia, *Moral Competence and the Limits of Reasonable Doubt: Perspectives from Wittgenstein*, Basingstoke: Palgrave, 2014.
Hertzberg, Lars, "Moral Escapism and Applied Ethics," *Philosophical Papers* 31, no. 3 (2002): 251–70.
Klagge, James, "Review of *Virtues and Reasons: Philippa Foot on Moral Theory*, ed. R. Hursthouse, G. Lawrence, and W. Quinn," *Ethics* 107, no. 4 (1997): 743–6.
Klagge, James, *Wittgenstein: Biography and Philosophy*, Cambridge: Cambridge University Press, 2001.
Klagge, James, *Wittgenstein as an Exile*, Cambridge, MA: MIT, 2011.
Künne, Wolfgang, *Conceptions of Truth*, Oxford: Clarendon Press, 2003.
Lovibond, Sabina, *Realism and Imagination in Ethics*, Oxford: Blackwell, 1983.
Lovibond, Sabina, *Ethical Formation*, Cambridge, MA: Harvard University Press, 2003.
Lurie, Yuval, *Wittgenstein on the Human Spirit*, Amsterdam: Rodopi, 2012.
Mackie, John L., *Ethics: Inventing Right and Wrong*, Harmondsworth: Penguin, 1977.
Malcolm, Norman, *Wittgenstein – A Memoir*, Oxford: Oxford University Press, 1984.
McDowell, John, *Mind and World*, Cambridge, MA: Harvard University Press, 1996.
McDowell, John, *Mind, Value and Reality*, Cambridge, MA: Harvard University Press, 1998.
Monk, Ray, *Wittgenstein: The Duty of Genius*, London: Cape, 1990.
Moore, George Edward, *Principia Ethica*, Cambridge: Cambridge University Press, 1903.
Mulhall, Stephen, "Ethics in the Light of Wittgenstein," *Philosophical Papers* 31, no. 3 (2002): 293–321.

Oberdiek, Hans, "Wittgenstein's Ethics: Boundaries and Boundary Crossings," in Hans-Johann Glock and John Hyman (eds.), *Wittgenstein and Analytic Philosophy: Essays in Honour of Peter Hacker*, 175–202, Oxford: Oxford University Press, 2009.

Pascal, Fania, "Wittgenstein: A Personal Memoir," in Rush Rhees (ed.), *Recollections of Wittgenstein*, 26–62, Oxford: Oxford University Press, 1984.

Platts, Mark, *Ways of Meaning*, London: Routledge & Kegan Paul, 1979.

Platts, Mark, *Reference, Truth and Reality*, London: Routledge & Kegan Paul, 1980.

Pleasants, Nigel, "Wittgenstein, Ethics and Basic Moral Certainty," *Inquiry* 51, no. 3 (2009): 241–67.

Price, Huw, *Naturalism without Mirrors*, Oxford: Oxford University Press, 2011.

Ramsey, Frank, "Facts and Propositions," Reprinted in *Philosophical Papers*, ed. D. H. Mellor, 34–51, Cambridge: Cambridge University Press, 1990.

Searle, John, *Speech Acts*, Cambridge: Cambridge University Press, 1969.

Stevenson, Leslie, "The Emotive Meaning of Ethical Terms," *Mind* 46, no. 181 (1937): 14–31.

Stevenson, Leslie, *Ethics and Language*, New Haven, CT: Yale University Press, 1943.

Szabados, Béla, *Ludwig Wittgenstein on Race, Gender, and Cultural Identity: Philosophy as a Personal Endeavour*, Lewiston, NY: Edwin Mellen Press, 2010.

Warnock, Mary, *Ethics Since 1900*, Oxford: Oxford University Press, 1966.

Weininger, Otto, *Sex and Character*, London: Heineman, 1906 (German edn. 1903).

Wiggins, David, *Needs, Values, Truth*, Oxford: Blackwell, 1991.

Wittgenstein, Ludwig, *Tractatus Logico-Philosophicus*, London: Routledge & Kegan Paul, 1961.

Wittgenstein, Ludwig, "A Lecture on Ethics," *Philosophical Review* 74 (1965): 3–12.

Wittgenstein, Ludwig, *Lectures and Conversations on Aesthetics, Psychology and Religious Belief* [1938–46], ed. Cyril Barrett, Oxford: Blackwell, 1966.

Wittgenstein, Ludwig, *Philosophical Investigations*, Oxford: Blackwell, 1967.

Wittgenstein, Ludwig, *Zettel* [1945–48, German-English parallel text], ed. Gertrude E. M. Anscombe and Georg Henrik von Wright, trans. G. E. M. Anscombe, Oxford: Blackwell, 1967.

Wittgenstein, Ludwig, *On Certainty*, ed. Gertrude E. M. Anscombe and Georg Henrik von Wright, trans. Danis Paul and G. E. M. Anscombe, Oxford: Blackwell, 1975.

Wittgenstein, Ludwig, *Remarks on the Foundations of Mathematics* [1937–44], ed. Georg Henrik von Wright, Rush Rhees, and Gertrude E. M. Anscombe, trans. G. E. M. Anscombe, rev. ed., Oxford: Blackwell, 1978.

Wittgenstein, Ludwig, *Wittgenstein and the Vienna Circle [1929–32]*. Shorthand notes recorded by Friedrich Waismann, ed. Brian F. McGuinness, Oxford: Blackwell, 1979.

Wittgenstein, Ludwig, *Wittgenstein's Lectures, Cambridge* 1932–35. From the notes of Alice Ambrose and Margaret MacDonald, ed. Alice Ambrose, Oxford: Blackwell, 1979.

Wittgenstein, Ludwig, *Notebooks* 1914–16 [German-English parallel text], ed. Gertrude E. M. Anscombe and Georg Henrik von Wright, trans. G. E. M. Anscombe, rev. ed., Oxford: Blackwell, 1979.

Wittgenstein, Ludwig, "Letters to Engelmann," in *Briefe*, ed. Brian F. McGuinness and Georg Henrik von Wright. In German, with original version of Wittgenstein's own letters (when in English), in an appendix; German translations Joachim Schulte, Frankfurt: Suhrkamp, 1989.

Wittgenstein, Ludwig, *Remarks on the Philosophy of Psychology* [1945–47, German-English parallel text], vol. I, ed. Gertrude E. M. Anscombe, Oxford: Blackwell, 1989.

Wittgenstein, Ludwig, *Philosophical Occasions* 1912–1951, ed. James Klagge and Alfred Nordmann, Indianapolis: Hackett, 1993.

Wittgenstein, Ludwig, *The Voices of Wittgenstein – The Vienna Circle, Ludwig Wittgenstein and Friedrich Waismann*, ed. Gordon Park Baker, trans. Gordon Baker, Michael Mackert, John Connolly, and Vasilis Politis, London: Routledge, 2003.

Wittgenstein, Ludwig, *The Big Typescript: TS 213*, ed. and trans. C. Grant Luckhardt and Maximilian A. E. Aue, Oxford: Wiley-Blackwell, 2005.

6

Wittgenstein and Moral Realism
The Debate Continues
Sabina Lovibond

1 Introduction: Recalling the 1980s

Can there really be such a position, in ethics or any other branch of philosophy, as "anti-anti-realism"? The term would not spontaneously have suggested itself to me, but I cannot avoid taking some responsibility for the view it denotes, since Hans-Johann Glock has named me—along with John McDowell—as one of its patrons.[1]

McDowell suggests this form of words rather lightly and deprecatingly in the introduction to his *Mind, Value, and Reality*. Some of the essays in that collection, he says, can be taken to defend a version of "moral realism." But they do so by inviting us to revisit a conception of the ethical that is rationalist or objectivist "in an unambitious sense involving no more than the idea of getting things right." Hence, McDowell regards the "moral realist" label as potentially misleading: it risks obscuring the fact that his stance is "more negative than positive," something "better described as 'anti-anti-realism' than as 'realism'"; he seeks to show simply that "anti-realist positions such as emotivism and its sophisticated descendants ... are responses to a misconception of the significance of the obvious fact that ethical, and more generally evaluative, thinking is not science."[2] This, then, is the source—whether or not McDowell ever seriously envisaged his double-negative mouthful being admitted to more general discussion—of the language used in Glock's title and projected back into the 1970s and 1980s, when "Oxford philosophers like McDowell and Lovibond invoked Wittgenstein's philosophy of language against the still prevailing non-cognitivist/anti-realist mainstream" in ethical theory.

It must be acknowledged that Lovibond—that is, the Lovibond of *Realism and Imagination in Ethics*,[3] to which Glock refers—is not so circumspect. The position I develop in that book is described without compunction as "a form of *moral realism* derived from the later philosophy of Wittgenstein"—though I do go on in the same paragraph to say that I will try to construct "an *idealized version* of this position as I understand it, so that my discussion will have as its object a philosophical theory rather than a specific philosopher or group of philosophers."[4] In fact, rereading the book with Glock's criticism in mind, I could see that circumspection is not its salient point. It is a "young person's book," fired off into the public domain as if there were no tomorrow and nothing to plan for, and probably containing numerous errors of taste and judgment.

But my business here is not to apologize or recant, because I don't feel that the underlying lessons drawn from my philosophical education up to (let's say) 1980 positively require to be unlearned. Much has since been added, many difficulties negotiated, but not in the manner of someone tearing up their opening pages and starting again. The "anti-non-cognitivism" which Glock[5] finds in Lovibond's *Realism* has continued to prove its worth as an intellectual compass, and the later Wittgenstein has continued to inform my thinking—not exactly *qua* moral mentor or cultural critic (a role in which, as Glock aptly observes, the man was a "loose cannon"[6]), but rather as an inward defense against certain kinds of mystification.

To begin, then, with a snapshot composed from a distance of thirty-odd years, but not yet accountable to Glock's recent commentary: the book is indeed designed to offer a somewhat systematic response to ethical noncognitivism. By this I mean the view that moral (and other) value judgments—in so far as they really are evaluative rather than descriptive—lack cognitive sense, or in other words, seek to express (not knowledge, but) a variety of positive or negative *attitudes*. The response is meant to work not just on a theoretical but also on an existential level: it addresses difficulties about the "meaning of life," which had already been identified as a weakness in noncognitivist approaches, with their implicitly infantilizing tendency to reduce the ethical subject to a locus of quasi-consumerist preferences—the bearer, so to speak, of a wish list in regard to the state of the world. Although some of the insights of noncognitivism emerge unscathed from critical inspection (see § 5), the book aims to dislodge any dogmatic or *a priori* conviction that evaluative discourse lies beyond the legitimate reach of the effort to *get things right*. In pursuing that aim, it draws extensively on ideas from Wittgenstein about the grounding of human powers of judgment in the life of a community. But also—and with an eye to the ideological pressures or temptations to which academic moral philosophy appeared susceptible at the time of writing—it devotes some close scrutiny to an emerging *authoritarian* application of "moral realist" views, and to the critique of an illiberal or sentimental "communitarianism." To that extent it is a politically motivated book; though of course it is nonetheless an attempt to achieve clarity about some strictly philosophical questions, in what I saw (and still see) as the therapeutic spirit of Wittgenstein's later work.

2 Questions of Method

The verdict of Glock—stated programmatically at the end of his introduction—is that "while AAR fails both exegetically and philosophically, its insights and errors provide crucial lessons for any attempt to use Wittgenstein's ideas in striking the delicate balance between realism and anti-realism concerning ethics."[7] My concern here will naturally be with the supposed errors. However, I remain more interested in philosophical than in exegetical correctness: not because accuracy of exposition is a value to which we can afford to show any disrespect, but because the attempt to learn from another writer for one's own heuristic purposes—to make fresh use of ideas "derived from" theirs—is always likely to involve a certain eclecticism, and possibly a certain one-sidedness.[8]

Glock also says that AAR, which he sees as a contribution to "neo-intuitionist" moral philosophy, "stands out from many other realist positions inspired by Wittgenstein in that it appeals to Wittgenstein's claims on particular topics—notably truth—rather than his method."[9] This is a characterization which I might or might not accept in relation to *Realism*, depending on how we understand "method." While the book is not devoid of examples or thought experiments drawn from actual linguistic practice, it is certainly not a specimen of detailed conceptual inquiry mediated by *what we might be inclined to say* about this or that problematic situation, or how we might teach or communicate particular moral ideas. Nor does it address itself (as Cora Diamond subsequently pointed out) to that important dimension of moral expression which *exceeds* or *bypasses* the verbal, relying instead on material that "speaks for itself": the restrained but powerful narrative, the dry observation.[10] Having sprouted from the soil of Davidsonian truth-conditional semantics, my discussion is indeed rather fixated on moral *discourse* and the truth-aptitude of moral *propositions* or *judgments*. On the other hand, it is (I would claim) attentive to the methodological principle that informs everything else in *Philosophical Investigations* (hereafter "PI") and in "later Wittgenstein" generally: that of the integration of language with activity, practice, technique, institutions, "forms of life." It takes seriously the question what, if anything, we can *do* with (for example) the kind of sentences that purport to make contact with a strongly recognition-transcendent moral reality—that is, with "a world containing moral circumstances which transcend the awareness, not just of individuals, but of the entire linguistic community."[11] It states explicitly that this is no longer a matter of the formal possibilities offered by a certain vocabulary and syntax, but of whether the resulting sentences have a use: whether we know "what it would be like" for everyone to be wrong about a moral issue. This problem takes up a good deal of space in the later sections of the book, and connects with the presence of the word "imagination" in its title.

"Meaning is a physiognomy," says Wittgenstein, epigrammatically.[12] This thought exerts a strong influence on Lovibond (1983), with respect both to linguistic meaning and, later, to the question of the "meaning of life" which frames the entire discussion. But again, should it be read as a "claim on a particular topic," or rather as a general-purpose methodological principle or "reminder"? Bearing in mind the systematic nature of Wittgenstein's determination to confine himself to the visible surfaces of expressive phenomena—not in the reductive sense of maintaining that behavior is "all there is," but by refusing to back away from strictly conceptual subject matter into psychological or physiological speculation (since "there must not be anything hypothetical . . ."[13])—I would place this feature too under the heading of Wittgensteinian *method*. The book's "neo-intuitionist" moves are not merely opportunistic but seek to show how ethics can benefit from an open-minded, phenomenological approach to debates about what sorts of thing can be "seen." For example, we can challenge the "physiological prejudices" that might lead us to find fault with perfectly ordinary idioms such as "I saw the way you looked at him." There is nothing wrong with this; though as Wittgenstein goes on to observe, there is no heavy-duty philosophy in it either; for "our naïve, normal way of expressing ourselves . . . does not show you a *theory* but only a *concept* of seeing."[14] In the same way—despite a few artless uses of the word "theory" to describe its own proceedings—the book's main concern in regard to metaethics is to free evaluative discourse from the prejudice it has suffered in the British empiricist tradition, and to promote appreciation of the "physiognomy" of such discourse. It is true that my account of ethical intuitionism, a view finding some fresh support at that time in writers like McDowell and Mark Platts, is designed to show how that view can defend itself against the familiar objection that "moral perception," "moral blindness," and so forth are mere bluster with no proper epistemological basis. But the defense proceeds—initially at least—by way of an appeal not to disregard the license contained in our *naive language* to talk, for instance, about "seeing moral aspects of a situation." So the proposed "modest form of intuitionism," while admittedly helping itself for purposes of orientation to a bit of philosophical jargon, still seems to me to be faithful in spirit to the later Wittgensteinian method—that method being applied here to the retrieval, and possible restoration to esteem, of some underrated elements in our *actual* concept (or conception) of "seeing."

3 The Idea of Truth-Aptitude

Let's now add some more detail to Glock's critique of AAR. He lists six claims which he takes to be definitive of this position, but I will focus on claim (1) since he describes this as "the central tenet, around which the others revolve." It says that "ethical judgements or statements can be true or false," or in other words that such statements, "at least those in the indicative mood, are truth-apt."[15] This claim rests, as Glock goes on to explain, on a "deflationary" view of truth in general—a view that renounces any substantive account of truth in terms of the relation between "truth-bearers" and "truth-makers" (e.g., propositions and states of affairs), and accepts instead that the essence of the matter is captured by Tarski-style truisms of the form "'p' is true iff p." And with regard to Wittgenstein, Glock agrees that "[t]hroughout his career, [his general perspective on truth] had a deflationary touch."[16] So to that extent Glock is in listening mode. He takes issue, however, with the "homogeneous or 'seamless' conception of language" attributed to (the later) Wittgenstein in *Realism*, § 6: with the suggestion that "[i]f something has the grammatical form of a proposition, then it *is* a proposition"; and that "the only way in which an indicative statement can fail to describe reality is by *not being true*"—a move in support of which I cite Wittgenstein on the temptation to find fault, by some supposedly philosophical criterion, with ordinary (and viable) forms of expression. ("As if, for example, the proposition 'he has pains' could be false in some other way than by that man's *not* having pains.")[17]

These remarks—the ones just cited from my 1983 text—certainly look like sweeping generalizations. Even here, Glock finds some common ground, since he thinks the idea of "seamlessness" correctly captures Wittgenstein's view that our language-game, or rather the sum total of our various language-games, is "not answerable to a purported essence of reality":[18] this picture of language as "autonomous," and of grammar as "arbitrary," is topic-neutral and thus no more threatening to evaluative talk than to any other kind. But Glock thinks I go wrong in the consequences I draw from the Wittgensteinian approach. For although "there is no *metaphysical* perspective from which one form of discourse could be disqualified as *less realistic* than another," it "does not follow that scientific and moral statements have the same role or function to begin with. It does not even follow that all statements that we call true or false have the same role or function."[19] These words contain a message for Lovibond, who (as Glock puts it) "*denies* that there is such a divergence in function [for example, the functions of description and expression] between different kinds of truth-apt propositions,"[20] since all of them may be said to refer to an objective reality.

4 Intellectual Authority-Relations

My book does lay stress, at least in its opening phase, on metaphysical considerations—or rather, on what it offers as therapeutically *anti*-metaphysical considerations—as distinct from the functional study of language-games. This is because, as noted earlier, the initial purpose of the discussion is to confront— and to resolve or "deconstruct"—the dogmatic fact-value opposition inherited from noncognitivist ethics. However, the pluralist (or as Glock puts it, "anti-formalist"[21]) aspect of Wittgenstein's thought is not forgotten even at this stage: thus § 9 spells out the point that

> [t]he homogeneity of language is not [being] asserted at the phenomenal level (the level at which we "describe language-games," cf. PI I § 486), for there are manifestly countless different kinds of use of what we call "symbols," "words," "sentences" (PI I § 23). It is asserted at the metaphysical level—the level at which empiricism drives a wedge between factual and evaluative meaning.[22]

I say that the pluralist aspect is not *forgotten*; and the varying functions that indicative sentences can perform in different regions of discourse are not forgotten either. The book takes up this point in a selective fashion governed by its own concerns: at any rate it soon discovers what Glock calls the "semantic ('grammatical') perspective from which one form of discourse can be described as *less descriptive* than another,"[23] and as he himself observes, is quite candid about the uneven prospects of securing consensus among competent participants in a conversation, depending on subject matter. Glock notes that McDowell has less to say than I do about such variation. But his supporting reference to me is to some fairly preliminary thoughts on this subject, which in fact permeates the book in its entirety from about §10 onward, moral consensus and its absence being among my central themes. Above all, someone approaching me through Glock would be unlikely to guess that my discussion attempts—however amateurishly—to connect the insights of nonfoundational epistemology in the analytical tradition, developed partly (though not exclusively) in a Wittgensteinian idiom, with those of critical theory. Particularly important here is the idea of "intellectual authority-relations" introduced in § 16.[24] Wittgenstein's treatment of rule-following has probably commanded more attention than anything else in PI; yet its material aspect (or so I suggest) has not been fully appreciated. Just as Quine will speak a few years later about a *"pull* toward objectivity" which induces us to match our linguistic responses correctly to sensory stimulation, so Wittgenstein brings to his account of the teacher-pupil relationship a characteristic physicality: "I let him go his way, or hold him back."[25]

Allusions of this kind to the phenomenon of social control, and to the speed with which we fall back (so to speak) on sheer muscle in any actual rule-following crisis, may sound reductive. There is, to be sure, nothing cosy about Wittgenstein's picture of the learning experience ("Stop interrupting me and do as I tell you. So far your doubts don't make sense at all."[26]) And in reporting on this picture in its application to ethics, Glock sometimes speaks in what might be taken for a reductionist voice: thus, "[a]n ethical proposition is true [he says on behalf of Wittgenstein] in so far as it accurately expresses the stance of the speaker's community and prescribes a course of action condoned by that stance."[27] But any such impression is dispelled when he goes on to warn that although Wittgenstein *connects* truth with consensus, he does not *equate* these things: a faithful reading will be one that steers a course between the "Scylla of anti-realist reductionism" (since the bearers of truth-values are nothing other than actual or possible *contents* of thought) and the "Charybdis of a realist disregard for the role of human thought and practice."[28] So here again Glock and I find ourselves in harmony, though my own number one piece of textual evidence suggests a slightly different way of putting the point. "Wittgenstein writes at RFM VI § 23: 'Not empiricism and yet realism in philosophy, that is the hardest thing.'"[29] Despite the obscurity or instability of the idea of "realism," I take it that the difficulty envisaged in this sentence is precisely the one mentioned by Glock—namely, that of holding on to the critical concepts by which our thought-contents are to be assessed (and thus refusing to disown the innocently realist attitude implicit in all truth-orientated thought), while at the same time declining to be drawn into the bad kind of "realism" which seeks to ground what we say and think in something external to the space of concepts (Glock's "Charybdis," aligned in my quoted text with the "empiricist" appeal to sense-data). In any event, Glock and I agree that in order to find a way between Scylla and Charybdis, one needs to do justice both to the (human) "language-game" as a natural phenomenon and to the claims of (at least some of) our talk to reach all the way out to its ostensible subject matter. ("When we say, and mean, that such-and-such is the case, we—and our meaning—do not stop anywhere short of the fact, but we mean: *this—is—so*"; PI I § 95.)

5 Degrees of Factuality

It's important, at this point, to notice once again how misleading it could be to attribute to my book the thesis that all truth-apt propositions have "the same role or function."[30] Taking the "function" of any given linguistic practice not in a purely formal sense, but—as Glock would presumably wish—in terms of its place in the nexus of social activity, I can readily agree (on behalf of *Realism*) that not all assertoric discourse involves de facto realist aspirations. That is: not all language-games in which we proceed by making assertions—by uttering sentences in the indicative mood—are equally beholden to an ideal of intersubjective agreement, or equally committed to treating disagreement as a symptom of error in some quarter. At one extreme in this respect would be the technique of counting, in which we are trained "with endless practice, with merciless exactitude";[31] at the other would be the kind of conversation that does not even seriously aim at the reconciliation of conflicting judgments. For example, "if you tell me . . . that it is great fun to ride on the big dipper [roller-coaster], and I then undertake to prove to you that you are mistaken and that in fact it is not really fun at all, you will be right to infer that (for whatever reason) I have failed to make myself at home with the concept of 'fun.'"[32] The use of "fun" and suchlike words is premised to some extent on our interest in the variety of individual perspectives and responses: it approaches these with curiosity rather than with dismay. So while my discussion seeks to undermine the "fact-value distinction" *qua* metaphysical dogma, it is certainly not meant to substitute a new dogma to the effect that there is nothing worth saying, at the phenomenal level, about the way language-games differ from one another in "factuality." I made an effort to tread carefully here because I was anxious to show that the position developed in my book could sustain a certain liberal-pluralist atmosphere which is one of the attractions of noncognitivist ethics, and which goes missing, in particular, in the moral realism of Platts (in *Ways of Meaning*).[33] If that is the atmosphere we favor, we will do well to acknowledge—and to make our peace with—the variable role of intellectual authority within different "games."

6 Recognition-Transcendent Moral Truth?

However, when it comes to the description or "perspicuous representation" of linguistic practice, all parties have an equal duty to avoid tendentiousness. And anyone not prejudiced in advance against the claims of an "unambitious" realism—against the idea of an implicit commitment to correctness in our thinking (cf. § 1)—can legitimately point out that we do not in general feel bound to set that commitment aside, or to regard it as discredited, wherever we come up against the limited power of discursive argument. Of course, one can easily be discouraged by the perceived moral stupidity of others. But there is no sound reason to presume that in the case of every question that admits of a correct (or good enough) answer, the correctness of that answer will be obvious without more ado. In fact, McDowell has argued in a more recent discussion that Plato's Forms are to be understood as an antidote to just this mistake. The Forms, he says, "are an image to enable us to sustain the idea that there is such a thing as getting things right, precisely in the absence of ways to make answers to ethical questions universally compelling."[34] Plato's dialogues set before us certain characters who are able—contingently, by virtue (for example) of not having their heads stuffed with sociobiological nonsense—to find their way to such answers, even if they are unable to take their opponents with them. We may be reminded here of Wittgenstein's remark about knowing how to judge the genuineness, or otherwise, of expressions of feeling: "Can one learn this knowledge? Yes; some can."[35] Only *some*. But what those people have is nevertheless *knowledge*.

As noted earlier (§ 2), my book does not shy away from the question whether a "Wittgensteinian realism" (or as Glock would put it, AAR) can accommodate recognition-transcendent moral truth—that is, whether it can make sense of the possibility that moral truth might spin free of any existing *doxa* or consensus. In envisaging this possibility, we are evidently distancing ourselves from the commitment of the historical Wittgenstein to a "non-cognitivist and loosely speaking existentialist morality" (though not necessarily from his personal "predilection for dogmatic-cum-authoritarian ideologies": Glock's words in both cases; he wisely holds back from trying to square this circle).[36] I think I can claim to have remained faithful, in my treatment of the problem of recognition-transcendence, to my declared intention of working at the level of what "lies open to view"—namely, the "physiognomy" of the moral language-game as revealed to a descriptive method; but it takes me more than one encounter with that problem to unpack all of what I want to say about it. My first attempt, in § 19, revolves around "what it is like for a community to change its mind about a moral issue,"[37] and concedes that there is no counterpart (or no *precise* counterpart) in ethics to the experience of acquiring *decisive new evidence*—for example, the kind of observational evidence which can lead to a more or less uniform and immediate change in the view taken by competent judges about a natural-scientific question. So this discussion continues to dwell on the rough-and-ready state of intellectual authority in ethics, by comparison with the sciences:[38] it concludes by granting that with regard to the totality of speakers (as distinct from the inevitably flawed individual), "moral facts have a non-metaphysical way of failing to be . . . recognition-transcendent, just as . . . moral judgements have a non-metaphysical way of failing (sometimes) to be objective."[39] We may or may not be enthusiastic about diversity of values for its own sake, but it may in any case be impossible to achieve that underlying condition of like-mindedness that would enable us to approach moral thinking, as we do arithmetic, with the feeling that "the steps are *really* already taken, even before *I* take them" in any given context.[40]

Now, to repeat, this is a *first* attempt—though despite the diligent cross-referencing practiced throughout the book, I don't actually seem to call attention to the moment when I embark, much later at § 35, on a second one with a rather different outcome. The later discussion switches to a more purely phenomenological, or "surface-grammar," approach for which it is essential to recognize the contrast between *truth* and *social acceptability* as an internal feature of the language-game. As Glock notes, while Wittgenstein *connects* truth with consensus, "this is not by way of a consensus or pragmatist theory of truth. Without consensus in the application of predicates, we would (could) not employ them, but this is *not part of their meaning*. Whether (it is true that) an object satisfies a predicate does not depend on human consensus."[41] This point is central to my second, more assertive treatment of recognition-transcendent moral truth, which takes comfort from the "absence [in ethics as elsewhere] of any logical (or 'grammatical') objection to statements of the form: 'I'm right and everyone else is wrong'"[42]—the legitimacy of which, as I go on to say, "belongs with" the use of critical or normative concepts such as truth, goodness, reality, and rationality.

7 The Power to Imagine Alternatives

"In ethics as elsewhere"—really? This may seem to invite the suspicion that we have after all lost interest in whether it is possible to "do anything" with the moral realist idiom I am trying to defend. Aren't we now heading back toward the dead end represented by old-fashioned ethical intuitionism, which was said to rely on bluster to distract attention from its epistemological poverty (cf. § 2)? I must answer: hopefully no, because the book is by this time well launched upon the application of its interim findings to the topic of *confrontation* between forms of life—not just in the synchronic mode reflected in discussions of cultural relativism[43] but also in a diachronic mode exemplified specifically by historical difference and change. In order to deal with these latter phenomena in a nonreductive fashion—to keep faith, as Glock and I both wish to do, with the principle that "truth is not a matter of consensus"—it is necessary to develop a more dialectical account of our practices of truth-orientated, or world-directed, thinking. Our aim must be to acknowledge the material *grounding* of those practices in consensus, but to avoid lapsing into what McDowell calls the "sideways-on" view[44]—rather, to show respect for the inbuilt commitment of our meanings *not* to "stop anywhere short of the fact" (cf. § 4; this of course remains subject to the qualification mentioned in § 5 about concepts like "fun").

"We're right and the other lot are wrong." The license to say this, or at least to entertain this thought—not merely for propaganda purposes, but as a putative landmark en route from objectively worse to better thinking—is located, I suggest, at the heart of the moral realist project. But what my book eventually posits as the (epistemologically) most precious thing is to know that one retains that license in a situation of difficulty or defeat. To this end, it argues—still by the method of "assembling reminders"—that just as (for example) pain-language has evolved toward a measure of autonomy in relation to the pain-behavior of which it is a sophisticated outgrowth, so our normative and critical concepts have attained to a measure of autonomy vis-à-vis the institutional basis (i.e., the means of enforcement) without which, in a general way, those concepts would not be viable. Thanks to the resources of self-mastery, the all-pervasive wealth of cool, that comes with civilization, we can suppose—not easily perhaps, but quite intelligibly—that someone who is laughing is really in pain; likewise, thanks to our culturally implanted power to imagine alternatives (different evaluative attitudes, different systems of social constraint), we can think—again perhaps not easily, but intelligibly: "People seem not to have a problem with this, but actually, it is wrong and we ought to change direction."[45]

This willingness to appeal proleptically to an imagined "form of life" that would validate our nonconsensual, yet at the same time nonarbitrary, judgment is the badge of the moral realist; it expresses faith in the possibility of "getting things right . . . in the absence of ways to make [our own views] compelling." However, it is first and foremost a practical orientation and only secondarily (and negatively) a matter of theory—only, that is, in so far as one refuses to be *dislodged* by theoretical (metaphysical) considerations from one's position "inside" the moral language-game. This, we may recall, was the point of the "homogeneous or seamless" conception of language which Glock finds problematic: not to project on to our linguistic behavior a misleading image of uniformity, but to suggest (or, to issue a "reminder") that if we find it possible to occupy the internal perspective on factual or scientific discourse, there is no properly *philosophical* reason—at any rate, no reason innocent of a quasi-empiricist "metaphysical favouritism"—why we should not be able to do this for moral discourse too. Consensus in that area can certainly be elusive at times, but (to echo Wittgenstein) why allow the occasional contradiction to wreck the game?[46] It is not as though nothing of importance would be lost if we did so.

I continue, therefore, to have my doubts about a reading of (the later) Wittgenstein that credits him with some kind of substantial, revisionist philosophical position—for example, one that "points in the direction of a communitarian variant of expressivism"[47]—and to find his thought more congenial to the purpose that governs my book: namely, the removal of certain intellectual obstacles to our thoroughgoing acquiescence in the "situated," human cognitive standpoint. Glock and I are agreed that to occupy that standpoint—to consent actually to *play* one of our assertoric language-games—is to draw a distinction between true propositions and (merely) socially acceptable ones. But for him the sticking point, the moment when AAR supposedly helps itself to "one 'anti' too many," comes with the idea that to insist on that distinction is simply to take seriously the possibility of really meaning what we think and say from within our own conceptual space; of meaning nothing less—even, for instance, in ethics—than: "*This—is—so.*" Glock, I take it, will refuse to say with McDowell that the deflationary view of truth as a "predicate of disquotation" is adequate in itself to support the AAR picture. ("If one has a *steadfast understanding of truth as disquotability*," writes McDowell, "one can be immune to philosophically induced anxiety about how thought and speech, undertaken from the midst of our local practices, can make contact with reality."[48]) I think he (Glock) will be the loser by this refusal, but I am unsure how to pursue the point any further.

8 Values and Secondary Qualities

Instead, as a coda, I will add a few words on the topic which also forms a coda to Glock's discussion of AAR—the analogy between values and secondary qualities (VSQ). This analogy rests on the idea that predicates which reflect or express human sensibilities can nevertheless denote real features of the objects we talk about—the word "sensibilities" being intended to embrace both physical sense-perception and ethical (or aesthetic) "intuition."

Glock identifies this as a place where "trouble lurks" for AAR;[49] but his diagnosis is unconvincing. He offers a reconstruction of the analogy in terms of *competent* judgment: "An object having secondary quality Q is [i.e., consists in] its being such as to appear Q to competent and well-placed observers.... An object having moral value V is [i.e., consists in] its being recognized as having V by competent members of a speech-community." And he thinks these claims do violence to the Wittgensteinian principle that consensus can play only an indirect role in our understanding of truth and falsehood, since they effectively "*define* their respective analysanda by reference to human reactions"—thus committing AAR "[i]n this respect, at least . . . [to a position] much closer to Blackburn-style anti-realism or projectivism than its adherents would be prepared to concede."[50] So AAR is supposedly in danger here of forfeiting its right to that crucial second "anti."

The problem with Glock's (admittedly rapid and impressionistic) account of the VSQ analogy is that it fails to acknowledge the normative implications of the reference to *competent* observers or judges. In the case of color-properties, for example, the competence in question will presumably just amount to a disposition to call things red (etc.) when they *are* red. That disposition will of course depend for its successful establishment on the (contingent) absence of handicaps such as color blindness. But if there is no difficulty of that kind, what one acquires is competence in describing a certain kind of (objective) feature of one's surroundings.[51] This element of normativity—the thing that enters with the requirement to *get it right*—is all the more evident in the case of value judgment, which calls upon dispositions to react to objects in the way that is *merited* by their various good or bad attributes. We may doubt whether McDowell does himself any favors here by talking about a *disanalogy* attendant upon the analogy between values and secondary qualities:[52] he would have done better, I think, to posit an *imperfect or qualified analogy*, the imperfection lying in the fact that "moral blindness" is a good deal more prevalent than color blindness, and the likelihood of going wrong in one's judgment correspondingly more acute. (This is what I have tried to capture by saying that the get-it-right constraint is "all the more evident" in the evaluative case.) However, my present concern is not to settle that question, but simply to dissent from the suggestion that AAR is committed to any reductive definition of value-properties "by reference to human reactions"—or, consequently, to any retreat into anti-realist or "projectivist" territory. Human reactions are of course involved in the deployment of evaluative vocabulary, just as the human perceptual apparatus is involved in talk about colors; but the realist (or AAR) character of the analogy comes out in the idea that our perspective on our own evaluative responses is an essentially critical one: that is, it contains a permanent *potential* for critical reflection. Thus, fear is a response to the (objectively) fearful, or failing that, it is "the *intelligibly defective* product of a propensity towards responses that *would be intelligible* in that way."[53] Admiration, likewise, is a response to the (objectively) admirable, or failing that, is an intelligibly defective by-product of our capacity for admiring what we ought to admire. In representing this critical function as internal to the powers we invoke when we say that "to have moral value V is to be recognized as having V by competent judges"—that, for example, "the good is what is loved by the good"—we ensure that although such judgment remains *ours* (being shaped, in some cases at least, by such obviously subjective tendencies as love or admiration), it accepts guidance from the *objective* presence of the properties that engage its interest. I persist, therefore, in the belief that AAR can avoid collapsing into any of the revisionary metaphysical theories (projectivism, "communitarian expressivism," or whatever) which one may be tempted to read into the later writings of Wittgenstein.

9 An Enduring Critical Realism

The foregoing discussion has probably sounded a bit intransigent as a response to Glock's thoughtful commentary. That impression would be accurate in that I have resisted his central suggestion about "one 'anti' too many"—though I have also tried to put to rest any suspicion that a Wittgensteinian moral realism of the kind I was advocating is doomed to be in denial about the actual (empirical) variety of our "language-games," or about the varied styles of authority relationship involved in them.

Still, the moment of AAR as reconstructed by Glock was some thirty or forty years ago. What, if anything, remains of it that can lay claim to the attention of present-day philosophy? I would answer in a nutshell that the thing of enduring interest is the critical attitude demanded by this kind of view toward the *totality* of our linguistic practice—irrespective of the degree to which this or that local discursive phenomenon happens to qualify, by the standards of an empiricist "metaphysical favouritism," as genuinely "descriptive."

"It is our *acting* which lies at the bottom of the language-game," writes Wittgenstein (OC § 204). To bring this idea to full consciousness is to add a dimension of *complicity* to our acquiescence not only in the overtly "moral" side of our ongoing form of life but also in its indebtedness to the discourses of scientific, technical, and managerial expertise; and with the recognition of complicity—or so I would optimistically suggest—comes a newly vigilant or critical relation to the "customs, uses, institutions" that regulate our lives as thinking beings.[54] But the critical perspective is not necessarily a skeptical one, in the sense of disavowing or abandoning the get-it-right constraint. Rather, to think critically is to seek to *correct* the faults in one's present state of understanding, whether theoretical or practical. It favors skepticism, not of a metaphysical or global kind, but of the worldly kind that teaches us to be careful where we bestow our trust.

The merit I still see in AAR—not that I am particularly keen to perpetuate this label—is that it offers a strategy for resistance to any specifically ethical skepticism, any conception of evaluative subject matter as in principle epistemically second-rate, by bringing such subject matter within the scope of a topic-neutral critical realism. The resulting view is set against the background of a (purportedly) sober acknowledgment of the limitations of discursive reason—limitations which that of course are liable, under modern (or postmodern) conditions, to look more forbidding in relation to ethics than to "factual" or scientific discourse. *Realism* may in fact have been regarded in some quarters as naive or out of touch in its deference to ideals of "universal reason"; and I did subsequently have a go at processing some of the postmodernist hostility to this idea which gained currency in the 1980s and 1990s.[55] However, it's worth mentioning that one of the incentives not to sneer at "universal reason" is the impending ecological crisis, the (contingent, historic) threat to our *collective* species-life, which already forms part of the intellectual landscape of my book and which is all the more inescapable today: this might in fact be regarded as a more valuable long-term point of reference than the paranoia about discursive "totalitarianism" that informs much late twentieth-century cultural theory. And I would also continue to give credit to AAR as a position that can motivate us not to stand by without protest while practical thinking—the pursuit of the good life, the negotiation of human problems—is expelled or excused from the domain in which noninstrumental standards of correctness apply.[56]

Notes

1 Hans-Johann Glock, "Wittgensteinian Anti-Anti-Realism: One 'Anti' Too Many?," originally published in *Ethical Perspectives* 22, no. 1 (2015): 99–129; hereafter "Wittgensteinian AAR": Glock uses the abbreviation "AAR" for "anti-anti-realism."

2 John McDowell, *Mind, Value, and Reality* (Cambridge, MA: Harvard University Press, 1998), viii.
3 Sabina Lovibond, *Realism and Imagination in Ethics* (Oxford: Blackwell, 1983); hereafter *Realism*.
4 Ibid., 25; emphasis added.
5 "Wittgensteinian AAR," 113.
6 Ibid., 100.
7 Ibid., 101.
8 These words may seem to identify me as one of Richard Rorty's "pragmatic Wittgensteinians," who do not set out to recapture what is "merely idiosyncratic in . . . Wittgenstein's own way of thinking, but rather to restate his best arguments in more effective ways" ("Wittgenstein and the Linguistic Turn," in *Wittgenstein's Philosophical Investigations: A Critical Guide*, ed. Arif Ahmed [Cambridge: Cambridge University Press, 2010], 134). My approach could perhaps be described, in this sense, as pragmatic (as distinct from "pragmatist"—that is, affiliated to a pragmatist *theory* of the kind favored by Rorty), but overall I find myself more in tune with the effort of Paul Horwich ("Rorty's Wittgenstein," in the same collection) to show that a therapeutic reading of *Philosophical Investigations* has greater merit than Rorty allows, and to commend the resulting metaphysical attitude as correct in itself. And to the extent that contemporary Wittgenstein studies comprise a "rationalist" and an "irrationalist" tendency, as suggested in another discussion by Glock, I would have to align myself predominantly with the former; see his "Perspectives on Wittgenstein: An Intermittently Opinionated Survey," in *Wittgenstein and his Interpreters: Essays in Memory of Gordon Baker*, ed. Guy Kahane, Edward Kanterian, and Oskari Kuusela (Oxford: Blackwell, 2007), esp. § IV.
9 "Wittgensteinian AAR," 112.
10 For this criticism of the treatment of ethics in *Realism*, see Cora Diamond, "Wittgenstein, Mathematics, and Ethics: Resisting the Attractions of Realism," in *The Cambridge Companion to Wittgenstein*, ed. Hans Sluga and David Stern (Cambridge: Cambridge University Press, 1996). My book is by no means neglectful of the wordless side of life since it builds upon the more general insight that all communication, linguistic or otherwise, presupposes a sublinguistic consensus attributable to our "insertion into the natural world": see esp. § 48, 211–12. However, I respond directly (and somewhat concessively) to Diamond in my *Ethical Formation* (Cambridge, MA: Harvard University Press, 2002), ch. 2, §§ 3–4. And for some more recent reflections on her view that there is no such thing as the subject matter of ethics—this being the thought with which I still find myself at variance—see "The Elusiveness of the Ethical: From Murdoch to Diamond," *Royal Institute of Philosophy Supplement* 87 (2020): 181–200.
11 *Realism*, 77.

12 Ludwig Wittgenstein, *Philosophical Investigations*, trans. G. E. M. Anscombe, 3rd ed. (Oxford: Basil Blackwell, 1967), I § 568.
13 Ibid., I § 109.
14 Ludwig Wittgenstein, *Zettel*, ed. G. E. M. Anscombe and Georg Henrik von Wright, trans. G. E. M. Anscombe, 2nd ed. (Oxford: Blackwell, 1981), § 223; cf. *Realism* § 12, 48–9. For the idea of the meaning of life as a "physiognomy," see § 50 of the book. Unless otherwise stated, emphasis in quotations is in the original text.
15 "Wittgensteinian AAR," 113; see in particular PI I § 136.
16 Ibid.
17 *Realism*, 25–6; cf. PI I § 402.
18 "Wittgensteinian AAR," 120.
19 Ibid., 121.
20 Ibid., 119; emphasis added.
21 Ibid., 117: "[T]he later Wittgenstein insists on just such differences [i.e., '"grammatical" differences between moral assertions or judgements on the one hand, factual assertions or judgements on the other'], as part of what one might call his *anti-formalism*."
22 *Realism*, 36.
23 "Wittgensteinian AAR," 121.
24 *Realism*, 63 and context.
25 PI I § 208.
26 Ludwig Wittgenstein, *On Certainty*, ed. G. E. M. Anscombe and Georg Henrik von Wright, trans. Denis Paul and G. E. M. Anscombe (Oxford: Blackwell, 1969), § 310; hereafter *OC*.
27 "Wittgensteinian AAR," 123.
28 Ibid., 126.
29 *Realism* § 11, 45. The reference is to Wittgenstein, *Remarks on the Foundations of Mathematics*, ed. Georg H. von Wright, Rush Rhees, and G. E. M. Anscombe, 3rd ed. (Oxford: Blackwell, 1978); hereafter *RFM*.
30 "Wittgensteinian AAR," 119; quoted in § 3.
31 Wittgenstein, *RFM* I § 4.
32 *Realism* § 17, 66.
33 See Mark Platts, *Ways of Meaning: An Introduction to a Philosophy of Language*, 2nd ed. (Cambridge, MA: MIT Press, 1997), ch. 10.
34 John McDowell, "Towards Rehabilitating Objectivity" (first published 2000), in his *The Engaged Intellect: Philosophical Essays* (Cambridge, MA: Harvard University Press, 2009), 210.
35 Wittgenstein, *PI* II 227.
36 Glock, "Wittgensteinian AAR," 106, 100.
37 *Realism*, 79.

38 Compare Glock, "Wittgensteinian AAR," 124: "The kind of consensus one can achieve in scientific discourse, however fallible, far outstrips the kind of consensus we appear capable of attaining concerning matters moral."
39 *Realism*, 81.
40 Cf. Wittgenstein, *PI* I § 188.
41 Glock, "Wittgensteinian AAR," 124–5.
42 *Realism* § 35, 148.
43 Ibid., § 32.
44 John McDowell, *Mind and World* (Cambridge, MA: Harvard University Press, 1994), for example, at 34–6.
45 Ibid., § 35, 150; cf. Wittgenstein, *PI* I § 393.
46 Cf. *Realism* § 42, 179; cf. Wittgenstein, *RFM* VII § 11.
47 Glock, "Wittgensteinian AAR," 123.
48 "Towards Rehabilitating Objectivity," 221; emphasis added.
49 See Glock, "Wittgensteinian AAR," 125.
50 Ibid., 126.
51 Compare Wittgenstein, *PI* I § 381: "How do I know that this colour is red?—It would be an answer to say: 'I have learnt English.'"
52 John McDowell, "Values and Secondary Qualities" (first published 1985), in his *Mind, Value, and Reality*, 143: "The disanalogy . . . is that a virtue (say) is conceived to be not merely such as to elicit the appropriate 'attitude' (as a colour is merely such as to cause the appropriate experiences), but rather such as to *merit* it." The term "metaphysical favouritism" in § 7 is borrowed from this essay (see 148, fn. 54; 149, fn. 57).
53 McDowell, "Values and Secondary Qualities," 144; emphasis added.
54 For this notion of complicity see *Realism*, 119.
55 See my *Ethical Formation*, esp. Part III; and for direct discussion of "universal reason," see Essays 1 and 2—first published 1989 and 1992, respectively—of my *Essays on Ethics and Feminism* (Oxford University Press, 2015), the second of which responds to criticism by Richard Rorty.
56 Thanks to Hanjo Glock for providing the stimulus to revisit *Realism*; to the organizers of the 2016 Zürich conference, "Doing Ethics after Wittgenstein"; and to all who took part in the discussion on that occasion.

Works Cited

Diamond, Cora, "Wittgenstein, Mathematics, and Ethics: Resisting the Attractions of Realism," in Hans Sluga and David Stern (eds.), *The Cambridge Companion to Wittgenstein*, 226–60, Cambridge: Cambridge University Press, 1996.

Glock, Hans-Johann, "Perspectives on Wittgenstein: An Intermittently Opinionated Survey," in Guy Kahane, Edward Kanterian, and Oskari Kuusela (eds.), *Wittgenstein and His Interpreters: Essays in Memory of Gordon Baker*, 37–65, Oxford: Blackwell, 2007.

Glock, Hans-Johann, "Wittgensteinian Anti-Anti-Realism: One 'Anti' Too Many?," *Ethical Perspectives* 22, no. 1 (2015): 99–129.

Horwich, Paul, "Rorty's Wittgenstein," in Arif Ahmed (ed.), *Wittgenstein's Philosophical Investigations: A Critical Guide*, 154–61, Cambridge: Cambridge University Press, 2010.

Lovibond, Sabina, *Realism and Imagination in Ethics*, Oxford: Basil Blackwell, 1983.

Lovibond, Sabina, *Ethical Formation*, Cambridge, MA: Harvard University Press, 2002.

Lovibond, Sabina, *Essays on Ethics and Feminism*, Oxford: Oxford University Press, 2015.

Lovibond, Sabina, "The Elusiveness of the Ethical: From Murdoch to Diamond," *Royal Institute of Philosophy Supplement* 87 (2020): 181–200.

McDowell, John, *Mind and World*, Cambridge, MA: Harvard University Press, 1994.

McDowell, John, "Values and Secondary Qualities," in John McDowell, *Mind, Value, and Reality*, 131–50, Cambridge, MA: Harvard University Press, 1998.

McDowell, John, "Towards Rehabilitating Objectivity," in John McDowell, *The Engaged Intellect: Philosophical Essays*, 204–24, Cambridge, MA: Harvard University Press, 2009.

Platts, Mark, *Ways of Meaning: An Introduction to a Philosophy of Language*, London: Routledge and Kegan Paul, 1979.

Rorty, Richard, "Wittgenstein and the Linguistic Turn," in Arif Ahmed (ed.), *Wittgenstein's Philosophical Investigations: A Critical Guide*, 129–44, Cambridge: Cambridge University Press, 2010.

Wittgenstein, Ludwig, *Philosophical Investigations*, trans. G. E. M. Anscombe, 3rd ed., Oxford: Basil Blackwell, 1967.

Wittgenstein, Ludwig, *On Certainty*, ed. G. E. M. Anscombe and Georg H. von Wright, trans. Denis Paul, and G. E. M. Anscombe, Oxford: Basil Blackwell, 1969.

Wittgenstein, Ludwig, *Remarks on the Foundations of Mathematics*, ed. Georg H. von Wright, Rush Rhees, and G. E. M. Anscombe, 3rd ed., Oxford: Basil Blackwell, 1978.

Wittgenstein, Ludwig, *Zettel*, ed. G. E. M. Anscombe and Georg H. von Wright, trans. G. E. M. Anscombe, 2nd ed., Oxford: Basil Blackwell, 1981.

7

Does It Pay to Be Good?

On D. Z. Phillips Having a Theory about Not Having a Theory in Ethics

Hartmut von Sass

1 In the Beginning Was . . . the Problem

Deciding to write on D. Z. Phillips's ethics leads rather quickly to a simple problem: there is no such thing as a proper Phillipsian ethics. Saying that Phillips was, primarily, a philosopher of religion who also worked as an ethicist is, thus, not quite correct. If one tries to pin down "the ethical" in Phillips, one will be mostly led to indirect considerations that have their disciplinary location originally in other fields, such as epistemology and philosophy of language—and only from here Phillips draws some consequences that may have to do with human behavior and the heterogeneity of our actions, values, virtues, or interests. You won't find something in Phillips that is traditionally called *applied ethics*, that is, no substantial work on peace, economics, environment, health, animals, sexuality, etc., but you won't find something that is traditionally called *normative (or general) ethics* either, that is, no effort to invest in justifying moral convictions, solving moral disagreements, or proposing suggestions on how to handle the ramified challenges today in bioethics, immigration, or of the precarious relationship between state and religion(s).

What Phillips is actually doing is—if one insists on labeling it—*metaethics*. Now, there are two different metaethical forms, one that represents the shift from morals to the language in which we express ourselves morally and another version that puts the stress on methodological issues in ethics. Although Phillips was, from time to time, also concerned with our moral discourses, their variety, and the normativity that is under pressure by this heterogeneity, he was essentially focused on *how to do ethics* in the first place. More precisely, Phillips is interested in describing and, in doing so, in defending the "hubbub of voices" (Rush Rhees)[1] within our moral practices without reducing them to one formula and without justifying them by reference to some "deeper" layer or nonmoral standard of general rationality.

Elaborating on what this methodological metaethics precisely amounts to is, again, not an easy task to fulfill. One reason for this difficulty is that Phillips stated how *not* to do ethics, rather than giving a constructive account of "his" ethics. At first glance, this reservation to present an ethical method seems to be completely consistent with his general reluctance against generalizations. He is—following Rhees, Ray Holland, and Peter Winch—interested in paying "attention to particulars,"[2] in giving the singular case its due, and in doing justice to the divergent responses, attitudes, and orientations within "the conversation of mankind."[3] Especially when it concerns the ethical, Phillips holds that general accounts could entail confusing results of moral ignorance and aspect-blindness.[4] Instead of sketching his ethical method, Phillips presents "interventions in ethics" in criticizing others—including his very best philosophical friends—by showing how their approaches suffer from following an agenda or proposing a (too) general claim.

Phillips, however, is about "to go nowhere."[5] This means he is not doing ethics to fulfill a task, to contribute to solve a problem, or, even worse, to advertise a philosophical program and metaphysical system. As soon as you do, Phillips (as long as he could) would not wait very long until trying to undermine the assumptions on which your systematic account has been based. "Interventions in . . ."—this is exactly what Phillips was concerned with, pretending to come from outside and take care to therapeutically clean and purify the discourse from allegedly severe confusions. His alternative was a philosophical contemplation—as a descriptive philosophy 2.0—that attempts to do justice—a moral term!—to reality or to the world.

Phillips's contemplative philosophy was, for the most and crucial part, developed in debates about genuine faith and existential orientations in life, about different, but equally vivid possibilities to understand (non-metaphysical or post-theist) religious practices.[6] This descriptive and, later on, contemplative endeavor was also applied and worked out in the field of ethics as clarification of how *not* to *do* ethics. Here, however, things start to turn problematic, since in order to defend a descriptive or contemplative ethics, one needs a methodological metaethics. Phillips does have such a general method—which is precisely the problem: to present his case for a contemplative ethics (as, itself, an ethical demand on the philosopher) he refers to a metaethics that suffers crucially from a lack of contemplation, which would have to be applied to itself. If contemplation opens the conceptual and hermeneutical space to appreciate divergent ways of dealing with a (ethical or philosophical) problem, the meta-philosophical question of how to philosophize calls for contemplation itself. This might imply that contemplation is only one possibility within the "hubbub of (philosophical) voices."

Unfortunately, it is one of the major difficulties in Phillips that he was blind to a contemplation applied to itself, that is, to a self-reflective contemplation.[7] In other words, Phillips had a theory about not having a theory; he presented (or sometimes at least presupposed) a generalized metaethics concerning ethics without any generalizations. Therefore, it is clear from the outset that this proto-program could not have turned out to be successful due to a deep inconsistency in Phillips's "system."[8] By "system" I mean his far-reaching semantic assumptions concerning the formation of our concepts and, combined with it, the relation between beliefs and the practices in which these beliefs have their context (see esp. section 4).

Therefore, the present study leads us to the very heart of Phillips's work by being dedicated to uncover these backgrounds that inform his view on ethics as well as create the dilemma of a noncontemplative contemplation. Hence, it will be asked what ethics could look like when appreciating Phillips's (and Wittgenstein's) serious concerns without taking his (or their) methodological metaethics—I know, they would dislike that term—at face value.

2 Ethics and Thinking Morally

It is well known that Ludwig Wittgenstein thought that his early masterpiece consists of two parts, the *Tractatus* itself and what he did not and could not say in it.[9] In this realm of silence belongs also the ethical (or mystical) that is not directly expressed (or expressible), but rather shown.[10] Something that is similar to this distinction can also be found in Wittgenstein's *Philosophical Investigations*. Clearly, this late collection is not a book on normative ethics as, traditionally, the "rational justification for moral judgements,"[11] and it has hardly anything to say about specific moral issues either. Nevertheless, one might hold that the *Investigations* are indeed an ethical volume in the sense of the mode of thinking they are depicting.[12] In them, one might find a way of interacting with reality and our understanding of it that is itself a moral lesson: the probing of different descriptions, the referring to singular cases and particular examples, the close reading of the language we are actually using, the reluctance to minimize this usage to one imperative. The form of the *Investigations* is, without an explicit structure, an aphoristic game of allusions, considerations, questions, and assumptions.

As much as the *Investigations* are a "book" on philosophical problems, they are also a "book" on philosophy as a problem. Wittgenstein is, thus—and *pace* Kripke and Hacker—not so much concerned with contributing to the question of rule-following or an anti-private-language argument; rather, by referring to these specific issues, he is showing how to think philosophically. This way of thinking, one might say, has itself ethical implications when dealing tentatively with its subjects, when giving a sensitive account of certain phenomena, when letting the contexts speak (for themselves?) while avoiding to integrate them into a general structure. Therefore, Wittgenstein's descriptive philosophy is an educational journey into doing justice to philosophy's topics.

Phillips is on the same page with Wittgenstein here. He subscribes to Wittgenstein's descriptive philosophy—that is not only "shown" in the course of the *Investigations* but also explicitly expressed in their §§ 89–132—and, hence, he follows the shift from ethics as a particular subject within philosophy to an ethical mode of thinking relevant to all endeavors of philosophy. There is, Wittgenstein and Phillips hold, a way in which one is thinking (un)morally, that is, our thinking is not per se innocent.

The danger of becoming philosophically guilty lies, for Phillips, in proposing (metaphysical) systems as the most prominent version of generalizing particulars and forgetting about or neglecting their very particularity. So, what Nietzsche celebrated as the condition for having concepts at all, namely to forget about the specific features of, say, *that* tree, in order to construct a usable notion of a tree, seems to lead to a morally not unimportant failure.[13] For Phillips as well as for Rhees, there is a strict alternative between presenting a general theory and appreciating the variety from which the theory should be inferred—*either/or*. Wittgensteinians (of a specific fashion: the "Swansea School") are very clear about going with the "or," meaning that they do not succumb to the theoretical temptations by sticking to particular cases.[14]

Philosophy, Phillips states, has primarily to do with seeing differences; it is not concerned with solving problems, but with elaborating on what these problems amount to in our lives. A contemplative philosophy shows what it means to have a worldview but does not advertise a particular version of them. In doing so, it tries to be just to divergent positions and entails a moral endeavor with all its obstacles of not showing the necessary allegiance to a phenomenologically sensitive approach and, instead, to present a solution, to defend a standpoint, or to put forward a program.[15] Accordingly, Phillips is highly critical of what he takes to be the Enlightenment idea(l) of justifying everything and of deciding generally (or even universally) between right and wrong. This evidentialism,[16] Phillips adds, is only possible at the price of elevating one discourse over others in order to judge them from one paradigmatic point—that is itself, of course, not truly "justified."[17] Contrary to these expectations, one has to admit that philosophy is not able (but not responsible either) to give general answers to theoretical or existential questions. Concerning the business of ethics, such a wrongheaded expectation would lead, Phillips fears, to simplifying life whereas literature (rather than philosophy itself—but what about film?)[18] could rescue us from this simplification by showing the real "difficulty of life."[19]

First of all, it is important to cherish this difference between ethics as a subject of philosophy and thinking morally in all philosophical subjects (and beyond), between ethics as a discipline and ethics as a moral performance in our intellectual dealings with reality. Characterizing Phillips as an ethicist appreciates his philosophy as being concerned with ethics as a methodological account of our thinking, that is, as metaethics. I will put here the aforementioned concern aside that a contemplative philosophy as openness for divergent ways of understanding would also entail leaving space for different ways of philosophizing, including "systems," "generalizations," and some distance to just the particular case (or even "clusters" of them).[20] For Phillips, however, this room does not exist; all these attempts seem to be, for him, mere "metaphysics" and, as such, incapable of doing justice to reality, which means that they are morally insufficient.

I am sure, Phillips himself would have to be the very first one to criticize this generalized account of how (not) to do ethics. It is, in its general ambition, untenable as criticism against other philosophical orientations, and it is a helplessly impoverished picture of ethics (and philosophy in general). There are times when Phillips seems to have seen this in asking whether his attack on theories and generalizations might undermine the ethical business altogether. He replies by saying that, what is general in ethics, is the investigation of particular cases in "struggling for conceptual clarity."[21]

My impression is that Phillips fails to pay heed to one of his own major principles, namely to see how we actually do something or apply a term, in that case doing ethics and speaking of "ethics," respectively. Phillips, indebted to Kierkegaard, is in danger of reducing ethics to the individual and, from there, to the particular understanding of the lonely man—before God. Without acknowledging, however, that ethics is a social endeavor that deals, mostly, not with single individuals, but with common demands and their internal tensions—including the necessity to find a practical solution for them—the room will remain locked to see that generalizing things is, not always, but often enough, not a moral failure, but precisely the moral demand on behalf of practicability.[22]

Phillips would dismiss this as letting ethics be governed by *non-moral* considerations. Even if that were true, one should answer to this concern by referring to the ramified contexts in which our ethical thinking is called for—and these contexts may involve the allegedly pure ethical thinking about political, economic, juridical, practical, even biological, and religious issues, demands, and interest. As much as it is important to pay heed to our highly divergent and, sometimes, incompatible responses to, for instance, the possibility of reproductive cloning, it is insufficient to leave it there, since facing this challenge between promise and danger calls for an ethically consistent solution. It is Phillips's own and highly important distinction between ethics as subject and ethics as mode of thinking that brings us back to contemplating divergent contexts, individual and social ones, in which ethics as subject and as modal determination of that subject gains its relevance for the shared life we live together.

3 Phillips and Philippa. The Case of Consequentialism

Following Phillips, we distinguished between ethics as a theory on morals and ethics as a mode of thinking morally. Now, it is not too difficult to see that the first version gets undermined by the second one. More precisely, the methodological and, insofar, ethical demand on the philosopher to pay "attention to particulars" (without "meddling" with them, which is apparently identified with giving a general account of them)[23] excludes the philosophically legitimate possibility to pursue a normative ethics from the outset. One striking example for this deeply rooted reservation—and the accompanying ambivalence—in Phillips is his critique of Philippa Foot's early work on virtues and their relation to the "good."

According to Phillips, Foot is basically concerned with the question of why one should act well and justly. Foot's answer to this normative quest is simply that it pays off, as if the old karma rule were still in place: "do good things—and good things happen to you."[24] Contrary to deontological ethics where the intention is the basic element here the results of an action should provide the basis for evaluating a deed. Foot, Phillips holds, emphasizes that those who act in a just way will benefit from that very acting.[25] Hence, Foot happens to be a thinker of thick consequentialism.

Instead of elaborating critically on consequentialism in general, I would like to show how Phillips reacts to what he presents as Foot's generalized rule concerning acting and benefiting. First of all, it does not come as surprise that Phillips excludes the normative gesture expressed in Foot. "There are no theories of goodness," he says.[26] Moreover, Foot reduced morality to "expediency" and moral principles to a pragmatic politics; she argued on empirical grounds, which would, Phillips replies, entail that the lucky wrongdoer leads the best life he can.[27] However, it is, for Phillips, not so much about the wicked who prosper, but rather about the architecture of Foot's approach. Foot introduced a standard for morality that lies *outside* morality by referring to the "fruits" of acting to appreciate this acting—which resembles the traditional Kantian critique against heteronomy. In Phillips's words: "Mrs. Foot has tried to find a non-moral justification for moral beliefs, and such an attempt always fails."[28] It might be right (or wrong) that a good (or bad) deed amounts to good (or devastating) results—but that is, Phillips underlines, irrelevant for the moral quality of that very action. If it were otherwise, then one would be incapable of drawing the line between someone for whom justice in itself is important and someone acting accidently in a just manner.[29] Foot's account suffers from this incapacity.

To Foot's credit one has to bear in mind that her considerations on acting and benefiting are embedded in a neo-Aristotelian virtue ethics. That means, that the good deed is necessarily a virtuous one and, accordingly, that there is an internal relation between a virtuous deed and their teleologically informed consequences.[30] There are times when Phillips seems to appreciate this *internal* connection,[31] but it is nevertheless more than doubtful whether his reduction of Foot's account to a rather sober consequentialism is really "doing justice" to her overall position.

This is unfortunate as well as unnecessary since the form of *internalism* Foot is presenting here possesses some family resemblances with what Phillips himself has to say. Now, there are two versions of Phillips's anti-consequentialism. The first and more prominent one denies the ethical legitimacy of thinking in means and ends altogether; this relation is, Phillips makes clear, utterly alien to morals; it turns out to be impossible to give an account of, say, remorse.[32] Also other kinds of behavior where it is fully evident that there is no benefit, in Foot's sense, turn here to be not understandable (or, even, irrational). Imagine a person who is ready to give up her life for the sake of justice. "Is there any pay-off?" Phillips asks rhetorically.[33]

Here, the second version of Phillips's anti-consequentialism emerges, insofar as he does not say farewell to the means-ends-language-game, but holds, that in martyrdom, for example, means and ends are the same.[34] This is an alternative expression for the Kierkegaardian claim in *Purity of Heart* according to which the benefit of an act lies precisely in the act itself. The death of a martyr has, then, no other sense than in itself without implying any further purpose beyond as a contribution leading somewhere. Instead of identifying means and ends Phillips can also say that (as a third anti-consequentialist form) they entertain an internal relation to one another.[35]

I think, Phillips is completely justified in undermining the general ambition with which consequentialism usually (and most forms of normative approaches in ethics) gets presented. Behind the gesture of all these ethical generalizations lies what Wittgenstein calls the "despicable attitude towards the particular case."[36] So far, so good—but what about Phillips's own Kierkegaardian proposal that means and ends are identical or, respectively, that means as acts are ends in themselves? It is not clear whether Phillips thinks here of what Kant calls "disposition" (*Gesinnung*) or "conscience" (*Gewissen*) and, moreover, what kind of status the reference to deeds as being significant and meaningful in themselves entertains. It is, however, obvious that the generalization of this Kierkegaardian figure would itself suffer from Phillips's previous criticism.

But there's another aspect: Phillips is not willing to contemplate the cases that call for paying heed to the consequences entailed by certain actions. In his own words: he did not "do justice" to particular circumstances whose evaluation is "consenquentialistically" structured. Take our aforementioned example, reproductive cloning (or other cases that imply technical possibilities with tremendous difficulties for an ethical evaluation): these are cases of an essential need to be informed about the biological facts, and to be aware of the practical demands included in that very technique where the current veil of knowledge is combined with the necessity to act immediately on the basis of a consistent regulation mirroring our moral values (despite their variety). It is, I think, fair to say that we rely in these bioethical questions, at least partly, on considerations having to do with the consequences of our ethical (and political) decisions in close view. We do not only do so but we *have* to.[37] Take another example, this time from individual ethics: imagine a man who gives his life for a child for the simple reason that he is so much older than that kid who, contrary to him, has his future ahead of him. That is a typically utilitarian way of putting the matter, but the man's reference to future states including likely consequences does not by any means keep his consideration from being morally unacceptable.

To summarize my reservation so far: First, Phillips does not remain loyal to his metaethical advice, namely, to give the particular case its due. Even if one refutes consequentialism as general agenda, one should not deny that there are also situations calling for a consequentialist (and utilitarian) thinking. Second, ethics as a mode of thinking creates, for Phillips, the obstacle to leave space for generalized ethical commandments. This, however, is at odds with a truly contemplative philosophy, since paying heed to particular cases does not entail the denial of general responses to certain moral problems—even knowing that one cannot be fair in every single case. Affording such a partial lack of fairness might precisely be the moral demand on those who have the (political) responsibility. Here, the practicability of an ethical consideration might override the ethical demand to attend to singular cases, and that might itself reflect a moral call. Third, Phillips's approach to ethics is based on a "one-sided diet of examples," to put it in Wittgensteinian terms.[38] As stated above, he refers exclusively to cases belonging to what is called *individual ethics*. His Kierkegaardian critique of consequences as being morally indifferent is informed by this focus—but it is a blind spot. Ethics is not only a social endeavor but often enough a response to *social challenges* that we have to face. Here, ethics might turn into something that Phillips is so fond of dismissing: solving problems. He could claim that here we leave the realm of pure ethics entering a political (or just practical) empire. But this will, of course, not do, because this claim would not only be a private stipulation but also be ignorant of the contexts in which we actually do ethics. Phillips fails, I fear, to appreciate the fine difference between consequentialism as omnipotent approach (as, for instance, in Peter Singer) and consequentialist thinking as part of our—not exclusively consequentialist—moral repertoire.[39]

4 Background or Abyss? Ordinary Realism and Descriptive Philosophy

In order to understand where Phillips's ethical appreciation for the singular case and his reluctance for general claims come from we will have to leave ethics for a moment. My suggestion is that one of the major sources for celebrating the particular is rooted in Phillips's view(s) on semantics and concept-formation. Here, Phillips defends a position—a highly generalized one—that might be called *semantic naturalism*. You could also call it *neo-behaviorist semantics* (again, it is obvious that Phillips and Phillipsians would eagerly protest against these technical tags, but you might take them to be just heuristically useful localizations). The basic assumption of this semantic naturalism is the following thesis:

> (T) The meaning of a proposition *p* is essentially dependent on the practical implications of that proposition *p*.

It has to be admitted that (T) needs further clarification, but this is what this section is dedicated to providing. There are two different philosophical debates in which Phillips discusses and defends (T). The one is his critique of a two-step (non)realism, the other is his evaluation of Peter Winch's papers on "primitive" reactions and the reaction of the Good Samaritan. I will discuss both problems subsequently.

Phillips's relation to realism is a complicated one, to say the least. In some papers, he is ready to dismiss "realism" as well as "anti-realism" as confused labels while searching for a third position beyond that duality.[40] Sometimes, however, he defends a position that is not labeled as realism, but belongs to the realist camp. This view is present in passages where Phillips underlines that there is no reality independent of our concepts to describe that reality: "The world is for us what is presented through those concepts," he states.[41] Phillips can also hold that "reality" is related to particular language-games we play whereas these games constitute a world-picture.[42] However, Phillips insists here on the crucial point that these world-pictures are the only frameworks in which it makes sense to use "right" or "wrong." Since there is no world-picture behind all world-pictures, the question of whether a specific world-picture is itself "right" or "wrong" remains without any meaning.[43] And, finally, Phillips can also adopt the realist label by adding an "ordinary." Thus, an ordinary realism, as an attempt to give an account of reality and the possibility of discourse, is a description that Phillips not only accepts but also uses himself to summarize what he is, following Rhees, up to and in his later work.[44] So, we could say that the first position is a general reluctance to -isms that contradict each other, while this contradiction is precisely the symptom of their shared common ground that appears to be so problematic; the second version is known as "internal realism" meaning that our access to reality is language-based with the far-reaching consequence that the change of linguistic capacities entails a change of what we take to be reality;[45] the third position, however, is Phillips's own and later attempt to combine the "realistic spirit"[46] (without the residual idealism that internal realism still embraces) with the metaethical gesture of doing justice to the variety of phenomena.[47]

It is primarily the first of these three versions that is connected to the debate on semantics and concept-formation. In one of his most important papers, "On

Really Believing" (from 1991), Phillips opens the scene by claiming that the traditional assumption according to which realism and nonrealism are the only alternatives we actually have is confused and "idle talk."[48] Now, Phillips does not understand these labels in the traditional manner, since he takes (non)realism not primarily to be an epistemological claim, but rather to be a thesis about the relation between a belief and the "fruits of belief," as Phillips puts it.

What Phillips refutes concerning the dual between belief and its fruits is what is usually described as "mentalism." He presents this position to be implying that the fruits of a belief are the consequences of a prior mental state, as Roger Trigg or Terence Penelhum have it. This would amount to a two-step logic with a propositional element and a secondary action. Moreover, Phillips holds that the mentalist thinks that only the first element, the mental state as proposition, is the instance that secures the meaning of what is expressed by the proposition. Hence, a dualism emerges between two ontologically separate realms, the semantic realm of inner mental states and the practical realm of attitudes and actions.[49]

Phillips is, following Wittgenstein, highly critical of this pervasive duality between inner and outer, between the mental and the practical, between propositions and deeds. More precisely, Phillips repudiates the traditional priority of the first element of that duality and holds it to be impossible to separate propositions, as (non)realists actually do, from their practical environment. Without these practical environments, Phillips says, propositions do not have any sense—and this claim is already similar to thesis (T).

What Phillips is criticizing concerning (non)realism is that both positions contradict (T). Both realists and their nonrealist counterparts would separate beliefs from their semantically relevant contexts. Phillips says,

> One way of referring to the criticisms Wittgenstein makes of realism, is to say that the realist wishes to speak of the relation of belief to its object, without specifying the context of application which specifies what the relation comes to.[50]

The result is, Phillips adds, that what the specific belief comes to or what it means remains completely obscure. He gives an example by referring to our color vocabulary and its meaning:

> But unless we agreed on our colour reactions, we would not know what it means to entertain beliefs about colours changing, fading or being renewed. But our reactions are what we do. They are not the consequences of our beliefs. Without our agreement in reactions there would be nothing to have beliefs about.[51]

Accordingly, Phillips fears that (non)realism implies just two forms of the same confusion, namely, to divide the beliefs from their context(s) of application. While realism, Phillips claims, holds that the propositionally structured belief is independent of these contexts by being constituted as mental state, nonrealism holds that the practical consequences are mere expressions of taste or preference without any beliefs referring to right and wrong. Hence, the aforementioned two-step logic means, realistically, that there is a belief being cognized, while that very logic means, nonrealistically, that there are actions being just expressive. But it will not do to separate logical beliefs from actions, since saying "I believe ...." is not a description of a mental state, but it is making an assertion, that is, itself a speech-*act*.[52] Moreover, the belief is connected to a deed—or: if it isn't, the belief lacks sense. Take, for example, someone who thinks that the world comes to its end tonight. If this belief does not mark a difference in the person's behavior, the presupposed belief is empty. Or imagine someone who believes in God while pretending not to care about God at all. Does this person trust his own words?[53]

The second context in which Phillips speaks of concept-formation and meaning is his discussion of what Wittgenstein called "primitive reactions."[54] The duality of beliefs and the fruits of beliefs is replaced by the relation between propositions and our common reactions, but Phillips's concern here is a similar one. In accordance with Wittgenstein, Phillips underlines that we do not decide to react to something in a certain way, but that our agreement is shown in our reactions.[55] Hence, our propositions get their sense by our ("primitive" or "natural") reactions. For instance, we cannot justify our reactions to other human beings by an underlying sense for the human element, since this sense is already itself informed by our reactions to others. We do not convince ourselves that the other is a human being first (as opposed to an automat), but what we take to be a person is shown in our reactions to and interactions with others.[56] There is, Phillips adds, no prior belief about, say, a man we are afraid of—a proposition whose truth we would prove first—rather, what fear comes to and really means is determined by our behavior toward that man.[57] The same is true, Phillips holds, in religious contexts:

> Believers do not praise God *because* he is the creator. To speak of "the Creator" is already to engage in praise.[58]

Accordingly, the semantic direction of justification is put upside down. Not a mental state or a logically separated proposition functions as the bearer of meaning, but it is the practical context that secures the possibility that there is meaning for the concepts embedded in them. Again, that is very close to the semantic thesis (T).

The most obvious problem of a claim like (T) is discussed extensively by Phillips himself in criticizing one of his best philosophical mates. It was Peter Winch who referred to the story of the Good Samaritan in the gospel of Luke to elaborate on the relation between beliefs and (re)actions.[59] For him, the Samaritan helped the man somewhere between Jerusalem and Jericho out of immediate compassion—without having any specific assumptions about that man or the scenario he encountered. Even if that were true, the difficulty remains that the other two people, the priest and the Levite, did not help the man who has fallen among thieves. It seems to be the case that we are dealing in these two cases with primitive reactions too. For Phillips, Winch gives the impression that the reaction of the Good Samaritan is the one we, as readers, would expect—and this is, at least, debatable.[60] Moreover, the thesis (T)—taken for granted—would force us to hold either (1) that the priest and the Levite did not recognize the man who desperately needed support as a human or (2) what the three different men coming along take to be human comes to highly different things or (3) their shared views on what is human (including situations of needing help) do not amount to the same or at least similar reactions.

Now, all three readings are at odds with (T) or are problematic interpretations of what happens in that story. Contrary to (1), the moral failure of the priest and the Levite consists precisely in *really* recognizing that human being without helping this person.[61] Version (2) is compatible with (T) insofar as different reactions go hand in hand with different meanings of "human," but compatibility is not correctness: it is not shown what (T) says, namely, that the (divergent) reactions (alone) determine the (divergent) meanings. Finally, version (3) could create a serious problem for (T) as well, because similar beliefs are not necessarily linked to similar reactions and the same reaction does not justify the claim that those showing that reaction are holding the same belief.

Now, if one is interested in defending a thesis like (T) one faces some serious difficulties.[62] First, it is one thing to say that there are prior beliefs and (secondary) actions, for example, believing in God and praying to Him every day; and it is quite another thing to say that this primary belief is prior to *all* possible fruits and independent of *every* context, for example believing in God while separating that belief from *all* religious actions. Hence, realists could subscribe to Wittgenstein's claim that meaning is bound to usage without implying that a (prior) belief is connected to a specific "fruit." Second, Phillips seems to insist on the further claim that a believer's action alone clarifies the meaning of a belief; nothing beyond that action like intentions, stipulations, or imagination, that is, something "mental," could contribute to that meaning. Third, Phillips takes it for granted that the actions or practical contexts giving a belief its sense are indeed among or even identical with what Phillips calls "fruits of belief."

What Phillips is actually doing is to connect beliefs and their fruits in a way that is far too direct. While it is important to underline the importance of the contexts for semantic questions it is semantically inappropriate to juxtapose a belief and an action. Phillips, however, seems to be doing this—and that allows for calling his position a neo-behaviorist one.[63] Having a belief does not lead immediately (or at all) to an action; holding the same belief does not go hand in hand with the same action; believing different (even incommensurable) things could be connected to similar actions; different actions could presuppose or be derived from the same belief; similar actions may be grounded in divergent beliefs. Accordingly, there is no "internal relation" between beliefs and fruits of beliefs, as Phillips thinks.[64] Here, it is also essential to see the differences and not to reduce the relation between a belief (or a proposition) and the fruits (or actions) to an internal link, since that move is based on a very small range of examples.

However, the main target of discussing Phillips's critique of (non)realism was not that ramified debate itself, but to sketch the philosophical background for his views on how (not) to do ethics. My initial claim was that Phillips's descriptive and, later on, contemplative philosophy is based on or informed by his critique of (non)realism. More precisely, his metaethical approach in characterizing ethics as a way of thinking—of "doing justice to the world in its variety"—is strongly connected to semantics and concept-formation. It means now that the discussion of a particular claim remains empty as long as one neglects what that claim comes to in practice. Doing justice to a specific belief implies now to pay attention to the consequences that this belief has in one's life. One could also say that an ethics informed by contemplation does not know mere beliefs and moral standpoints, because they remain semantically void without their practical environment.

This is exactly what Phillips is doing, primarily in his philosophy of religion. When a realist claims that we have to clarify, first, that God exists in order to continue with the fruits of faith such as prayer, confession, and service, Phillips reacts by saying it is this cluster of existential involvement that gives sense and significance to the sentence "I know my redeemer liveth."[65] And from here, Phillips tries to show that the theistic interpretation of religious utterances is not only a reduction to one out of several possible interpretations but also a confused one.[66]

Now, as we have seen, there is a peculiar connection between Phillips's view of ethics as a determination of our thinking and the practical formation of our concepts. We have also seen that Phillips defends the thesis (T) as semantic background to clarify how concepts get their meaning. Hence, we have to ask what it means for a contemplative ethics to deal truly contemplatively with the problematic claim (T)? Or the other way around: what might be the consequence of correcting (T) for Phillips's contemplative ethics?

5 Finally: Does It Pay to Be Good?

Where do we go from here? There are some argumentative moves that are still open to us; and in this short final section I will not do anything other than seeing where they may lead us. The first thing we should do is to take the thesis (T) at face value and to apply it to itself. Remember (T), it says,

> The meaning of a proposition p is essentially dependent on the practical implications of that proposition p.

Now, it is obvious that (T) is itself a proposition, more precisely, a propositional claim. Hence, its meaning is dependent on the practical implications that (T) has. Expressed in more Phillips's fashion, one might say that it is the context that shows to what the proposition really comes. Or put critically, the realist thinks that (T) expresses a mental state that could logically be separated from its surrounding, whereas the nonrealist reduces (T) to an expression of a general attitude without the ambition of making true claims. Accordingly, if there is no practical implication and consequence of this semantic claim, (T) lacks any sense following its own standards. Now, the interesting thing to recognize is that Phillips guards (T) against that danger precisely by being contemplative. Being contemplative—and ethical as a description of the mode in which the philosopher shows loyalty to the moral demand on her (or him)—is exactly the difference that could give (T) meaning and significance. Insofar as the contemplative philosopher dedicates her descriptive eagerness to the "practical implications," that is, the divergent contexts and ramified practices, this eagerness marks the difference (T) calls for when it should not remain semantically empty.

Let us turn to the second move open to us, which brings us back again to ethics and the metaethical presuppositions. There is a tension or even a contradiction between Phillips's anti-consequentialism (see section 3) and the semantic claim (T). We have seen that (T) underlines the consequences of a proposition as internally related to its meaning or even as the condition of the possibility for that very proposition to have meaning at all. While Phillips stresses the consequences in semantics, he is interested in avoiding the integration of them with the ethical evaluation of a particular action. As we have seen, Phillips tries to give an ethical absoluteness its place, an absoluteness that lies in an action itself, not in its implications and practical follow-ups.

> I have suggested that it is to be found in a devotion to the moral character of one's actions, a concern which imposes itself on purposive actions, to which means and ends alike are answerable. (. . .) The demands of morality, however, are unconditional, in that they cannot be put aside for considerations of another kind.[67]

However, it is not only this, say, negative parallel between stressing the consequences of a proposition semantically and avoiding the consequences of an action ethically (not: morally, of course) that is essential. Essential is that the unconditional value of an action, its end in itself, as Phillips can also say, is at odds with the semantic thesis (T). As soon as we express that value propositionally, it falls under the radar of (T). Thus, we are faced, as it seems, with an intriguing predicament in Phillips between semantic claims about propositional meaning and ethical claims about moral values—with the result that either (T) as general thesis is not correct or the (post-)Kantian defense of moral actions that have their value in themselves turns out to be problematic.

Or both alternatives hint to a serious difficulty—and, I think, that is precisely the case. In both cases, ethics and semantics, that is, anti-consequentialism and semantic naturalism, Phillips presents claims that are not meant to be possibilities "in the conversation of mankind," but highly general theses about values and meanings. While it is true that we need, sometimes, general accounts, especially in ethics, it is not a good idea to generalize that possibility about general accounts. Anti-consequentialism in ethics and naturalism in semantics are forms of general accounts, but, moreover, in contradicting each other they mutually reveal the perils and pitfalls of a generality Phillips could not have afforded as long as he follows his own standards.

Instead of claiming the importance of contemplating contemplation, I have attempted to show that Phillips's work leads to this moral demand by its own internal correction. Paying attention to this particularity is, then, a good that really pays off.

Notes

1 See D. Z. Phillips, "Religion, Philosophy, and the Academy," *International Journal for Philosophy of Religion* 44, no. 1 (1998): 129–44, esp. 142.
2 D. Z. Phillips, "Introduction: Attention to Particulars," in *Wittgenstein: Attention to Particulars. Essays in honour of Rush Rhees (1905-1989)*, ed. D. Z. Phillips and Peter Winch (New York: St. Martin's Press, 1990), 1–11.
3 Cf. D. Z. Phillips, "Reclaiming the Conversations of Mankind," *Philosophy* 69, no. 1 (1994): 35–53.
4 D. Z. Phillips, *Interventions in Ethics* (Albany: State University of New York Press, 1992), viii.
5 D. Z. Phillips, *Philosophy's Cool Place* (Ithaca and London: Cornell University Press, 1999), 158.
6 See *The Contemplative Spirit: Dewi Z. Phillips on Religion and the Limits of Philosophy* (*Religion in Philosophy and Theology* vol. 49), ed. Ingolf U. Dalferth and Hartmut von Sass (Tübingen: Mohr Siebeck, 2010), part III.
7 Cf. Hartmut von Sass, *Sprachspiele des Glaubens. Eine Studie zur kontemplativen Religionsphilosophie von Dewi Z. Phillips mit ständiger Rücksicht auf Ludwig Wittgenstein* (*Religion in Philosophy and Theology* vol. 47) (Tübingen: Mohr Siebeck, 2010), 83–92.
8 See Richard Amesbury, "In the Temple of Passions: D.Z. Phillips and the Possibility of Philosophical Contemplation," *Philosophical Investigations* 30, no. 3 (2007): 201–18, esp. 212–14.
9 In a letter to Ludwig von Ficker (a *very* unhappy name to have in German); see Joachim Schulte, "Was man nicht sagen kann. Der Sinn des Schweigens bei Wittgenstein," in *Stille Tropen. Zur Rhetorik und Grammatik des Schweigens*, ed. Hartmut von Sass (Freiburg im Br. and München: Karl Alber, 2013), 174–95.
10 Not everything that is not expressible has to be ethical (or mystical), of course; what Michael Polanyi calls "tacit knowing" is, by definition, not completely graspable by language, and yet it has, mostly, nothing to do with morals; see Michael Polanyi, *The Tacit Dimension* (1966). With a New Foreword by Amartya Sen (Chicago and London: Chicago University Press, 2009), 8–9 and 20–1.
11 Cf. for a Wittgensteinian critique of this claim, Johannes Fischer, *Verstehen statt Begründen. Warum es in der Ethik um mehr als nur um Handlungen geht* (Stuttgart: Kohlhammer, 2012), ch. 1.
12 See Stanley Cavell, "The Wittgensteinian Event," in idem, *Philosophy: The Day After Tomorrow* (Cambridge, MA and London: Belknap Press, 2005), 192–212, esp. 195 and 206.
13 Concerning Nietzsche see Renate Lachmann, "Gedächtnis und Weltverlust. Borges' *memorioso*—mit Anspielungen auf Lurijas *Mnemonisten*," in *Memoria. Vergessen*

und Erinnern, ed. Anselm Haverkamp and Renate Lachmann (München: Wilhelm Fink, 1993), 492–519, esp. 512.

14 See D. Z. Phillips and Howard O. Mounce, *Moral Practices* (*Studies in Ethics and the Philosophy of Religion Vol. VI*) (London: Routledge & Kegan Paul, 1970), 112; D. Z. Phillips, "Ethics, Faith and 'What Can Be Said,'" *Wittgenstein. A Critical Reader*, ed. Hans-Johann Glock (Oxford: Blackwell, 2001), 348–66, 355.

15 See Phillips, *Philosophy's Cool Place*, 2, 54, 100; idem, *Religion and the Hermeneutics of Contemplation* (Cambridge: Cambridge University Press, 2001), 319 and 323—following Peter Winch, "What Has Philosophy To Say To Religion?," *Faith and Philosophy* 18, no. 4 (2001): 416–30.

16 See William James's critique of evidentialists like William K. Clifford; cf. his "The Will to Believe," idem, *Pragmatism and Other Writings*, ed. Giles Dunn (New York: Penguin Books, 2000), 198–218, esp. 202 and 204–5.

17 See Phillips, *Philosophy's Cool Place*, 159–60.

18 On Phillips's and Rorty's account of literature as essential for philosophy, see Hartmut von Sass, "Broken Mirrors—Contemplative Nowheres. Rorty and Phillips on Description, Imagination, and Literature," in *The Contemplative Spirit. Dewi Z. Phillips on Religion and the Limits of Philosophy* (*Religion in Philosophy and Theology vol. 49*), ed. Ingolf U. Dalferth and Hartmut von Sass (Tübingen: Mohr Siebeck, 2010), 55–95.

19 D. Z. Phillips, *Trough a Darkening Glass: Philosophy, Literature & Cultural Change* (Notre Dame: University of Notre Dame Press, 1982), 29; see also Cora Diamond, "The Difficulty of Reality and the Difficulty of Philosophy," in *Philosophy and Animal Life* (New York: Columbia University Press, 2008), 43–89; Richard Eldridge, "Philosophy and the Achievement of Community: Rorty, Cavell and Criticism," *Richard Rorty* (*Sage Masters of Modern Social Thought*), vol. IV, ed. Alan Malachowski (London: Sage Publishers, 2002), 5–23.

20 See Ludwig Wittgenstein, *Philosophical Investigations* (Oxford: Blackwell, 1967), § 122, hereafter *PI*.

21 Phillips, *Interventions in Ethics*, xiv.

22 See Henk Vroom, "Philosophy of Religion in a Pluralistic Culture," in *D.Z. Phillips' Contemplative Philosophy of Religion. Questions and Responses*, ed. Andy F. Sanders (Aldershot and Burlington: Ashgate, 2007), 181–96.

23 D. Z. Phillips, *Wittgenstein and Religion* (Basingstoke and London: Macmillan, 1993), 254; idem, "Wittgenstein: Contemplation and Cultural Criticism," in Kai Nielsen and D. Z. Phillips, *Wittgensteinian Fideism?* (London: SCM Press, 2005), 347–71, 367.

24 Where this simple rule might lead is shown in the TV serial *My Name Is Earl* (2005–9 on HBO). There, the good will of the protagonist (who believes, after an accident, in the karma rule and wants to annihilate his former bad deeds by good ones) leads only to new challenges to his good will.

25 Cf. Phillips and Mounce, *Moral Practices*, 23; idem, "Does It Pay to Be Good?," *Proceedings of the Aristotelian Society*, New Series 65, no. 1 (1964/65): 45–60, 48.
26 Phillips and Mounce, *Moral Practices*, 60.
27 "Does It Pay to Be Good?," 45 and 48.
28 Ibid., 48.
29 Cf. ibid., 55.
30 See Philippa Foot, *Virtues and Vices and Other Essays in Moral Philosophy* (Berkeley: University of California Press; Oxford: Blackwell, 1978), 78–83; also Iris Murdoch, *The Sovereignty of Good* (1970) (London and New York: Routledge, 2001), esp. 90; for a highly nuanced critique of Foot (and Murdoch) cf. Christoph Halbig, *Der Begriff der Tugend und die Grenzen der Tugendethik* (Berlin: Suhrkamp, 2013), 103–6.
31 See "Does It Pay to Be Good?," 45; D. Z. Phillips, "In Search of the Moral 'Must': Mrs Foot's Fugitive Thought," *The Philosophical Quarterly* 27, no. 107 (1977): 140–57, 156.
32 Cf. "Does It Pay to Be Good?," 56–7.
33 See ibid., 50–1.
34 Cf. ibid., 57.
35 See ibid., 46; Phillips also discusses (in dialogue with John Stocks) the counter-critique that the acting of a martyr just shows the allegiance to a higher good (of moral perfection or so); accordingly, it would fit the consequentialist story of trying to benefit from a particular acting (Ibid., 59).
36 Ludwig Wittgenstein, *The Blue and Brown Books*, ed. Rush Rhes (Oxford: Blackwell, 1958), 35; the German original reads: "die verächtliche Haltung gegenüber dem Einzelfall."
37 For a theological approach on cloning that is also informed by Wittgenstein, see Stanley Hauerwas, *Approaching the End: Eschatological Reflections on Church, Politics, and Life* (Grand Rapids, MI and Cambridge: Eerdmans, 2013), 192–9.
38 Wittgenstein, *PI* § 595.
39 Phillips would, by the way, rightly insist on that important distinction between consequentialism (as general moral approach) and consequentialist thinking (applied under particular circumstances). However, I have the impression that his critique of the first one closes de facto the door for appreciating the possibility of the second.
40 See D. Z. Phillips, "Where We Are: At the Mercy of Method," in idem, *Recovering Religious Concepts: Closing Epistemic Divides* (Basingstoke and London: Macmillan, 2000), 1–15, esp. 3–5.
41 D. Z. Phillips, *Faith and Philosophical Enquiry* (New York: Schocken Books, 1970), 143.
42 See D. Z. Phillips, *Faith after Foundationalism: Plantinga—Rorty—Lindbeck—Berger. Critiques and Alternatives* (Boulder, San Francisco and Oxford: Westpoint 1995) (originally published by Routledge 1988), 55.

43 Cf. D. Z. Phillips, "Epistemic Practices: The Retreat from Reality," in idem, *Recovering Religious Concepts*, 24–44, esp. 34; idem, *Religion and the Hermeneutics of Contemplation*, 17.
44 See D. Z. Phillips, "Epistemic Practices: A Replay to William Wainwright," *Topoi* 14 (1995): 95–105.
45 Cf. Tage Kurtén, "Internal Realism: A Joint Feature by Dewi Z. Phillips and Paul Tillich?," in *D.Z. Phillips' Contemplative Philosophy of Religion: Questions and Responses*, ed. Andy F. Sanders (Aldershot and Burlington: Ashgate, 2007), 95–110; Hilary Putnam, *The Many Faces of Realism: The Paul Carus Lectures* (LaSalle, IL: Open Court, 1987); see also John Haldane, "Realism with a Metaphysical Skull," *Hilary Putnam: Pragmatism and Realism*, ed. James Conant and Urszula M. Zeglen (London and New York: Routledge, 2002), 97–104.
46 Cf. Cora Diamond, "Realism and the Realistic Spirit," in idem, *The Realistic Spirit* (Cambridge, MA: MIT Press, 1991), ch. 1.
47 See Phillips, *Religion and the Hermeneutics of Contemplation*, esp. chs. II and IV.
48 See D. Z. Phillips, "On Really Believing," in idem, *Wittgenstein and Religion*, 33–55, here 33 and 35; see also idem, "How Real Is Realism? A Response to Paul Badham," in *Is God Real?*, ed. Joseph Runzo (Basingstoke and London: Macmillan, 1993), 193–8.
49 Cf. Phillips, "On Really Believing," 40.
50 Ibid., 37.
51 Ibid., 39.
52 Cf. ibid., 36.
53 Cf. ibid., 51.
54 See Ludwig Wittgenstein, *On Certainty*, ed. Gertrude E. M. Anscombe and Georg Henrik von Wright, trans. Danis Paul and G. E. M. Anscombe (Oxford: Blackwell, 1975), § 475; D. Z. Phillips, "Afterword: Rhees on Reading On Certainty," in Rush Rhees, *Wittgenstein's On Certainty. There—Like our Life*, ed. D. Z. Phillips (Oxford: Blackwell, 2003), 133–82, 161–3.
55 See D. Z. Phillips, "Review Article: Martha C. Nussbaum, Poetic Justice: The Literary Imagination and Public Life," *Studies in Philosophy and Education* 17 (1998): 193–206, 195.
56 Cf. Phillips, *Trough a Darkening Glass*, 14; idem, *Recovering Religious Concepts*, 202; idem, *Philosophy's Cool Place*, 73.
57 See *Recovering Religious Concepts*, 201–2.
58 Ibid., 204.
59 For a discussion of Winch's reading see Hartmut von Sass, "Spontane Reaktionen und menschliches Mitleid. Über die Allgemeinheit und Verschiedenheit unseres Handelns im Gespräch mit Peter Winch," in *Mitleid. Konkretionen eines strittigen Konzepts* (*Religion in Philosophy and Theology vol. 28*), ed. Ingolf U. Dalferth and Andreas Hunziker (Tübingen: Mohr Siebeck, 2007), 161–80.

60 See D. Z. Phillips, "My Neighbour and My Neighbours," in idem, *Interventions in Ethics*, 229–51, esp. 246 and 250.
61 In an interview, Quentin Tarantino made a similar argument discussing American slavery (that is the topic of his movie *Django Unchained*). According to him, it is important to recognize that the slaves were actually seen as humans; the perverse element of slavery is eliminated if one holds that slaves were considered to be "something else."
62 See for a detailed critique of Phillips' position Michael Scott and Andrew Moore, "Can Theological Realism be Refuted?," *Religious Studies* 33, no. 4 (1997): 401–18; see also the reactions to "On Really Believing" by Alfred Louch, John Hick, and Don Cupitt, in Joseph Runzo (ed.), *Is God Real?* (Basingstoke and London: Macmillan, 1993); and D. Z. Phillips, "Great Expectations: Philosophy, Ontology and Religion," in Runzo (ed.), *Is God Real?*, 203–7.
63 Scott and Moore, "Can Theological Realism be Refuted?," 406.
64 Phillips, "On Really Believing," 46.
65 See D. Z. Phillips, *Belief, Change, and Forms of Life* (Basingstoke and London: Macmillan, 1986), 80–6; idem, *Religion and Friendly Fire: Examining Assumptions in Contemporary Philosophy of Religion* (Aldershot and Burlington: Ashgate, 2004), Ch. 1: "Philosophical Method and Friendly Fire."
66 See, for instance, Phillips, *Recovering Religious Concepts*, Ch. 5: "The Friends of Cleanthes: a Case of Conceptual Poverty."
67 Phillips, "In Search of the Moral 'Must': Mrs Foot's Fugitive Thought," 140–57, 155 and 150; Phillips adds, "To say that moral considerations constitute a reason for the indifferent man because of their formal characteristics, because they are necessarily connected with his self-interest, because to ignore them involves one in irrationality, or because the existence of a moral point of view itself provides a reason for action, seems to have no substance" (Ibid., 145).

Works Cited

Amesbury, Richard, "In the Temple of Passions: D.Z. Phillips and the Possibility of Philosophical Contemplation," *Philosophical Investigations* 30, no. 3 (2007): 201–18.

Cavell, Stanley, "The Wittgensteinian Event," in Stanley Cavell, *Philosophy: The Day After Tomorrow*, 192–212, Cambridge, MA and London: Belknap Press, 2005.

Dalferth, Ingolf U., and Hartmut von Sass (eds.), *The Contemplative Spirit: Dewi Z. Phillips on Religion and the Limits of Philosophy* (*Religion in Philosophy and Theology* vol. 49), Tübingen: Mohr Siebeck, 2010.

Diamond, Cora, "Realism and the Realistic Spirit," in Cora Diamond, *The Realistic Spirit*, Cambridge, MA: MIT Press, 1991.

Diamond, Cora, "The Difficulty of Reality and the Difficulty of Philosophy," in *Philosophy and Animal Life*, 43–89, New York: Columbia University Press, 2008.

Eldridge, Richard, "Philosophy and the Achievement of Community: Rorty, Cavell and Criticism," in *Richard Rorty (Sage Masters of Modern Social Thought)*, vol. IV, ed. Alan Malachowski, 5–23, London: Sage Publishers, 2002.

Fischer, Johannes, *Verstehen statt Begründen. Warum es in der Ethik um mehr als nur um Handlungen geht*, Stuttgart: Kohlhammer, 2012.

Foot, Philippa, *Virtues and Vices and Other Essays in Moral Philosophy*, Berkeley: University of California Press, 1978.

Halbig, Christoph, *Der Begriff der Tugend und die Grenzen der Tugendethik*, Berlin: Suhrkamp, 2013.

Haldane, John, "Realism with a Metaphysical Skull," in James Conant and Urszula M. Zeglen (eds.), *Hilary Putnam: Pragmatism and Realism*, 97–104, London and New York: Routledge, 2002.

Hauerwas, Stanley, *Approaching the End: Eschatological Reflections on Church, Politics, and Life*, Grand Rapids, MI and Cambridge: Eerdmans, 2013.

James, William, "The Will to Believe," in William James, *Pragmatism and Other Writings*, ed. Giles Dunn, 198–218, New York: Penguin Books, 2000.

Kurtén, Tage, "Internal Realism: A Joint Feature by Dewi Z. Phillips and Paul Tillich?," in Andy F. Sanders (ed.), *D.Z. Phillips" Contemplative Philosophy of Religion: Questions and Responses*, 95–110, Aldershot and Burlington: Ashgate, 2007.

Lachmann, Renate, "Gedächtnis und Weltverlust. Borges' *memorioso*—mit Anspielungen auf Lurijas *Mnemonisten*," in Anselm Haverkamp and Renate Lachmann (eds.), *Memoria. Vergessen und Erinnern*, 492–519, München: Wilhelm Fink, 1993.

Louch, Alfred, John Hick, and Don Cupitt, in Joseph Runzo (ed.), *Is God Real?* Basingstoke and London: Macmillan, 1993.

Murdoch, Iris, *The Sovereignty of Good*, London and New York: Routledge, 2001.

Phillips, Dewi Z., "Does It Pay to Be Good?," *Proceedings of the Aristotelian Society*, New Series 65, no. 1 (1964/5): 45–60.

Phillips, Dewi Z., *Faith and Philosophical Enquiry*, New York: Schocken Books, 1970.

Phillips, Dewi Z., "In Search of the Moral 'Must': Mrs Foot's Fugitive Thought," *The Philosophical Quarterly* 27, no. 107 (1977): 140–57.

Phillips, Dewi Z., *Trough a Darkening Glass: Philosophy, Literature & Cultural Change*, Notre Dame: University of Notre Dame Press, 1982.

Phillips, Dewi Z., *Belief, Change, and Forms of Life*, Basingstoke and London: Macmillan, 1986.

Phillips, Dewi Z., *Faith After Foundationalism: Plantinga—Rorty—Lindbeck—Berger. Critiques and Alternatives*, Boulder, San Francisco and Oxford: Westpoint 1995 (originally published by Routledge 1988).

Phillips, Dewi Z., "Introduction: Attention to Particulars," in D. Z. Phillips and Peter Winch (eds.), *Wittgenstein: Attention to Particulars: Essays in Honour of Rush Rhees (1905-1989)*, 1–11, New York: St. Martin's Press, 1990.

Phillips, Dewi Z., *Interventions in Ethics*, Albany: State University of New York Press, 1992.
Phillips, Dewi Z., "Great Expectations: Philosophy, Ontology and Religion," in Joseph Runzo (ed.), *Is God Real?*, 203–7, Basingstoke and London: Macmillan, 1993.
Phillips, Dewi Z., "How Real Is Realism? A Response to Paul Badham," in Joseph Runzo (ed.), *Is God Real?*, 193–8, Basingstoke and London: Macmillan, 1993.
Phillips, Dewi Z., *Wittgenstein and Religion*, Basingstoke and London: Macmillan, 1993.
Phillips, Dewi Z., "Reclaiming the Conversations of Mankind," *Philosophy* 69, no. 1 (1994): 35–53.
Phillips, Dewi Z., "Epistemic Practices: A Reply to William Wainwright," *Topoi* 14 (1995): 95–105.
Phillips, Dewi Z., "Religion, Philosophy, and the Academy," *International Journal for Philosophy of Religion* 44, no. 1 (1998): 129–44.
Phillips, Dewi Z., "Review Article: Martha C. Nussbaum, Poetic Justice: The Literary Imagination and Public Life," *Studies in Philosophy and Education* 17 (1998): 193–206.
Phillips, Dewi Z., *Philosophy's Cool Place*, Ithaca and London: Cornell University Press, 1999.
Phillips, Dewi Z., *Recovering Religious Concepts: Closing Epistemic Divides*, Basingstoke and London: Macmillan, 2000.
Phillips, Dewi Z., "Ethics, Faith and "What Can Be Said,"" in Hans-Johann Glock (ed.), *Wittgenstein: A Critical Reader*, 348–66, Oxford: Blackwell, 2001.
Phillips, Dewi Z., *Religion and the Hermeneutics of Contemplation*, Cambridge: Cambridge University Press, 2001.
Phillips, Dewi Z., "Afterword: Rhees on Reading On Certainty," in Rush Rhees, *Wittgenstein's On Certainty: There—Like Our Life*, ed. Dewi Z. Phillips, 133–82, Oxford: Blackwell, 2003.
Phillips, Dewi Z., *Religion and Friendly Fire: Examining Assumptions in Contemporary Philosophy of Religion*, Aldershot and Burlington: Ashgate, 2004.
Phillips, Dewi Z., "Wittgenstein: Contemplation and Cultural Criticism," in Kai Nielsen and D. Z. Phillips, *Wittgensteinian Fideism?*, 347–71, London: SCM Press, 2005.
Phillips, Dewi Z., and Howard O. Mounce, *Moral Practices* (*Studies in Ethics and the Philosophy of Religion Vol. VI*), London: Routledge & Kegan Paul, 1970.
Polanyi, Michael, *The Tacit Dimension*. With a New Foreword by Amartya Sen, Chicago and London: Chicago University Press, 2009.
Putnam, Hilary, *The Many Faces of Realism: The Paul Carus Lectures*, LaSalle, IL: Open Court, 1987.
Schulte, Joachim, "Was man nicht sagen kann. Der Sinn des Schweigens bei Wittgenstein," in Hartmut von Sass (ed.), *Stille Tropen. Zur Rhetorik und Grammatik des Schweigens*, 174–95, Freiburg im Br. and München: Karl Alber, 2013.
Scott, Michael, and Andrew Moore, "Can Theological Realism be Refuted?" *Religious Studies* 33, no. 4 (1997): 401–18.

von Sass, Hartmut, "Spontane Reaktionen und menschliches Mitleid. Über die Allgemeinheit und Verschiedenheit unseres Handelns im Gespräch mit Peter Winch," in Ingolf U. Dalferth and Andreas Hunziker (eds.), *Mitleid. Konkretionen eines strittigen Konzepts* (*Religion in Philosophy and Theology vol. 28*), 161–80, Tübingen: Mohr Siebeck, 2007.

von Sass, Hartmut, "Broken Mirrors—Contemplative Nowheres. Rorty and Phillips on Description, Imagination, and Literature," in Ingolf U. Dalferth and Hartmut von Sass (eds.), *The Contemplative Spirit: Dewi Z. Phillips on Religion and the Limits of Philosophy* (*Religion in Philosophy and Theology vol. 49*), 55–95, Tübingen: Mohr Siebeck, 2010.

von Sass, Hartmut, *Sprachspiele des Glaubens. Eine Studie zur kontemplativen Religionsphilosophie von Dewi Z. Phillips mit ständiger Rücksicht auf Ludwig Wittgenstein* (*Religion in Philosophy and Theology vol. 47*), Tübingen: Mohr Siebeck, 2010.

Vroom, Henk, "Philosophy of Religion in a Pluralistic Culture," in Andy F. Sanders (ed.), *D.Z. Phillips" Contemplative Philosophy of Religion: Questions and Responses*, 181–96, Aldershot and Burlington: Ashgate, 2007.

Winch, Peter, "What Has Philosophy to Say To Religion?," *Faith and Philosophy* 18, no. 4 (2001): 416–30.

Wittgenstein, Ludwig, *The Blue and Brown Books*, ed. Rush Rhes, Oxford: Blackwell, 1958.

Wittgenstein, Ludwig, *Philosophical Investigations*, Oxford: Blackwell, 1967.

Wittgenstein, Ludwig, *On Certainty*, ed. Gertrude E. M. Anscombe and Georg Henrik von Wright, trans. Danis Paul and G. E. M. Anscombe, Oxford: Blackwell, 1975.

Part Three

After Wittgenstein

8

"A Certain Purity of Attention to the World"

The Ethical Demands of Wittgensteinian Philosophizing

Mikel Burley

> I do not want to deny, for a moment, that practising a contemplative conception of philosophy is, in an important sense, personal. The reason why is obvious: the enquiry makes ethical demands of the enquirer. It calls for a certain purity of attention to the world which shows character.
>
> D. Z. Phillips[1]

1 Ethics in Wittgenstein's Wake

Ludwig Wittgenstein's philosophical methods have been adopted and adapted in various ways in the field of ethics or moral philosophy. There is, it seems, no single answer to the question of what implications Wittgenstein's thinking has for this field. Some interpreters have proposed that Wittgenstein, even in his later work, held that philosophy can say nothing at all *about* ethics, though it can itself *be* ethical.[2] Others have maintained that, although a Wittgensteinian approach would indeed refrain from theorizing (whether about normative ethics, applied ethics, or metaethics), such an approach can contribute usefully to the task of clarifying ethical concepts, which is itself a kind of ethical philosophizing.[3] Still others, especially in recent years, have looked to Wittgenstein's late epistemological writings for ideas that might disclose important features of our moral lives, most notably the fact that, amid the shifting sands of our attitudes and actions, there are "basic moral certainties" that stand fast for us, perhaps for all human beings.[4]

An issue that has been central to debates surrounding whether, or how, philosophizing about ethics is to be done in the light of Wittgenstein's work is that of the relation between philosophy and other areas of life. More specifically, it concerns the relation between the "philosophical" and the "personal" dimensions of the life of someone who is doing philosophy. It is this issue that D. Z. Phillips is addressing when he describes "a contemplative conception of philosophy" as being, "in an important sense, personal." Phillips concurs with his friend and mentor Rush Rhees that "there is something . . . like an internal connexion between what you are engaged on in philosophy, and the sort of life you lead."[5] In view of the close attention that Rhees gives in his work to philosophical methods, what he means by "what you are engaged on" is unlikely to be merely the subject matter that one is philosophizing about but also, and perhaps primarily, the approach that one takes to that subject matter—*how* one engages with it.

Phillips's way of adopting the methods of Wittgenstein and Rhees was to formulate the mode of philosophizing that he termed "contemplative." My purpose in this chapter is to examine that mode with regard to its ethical implications. In particular, I shall consider what it means to say, as Phillips does, that a contemplative inquiry "makes ethical demands of the enquirer." Phillips is not alone in proposing that an approach influenced by Wittgenstein makes such demands,[6] but what do the demands amount to, how do they relate to the idea of "a certain purity of attention to the world," and are they demands that can feasibly be met? In addressing these questions, my concern will not be merely the exegetical one of clarifying what Phillips means by declaring that contemplative philosophizing places ethical demands upon the philosopher. Rather, I shall also be investigating what a contemplative approach to philosophy allows and enables us to say about ethically relevant topics, and especially about forms of life that, in certain respects, the inquirer finds morally troubling or repulsive. In fact, there are not two distinguishable tasks here, since examining Phillips's meaning necessarily involves examining examples of contemplative philosophizing in practice.

My discussion will proceed as follows. I begin by explicating the debate between Phillips and certain other philosophers influenced by Wittgenstein over how the philosophical and the personal are related. The debate is complicated because although Phillips wants to defend a distinction between these elements in one respect, there is, as we have already seen, another respect in which he acknowledges that philosophical and personal aspects of a philosopher's life cannot be separated. Second, I place purity of attention alongside the imperative to "do conceptual justice" to one's philosophical subject matter, and examine the significance of these impulses for contemplative philosophy. Third, I turn to instances of contemplative philosophizing in action, principally from the work of Wittgenstein and Rhees, which Phillips held to be exemplary. By focusing on the thought of these philosophers in relation to what is "deep and sinister" in human life, I bring out the role of emotional and moral response in philosophical reflection. In conclusion I propose, in short, that the ethical demands of Wittgensteinian philosophizing—at least as envisaged by Phillips and embodied in the work of Wittgenstein and Rhees—are a complex matter, involving not a relinquishing of one's emotional and moral responses, but a careful integration of those responses into one's philosophical reflections.

2 The Philosophical and the Personal

The remark of Phillips's that I quoted as the epigraph to this chapter occurs in the context of a response to Stephen Mulhall, who questions the viability of the distinction that Phillips draws between the "philosophical" and the "personal."[7] The distinction is central to Phillips's formulation of the contemplative conception of philosophy that he claims to derive from Wittgenstein, for that conception is one according to which the task of philosophy is to contemplate "possibilities of human life" and to "wonder at the world in all its variety" without, in one's philosophizing, personally appropriating or advocating—or indeed rejecting—any of the possibilities that one encounters: "we appreciate more than we appropriate," as Phillips puts it.[8] Remarks of Wittgenstein's from which Phillips draws inspiration include especially the parenthetical comment that what makes someone "into a philosopher" is that he or she "is not a citizen of any community of ideas"[9] and the affirmation that his "ideal is a certain coolness. A temple providing a setting for the passions without meddling with them."[10] Phillips understands the foregoing remarks—along with Wittgenstein's more explicitly methodological injunctions that philosophy's purpose is not to explain, deduce, or justify anything but merely to describe what is already "open to view"[11]—to mean that developing a Wittgensteinian sensibility involves aspiring to separate one's philosophical endeavors from one's personal commitments, at least insofar as those commitments are ethically, politically, religiously, or aesthetically inflected. The philosopher, *qua* philosopher, is to "seek a perch above the fray" from which to undertake not a discriminating evaluation between different "beliefs and convictions in the name of rationality," but "a contemplation of the world from the vantage point which comes from philosophy's disinterested concerns."[12]

Against Phillips's attempt to demarcate philosophical from personal pursuits, Mulhall follows James Conant in questioning whether any such demarcation is tenable. As Conant sees it, the proper Wittgensteinian philosophical task of untying knots of conceptual confusion cannot be extricated from personal issues concerning how one lives, for philosophizing is itself a component of the philosopher's life; due vigilance to one's understanding of words and concepts is inseparable from vigilance to one's behavior and discourse more generally.[13] Mulhall summarizes the point by noting that "the philosophical difficulties are a species of personal difficulties" and, by failing to acknowledge this fact, Phillips loses sight of an incisive reminder from Kierkegaard, "that philosophers are human beings too—that philosophy cannot arrogate to itself a perspective upon the human condition that is external to it."[14]

In responding to the criticisms of Conant and Mulhall, Phillips maintains a combative stance while at the same time appearing to concede the central point. What Phillips emphasizes is the need for philosophers to survey a range of competing perspectives on life and the world without, in their philosophical endeavors, aligning themselves with any one of those perspectives;[15] that is, Phillips urges us to recognize the difference between elucidating someone else's words and appropriating those words for oneself. But Conant's point is not to deny that this difference obtains; it is, rather, to remind us of the need for attention to our *own* words, to the ways of thinking and speaking to which we are already—more or less wittingly—committed. We have, as it were, already appropriated certain perspectives on the world; as human beings, this is something we cannot avoid. To characterize the philosophical task as requiring a transcendence of all such appropriations is thus not only out of step with both a Kierkegaardian and a Wittgensteinian spirit but is also a confused aspiration—an aspiration to lay aside one's humanity, which is something no philosopher can realistically hope to do.[16]

Phillips's observation that philosophizing contemplatively "is, in an important sense, personal" appears to acknowledge the point that the personal and the philosophical cannot be rent apart, for it recognizes the need for attention to one's own preexisting appropriations as well as to the words and lives of others. The point also seems to be acknowledged when Phillips notes that "the perch above the fray" toward which the contemplative philosopher aspires is not "a view from nowhere."[17] We might add—although Phillips does not put it in exactly these terms—that what Thomas Nagel famously dubbed "the view from nowhere"[18] is a philosopher's fantasy, since the person doing the philosophizing is always somewhere, always enmeshed in a complex network of sociocultural and epistemic relations with other people and with whatever is being contemplated. The ethical demands that Phillips speaks of are thus demands for "a certain purity of attention to the world" in the sense that they call on us to cultivate and sustain a high degree of self-awareness, what Conant calls "vigilance which is directed towards how we live."[19] While Phillips is wary of the suggestion that philosophy can offer a guide to life, this is not what Conant or Mulhall is advocating. They are merely offering reminders that the call to enhance one's self-awareness is itself, in part, directed toward the life of the one who is doing the contemplating. A change in philosophical orientation is eo ipso a change in one's life. Phillips is not obviously disagreeing with that point.

3 Justice and Purity

Notwithstanding the difficulty of distinguishing between how the philosophical-personal relation is construed by Phillips and how it is construed by the critics of his whom I have mentioned, what Phillips sees as an implication of his own way of inheriting Wittgenstein's methods is that one should actively seek out contrastive perspectives on life and the world, including—and perhaps especially—perspectives that, when speaking for oneself, one would find morally unsettling. This is where the imperative to maintain "a certain purity of attention" comes into play, an imperative that itself has ethical, and indeed spiritual, dimensions. Though Phillips would probably have felt uncomfortable with the connections I am making here, the ethical dimension—which is, in a sense, also political—consists in the ideal of justice, which comes through in the injunction to do "conceptual justice to the world in all its variety."[20] Alongside this, the spiritual dimension consists in the impulse toward self-purification, which is closely analogous to the call for self-renunciation or "dying to the self" that one hears in the work of certain religious thinkers whom Phillips clearly admires—figures such as Kierkegaard, Tolstoy, and especially Simone Weil. I shall briefly elaborate these points concerning justice and purification below.

First, the idea of *doing conceptual justice* is one that recurs explicitly throughout Phillips's work from the late 1990s onward but is implicitly present before then. It is directed toward the goal of clarity and deepening one's understanding of particular forms of life, whether they be moral, religious, or political, while preventing, as far as is possible, one's own evaluative preferences from interfering with that understanding. "Neither Wittgenstein nor Rhees is concerned to stop us making moral, political, aesthetic or religious judgements," Phillips writes. "Both were men of strong personal convictions. But in philosophy, their interest was different. They had a contemplative interest in doing conceptual justice to the world in all its variety."[21] By doing conceptual justice to the world, one is doing conceptual justice to other people, to the lives that they lead and the outlooks they take. The purpose of the endeavor is to ensure both that one's own comprehension is as sharp as it can be and that the person or people into whose lives one is inquiring are not misinterpreted or misrepresented; it is to allow alternative points of view to "be themselves in face of deep tendencies to confuse them."[22]

Second, the idea of self-renunciation, which I am linking here with purity of attention, is especially emphasized in Phillips's thinking about Christian soteriology. From his earliest publications onward, he evinces a deep appreciation of the religious thought of Simone Weil in particular, who writes in her notebooks and essays of the need to renounce the assumption that we are entitled to anything by right. "In every claim which we think we possess there is always the idea of an imaginary claim of the past on the future," she observes. "That is the claim which we have to renounce."[23] Having quoted a long passage of Weil's that ends with these sentences, Phillips encapsulates the gist by noting, "To renounce these claims is to renounce one's personality."[24] Elsewhere, Phillips again draws heavily on the thought of Weil when offering an account of what, for the Christian, it means to aspire to eternal life. Far from longing for unending survival, what this means for Weil is "dying to the self," for it is in dying to self-orientated desires that one is able to love neighbor and God and to thereby participate in God's life, which is the life of eternity.[25] Although Phillips would not explicitly align his contemplative conception of philosophy with any specific religious orientation, I am proposing that there is a strong affinity between the form of self-renouncing religiosity that Phillips finds so eloquently expressed in the writings of Weil, on the one hand, and the ethical demands that, according to Phillips, are made upon the contemplative philosopher, on the other. The affinity consists in the requirement to relinquish one's own desires and preferences lest they interfere with the purity of one's relationship with the other.

There are, of course, also differences, for in the case of Christian faith, the relationship to be fostered is one of love or charity, whereas in the case of philosophical inquiry, the relationship involves a more detached observation. Moreover, the Christian commandments to love one's neighbor and to love God are injunctions for the whole of life whereas the philosophical imperative to purify one's attention to the forms of life and language one investigates covers only, or primarily, the philosopher's life *qua* philosopher, and not *qua* human being more generally. But again the distinction is not a sharp one, for as Phillips affirms, the purity of attention that is developed reveals something about the character of the one who develops it, and it is difficult to see what this could mean other than that contemplative philosophizing is itself rooted in a certain ethically infused form of life.

4 Contemplating the Deep and Sinister

The purity of attention that Phillips considers contemplative philosophizing to call for is exhibited most starkly when the inquiry concerns forms of life not only very different from one's own, but which, on the face of it, manifest values profoundly at odds to those with which one feels at home. It is thus no accident that one of the principal examples adduced by Phillips to illustrate contemplative philosophizing in action is an inquiry into religious practices that involve human sacrifice, for the ritual killing of human beings is, we might suppose, paradigmatically a mode of activity that runs counter to anything with which most of Phillips's readers would feel much sympathy, at least in their nonphilosophical moods. One direction in which such an inquiry might go is exemplified both in some of Wittgenstein's *Remarks on Frazer's "Golden Bough"* and in comments made by Rhees, which were, in large part, prompted by those of Wittgenstein.

A central theme of Wittgenstein's reflections is what he calls the *Tiefe und Finstere*—the "deep and sinister" nature of human sacrifice. "What makes human sacrifice something deep and sinister anyway?" he asks:

> Is it only the suffering of the victim that impresses us in this way? All manner of diseases bring just as much suffering and do *not* make this impression. No, this deep and sinister aspect is not obvious just from learning the history of the external action, but *we* ascribe it [*wir tragen es wieder*] from an experience in ourselves.[26]

Wittgenstein is not only resisting the tendency displayed by James Frazer to seek explanations for the rituals by turning to supposed historical precursors or to beliefs that purportedly underlie the practices; he is also resisting the tendency on the part of many Western readers of Frazer's accounts to assume a position of moral and intellectual superiority over the peoples whose rituals are being described. We find this latter tendency typified in comments from philosophers of religion such as John Hick, who characterizes "[t]he main changes between the ages of ritual human sacrifice and our own day" as consisting "in our understanding of the workings of nature, and in the enlargement of moral vision."[27] In place of condescending attitudes of this sort, Wittgenstein urges us to recognize a more instinctual level of our response—a level at which rituals involving human sacrifice are seen to be significant, even if, or perhaps precisely because, no neat instrumental account can be offered to explain them. "[T]he answer to the question 'why is this happening?,'" Wittgenstein proposes, is simply "Because it is terrible. In other words, what strikes us in this course of events as terrible, impressive, horrible, tragic, &c., anything but trivial and insignificant, *that* is what gave birth to them."[28]

When an English translation of Wittgenstein's *Remarks on Frazer's "Golden Bough"* was first published in 1971, Rhees sent a copy to his friend Maurice O'Connor Drury, who had read portions of Frazer's text with Wittgenstein in the early 1930s. In a letter thanking Rhees for the edition, Drury picks up certain points that Wittgenstein makes and ventures some thoughts of his own. At one place in the letter, Drury (who had once seriously considered becoming an Anglican priest) writes,

> I am shocked when I read about human sacrifice, even too about the ritual slaughter of animals. And the Covenanters going into battle with the cry "Jesus and no quarter." But I needn't add to the list for you to know what I would go on saying.[29]

Rhees's reply to Drury's letter reflects on this reaction, especially on Drury's claim to be shocked by human sacrifice. Among these comments, Rhees says of himself that he would not speak of being shocked if he were to learn that child sacrifice is being practiced "in a really living religion, say in some part of Africa."[30] While certainly regarding the practice as "terrible," Rhees says that he would "have a deep respect for it," though in saying this he is "assuming that the practice of child sacrifice *means* something deep to the people who take part in it; and, generally, to the victim."[31] He contrasts this both with massacres such as those carried out by the Nazis at Lidice in 1942 and by the US Army at Mỹ Lai, South Vietnam, in 1968, and with the hypothetical example of a group "practising child sacrifice in some house in London at the present day." The latter, he says, would be something "entirely—repeat: *entirely*—different" from the African case that he imagines.[32]

The central point that Rhees is emphasizing, and which he takes also to be Wittgenstein's point, is the familiar one of needing to view ritual practices in relation to their cultural surroundings. Although military massacres of unarmed civilians and ritual human sacrifice both involve the killing of human beings, sometimes in excruciating ways, Rhees is keen that they not be simplistically conflated. Contrasting the treatment of Communist resisters by Chiang Kai-shek in the 1920s with the sacrificial practices widely alleged to have been part of the worship of Moloch in ancient times, Rhees writes to Drury, "If you were to say that there was no difference between the two cases, then I do not see how we could discuss it."[33] The difference consists precisely in the contextual factors that enable the events to have the complex meanings that they do have—and hence to be the events that they are—for the people involved in them.

A notable feature of Wittgenstein's and Rhees's respective treatments of human sacrifice is that they do not seek to leave their own emotional reactions out of their philosophical considerations. On the contrary, the reactions become part of the analysis in the sense that how they react to different kinds of phenomena are included among the indicators of important differences between the phenomena themselves. Thus, when Wittgenstein speaks of the "deep and sinister" impression made upon "us" when we learn of human sacrifice, and contrasts this with the different impressions engendered by our learning of the effects of painful diseases, it is clear that he is drawing upon his own emotionally suffused experience. And Rhees, with reference to the sacrifices allegedly performed to Moloch, notes, "I should not have at all the sort of *disgust* that I have when I read of Chiang's treatment of his prisoners—although I might have a strong sense of something terrible in the Moloch rites."[34] The feeling of disgust is, as it were, among the sources that Rhees draws upon in discerning the salient differences between military atrocities and religious sacrifices. Meanwhile, the "sense of something terrible" can, for Rhees, take the form of recognizing the presence of an object of wonder, for it is in sacrificial rites, he suggests elsewhere, that certain peoples express their "wonder at what is terrible and what is evil . . . treating what is terrible as a sacrament."[35]

If, then, we are to take these examples from Wittgenstein and Rhees to illustrate what is required of the contemplative philosopher—and Phillips does cite them as exemplary in this regard[36]—we must be cautious about assuming that the purity of attention at issue precludes any expression of emotion on the philosopher's part. With Phillips's distinction between philosophical contemplation and personal advocacy in view, one might be tempted to suppose that felt emotions cannot enter into the philosophical activity. Indeed, if the "ideal is a certain coolness," which abjures any meddling with the passions, then it might be assumed that purity of attention requires passionless detachment. This need not be the case, however, if we envisage the philosopher as capable both of undergoing passionate emotional responses to the objects of contemplation and of disengaging from those very responses in order to reflect dispassionately upon them. This, I presume, is precisely what many philosophers do aspire to do, and is what Wittgenstein and Rhees are doing in their remarks about their emotional responses to the forms of human killing they discuss. When Rhees acknowledges his disgust at the acts of Chiang's forces, he is reporting rather than expressing his disgust. He can thus have this reaction without its interfering with his philosophical judgment.

Or can he? We might wonder whether the feeling of disgust is not itself internal to the philosophical judgment. Given that the distinction Rhees is making—concerning what it means to kill human beings in the two kinds of context he is considering—is in part articulated in terms of the feeling of disgust that the one engenders and the other does not, it is difficult to see how the reaction can be separated from the contemplative procedure. The same is true of Wittgenstein's remarks on human sacrifice; his inquiry into the meaning of such rites is significantly informed by the deep and sinister impression that they make. It is, he seems to be saying, because they make that impression on him—and, he supposes, upon many other people as well—that we are able to see what gave rise to the rites and what they meant for those who performed them. It would thus be disingenuous to suggest that personal responses are not operative in these remarks of Wittgenstein's and Rhees's. The responses are entering very directly into the philosophical analysis of what particular activities mean in human life.

5 Are There Limits to Conceptual Justice?

The attention that I have just been giving to the place of emotional responses in contemplative philosophizing generates some difficult questions concerning what disinterestedness and "doing justice" amount to in this context. What would it mean, for instance, to do conceptual justice to a practice, or to a whole way of life, by which one finds oneself repulsed and disgusted? Are there limits to the Wittgensteinian project of seeking commonalities of reaction that provide a bridge of understanding between oneself and another community whose behavior one is endeavoring to understand? In this connection, it might be important to recall Wittgenstein's reminder that human beings can sometimes be complete enigmas to one another. "One learns this," he suggests,

> when one comes into a strange country with entirely strange traditions; and, what is more, even though one has mastered the country's language. One does not *understand* the people. (And not because of not knowing what they are saying [among] themselves.) We cannot find ourselves in them.[37]

It is also important to acknowledge that this inability to understand can take different forms. One form of understanding, which we might call *cognitive* understanding, is absent when we say of a people's behavior that we simply cannot understand what they are doing. Another form, however, would be *moral* understanding. This is lacking in instances when, although there is a sense in which we see very well *what* the people are doing, we cannot understand them morally. On these occasions, to exclaim "I cannot understand how anyone could behave like that!" is to express moral exasperation; one cannot find oneself "in" the other person because one cannot imagine oneself being motivated to behave as he or she has done.[38]

What Rhees's way of adumbrating a distinction between religious human sacrifice and military massacres reminds us is that personal morality has a role in conceptual elucidation. To draw the distinction in terms of one of these activities evoking disgust and the other evoking a quite different response, which might even involve an appreciation of depth, is for moral evaluation to play a part in the making of the distinction. To be disgusted by an action is to feel morally distanced from it, and to acknowledge one's disgust in offering a characterization of the action is to express a moral judgment. It would thus be difficult to maintain that no advocacy or condemnation has taken place in such an instance.

There is, then, good reason for questioning whether the philosophical approach typified in Wittgenstein's *Remarks on Frazer's "Golden Bough"* and in Rhees's reflections on human sacrifice and military massacres is well described in terms of "disinterested concerns." For what we see in both Wittgenstein's and Rhees's treatment of religious rites involving human sacrifice is an effort to enunciate what they instinctively find impressive about the rites, whereas in the case of massacres or other wartime atrocities Rhees draws attention to what he finds repugnant and disgusting. While the judgments manifested in these descriptions are likely to have some resonance with many who read the remarks, this hardly makes the descriptions disinterested. They express a *human* interest: an interest in what people are doing to one another in these acts.

To focus more sharply the question of what it means to do conceptual justice to a practice that one finds morally repellent, let us consider a specific event in recent history. On December 24, 2014, Moaz al-Kasasbeh, a 26-year-old Jordanian air force pilot, was taken captive by soldiers from the group variously known as ISIS, ISIL, IS ("Islamic State") or Daesh.[39] Sometime in January 2015 al-Kasasbeh was placed outdoors in a steel cage, wearing an orange jumpsuit doused in petrol. In a high-quality video made by his captors he is shown being set alight by men wearing army fatigues and sand-colored balaclavas.[40] The video was incorporated into a twenty-two-minute IS propaganda film entitled *Healing of the Believers' Chests*, which was widely distributed in early February 2015.[41]

If talk of "doing conceptual justice" has any legitimacy in a case such as the killing of Moaz al-Kasasbeh, it must involve giving an account that does not shy away from the horror of the event depicted in the video. It means recognizing that al-Kasasbeh was anything but a willing participant, that his execution was, apparently, orchestrated not only to inflict maximal agony upon the victim but also to be exploited for propaganda purposes—to promote the interests of a warrior group by accentuating its ruthless image and instilling fear into its enemies. The video represents the killing as a solemn ritualized act: the fire is started not by the mere throw of a match, but by a hooded man ceremonially igniting with a wooden torch the trail of petrol leading to the cage in which al-Kasasbeh is locked. Several cameras have evidently been used to take shots of both al-Kasasbeh and the armed onlookers from different angles, and a soundtrack has been added of passages from the Qur'ān being chanted in Arabic. These theatrically ritualized elements allude to the long history in which burning people alive has been used as a deliberately spectacular form of punishment, not least in the context of religious persecution of alleged heretics, albeit far more commonly by purportedly Christian authorities than by Muslims.[42]

Are we to say of al-Kasasbeh's execution what Wittgenstein said of the ritual killing of the King of the Wood at Nemi, "that something strange and terrible is happening here" and that it is happening *because* it is terrible? Both Wittgenstein and Rhees saw in religious rituals something irreducible and unamenable to explanation in terms of underlying beliefs or purposes; to attempt to explain why the rituals are performed would be to miss the important point—that their meaning and purpose is internal to the performance itself. This is why Phillips, picking up a phrase that Wittgenstein uses in connection with genre paintings, says of religious ritual that it "says itself."[43] Whatever we think of that description of religious rituals, it would be implausible to apply it to the killing by IS of Moaz al-Kasasbeh. While it was undoubtedly carried out in the way it was because the burning of a human being is terrible, the terror served an instrumental purpose that was external to the act, the purpose being to further the military ambitions of the IS regime. We see this instrumentality in the surroundings—in the rapid distribution of the film, for example, and in the calls within the film itself for the killing of other Jordanian "Crusader" pilots.[44] In light of these instrumental motivations, it would seem that any analysis based on the approach demonstrated by Wittgenstein, Rhees, and Phillips should resist conflating the IS killing with the religious rites of human sacrifice to which these philosophers refer.

By identifying an end that the killing of al-Kasasbeh was intended to serve, we are enabled to see the act in a certain light and to situate it in relation to other acts, both religious and political, for the purposes of comparative analysis. We should not, however, be too quick to assume that we have thereby understood it. Even if there is a sense in which we have comprehended *what* was going on, we may remain baffled by a gulf of unintelligibility that prevents our appreciating how people could act in that way. This is where one runs up against the limits of moral understanding. In a case such as this, we (or many of us) would be with Drury in reacting with shock to the execution, and with Rhees in regarding it with disgust. Were someone to treat it lightly, responding with nonchalance or flippancy, we might wonder how he or she could fail to perceive the enormity of the violation that had been committed.[45] Seeing that those who carried out the act are human beings, one is left able only to "*describe* and say: that is what human life"—sometimes—"is like."[46]

6 Finding, or Not Finding, Oneself in the Other

At the end of this inquiry, it must be admitted that there is no straightforward answer to the question of what the ethical demands of Wittgensteinian philosophizing consist in. D. Z. Phillips highlights particular examples from Wittgenstein and Rush Rhees in which these philosophers are contemplating the meaning of ritual acts that involve burning human effigies or the actual sacrifice of human beings. The "purity of attention to the world" that Phillips praises is a mode of attention that exhibits an attitude of hermeneutical charity. This attitude seeks possibilities of sense within human activities that bring the participants in those activities closer to us, showing how their behavior can be understood to embody reactions to the world with which we are able to identify, even if the specific forms that the behavior takes are ones that leave us morally unsettled. When Phillips asserts that such purity of attention "shows character," he seems to have in mind the thought that abstaining from value judgments in one's philosophizing is a virtue that requires effort to cultivate. On this view, the temptation to be resisted is that of allowing personal preferences, including one's emotional and moral reactions, to contaminate one's philosophical contemplations.

When we look more closely at the very examples that Phillips cites, however, we see that the relation between philosophical contemplation, on the one hand, and emotional and moral reactions, on the other, is a complicated one. Neither Wittgenstein nor Rhees remains emotionally neutral in the face of acts of human killing. On the contrary, their natural responses to these acts constitute an access point for penetrating more deeply into what, in the case of religious rituals, these acts might mean for the people who perform them. Moreover, when Rhees contrasts religious sacrificial killings with the atrocities of war and political violence, it is to the disparity in his emotional reactions that he looks in order to find a vocabulary for articulating a difference between the phenomena.

The example that I cited of the killing of a Jordanian hostage by IS combatants in January 2015 is itself highly ramified, not least because the perpetrators deliberately amalgamate political execution and ostentatiously religious ritual. What doing conceptual justice to an act such as this would amount to cannot be determined independently of the particular questions about the phenomenon that one is seeking to address. One direction that the philosophical inquiry could take would involve showing how the immolation of a human being goes together with a perspective on life according to which it is the duty of the faithful to punish apostates and infidels and to use them as a means to the end of establishing a global caliphate. Taking the inquiry in that direction could, in a certain sense, help one to understand the act, and yet, I have suggested, there may remain another sense—a moral sense—in which one cannot understand the act at all. We might, as it were, know very well what the perpetrators are saying to themselves—to one another—and yet be unable to "find ourselves in them."[47]

Notes

1 D. Z. Phillips, "Locating Philosophy's Cool Place—A Reply to Stephen Mulhall," in *D. Z. Phillips' Contemplative Philosophy of Religion: Questions and Responses*, ed. Andy F. Sanders (Aldershot: Ashgate, 2007), 29–54, 38.

2 "Wittgenstein's later method is very much in keeping with his earlier remarks about ethics and is ethical without being about ethics" (Duncan Richter, "Nothing to Be

Said: Wittgenstein and Wittgensteinian Ethics," *Southern Journal of Philosophy* 34, no. 2 [1996]: 243–56, at 251). (This statement seems paradoxical. Are we to understand that Wittgenstein's "earlier remarks about ethics" were not really *about* ethics? I shall not pursue that question here.)

3 "[E]thics should be viewed as clarificatory, and not assertoric, in nature" (J. Jeremy Wisnewski, *Wittgenstein and Ethical Inquiry: A Defense of Ethics as Clarification* [London: Continuum, 2007], xiii). "[A]n investigation of Wittgenstein's remarks on ethics does not present a theory of ethics; rather, it clarifies what it is we do when we use words with an ethical point and elucidates the characteristic features of such a use" (Anne-Marie S. Christensen, "Wittgenstein and Ethics," in *The Oxford Handbook of Wittgenstein*, ed. Oskari Kuusela and Marie McGinn [Oxford: Oxford University Press, 2011], 796–817, 797).

4 See, for example, Nigel Pleasants, "Wittgenstein, Ethics and Basic Moral Certainty," *Inquiry* 51, no. 3 (2008): 241–67; Julia Hermann, *On Moral Certainty, Justification and Practice: A Wittgensteinian Perspective* (Basingstoke: Palgrave Macmillan, 2015); Neil O'Hara, *Moral Certainty and the Foundations of Morality* (New York: Palgrave Macmillan, 2018).

5 Rush Rhees, "The Fundamental Problems of Philosophy," *Philosophical Investigations* 17, no. 4 (1994): 573–86, 577.

6 See, for example, Paul Johnston, *Wittgenstein and Moral Philosophy* (London: Routledge, 1989), 25: "[I]n so far as Wittgenstein's later work does impose an ethical demand, it does this not because it draws the limits to what can be said, but rather because it imposes that process of self-discipline needed to restrict oneself to 'mere' description." See also Peter Winch, "Doing Justice or Giving the Devil His Due," in *Can Religion Be Explained Away?* ed. D. Z. Phillips (Basingstoke: Macmillan, 1996), 161–74, 173.

7 See Stephen Mulhall, "Wittgenstein's Temple: Three Styles of Philosophical Architecture," in *D.Z. Phillips' Contemplative Philosophy of Religion*, 13–27.

8 D. Z. Phillips, "Epistemic Practices—A Reply to William Wainwright," *Topoi* 14, no. 2 (1995): 95–105, 104; idem, *Religion and the Hermeneutics of Contemplation* (Cambridge: Cambridge University Press, 2001), 325. See also, among other places, D. Z. Phillips, *Philosophy's Cool Place* (Ithaca, NY: Cornell University Press, 1999), 163; idem, "Just Say the Word: Magical and Logical Conceptions in Religion," in *Religion and Wittgenstein's Legacy*, ed. D. Z. Phillips and Mario von der Ruhr (Aldershot: Ashgate, 2005), 171–86, 180.

9 Ludwig Wittgenstein, *Zettel*, ed. G. E. M. Anscombe and G. H. von Wright, trans. G. E. M. Anscombe, 2nd ed. (Oxford: Blackwell, 1981), § 455.

10 Ludwig Wittgenstein, *Culture and Value*, ed. G. H. von Wright and Heikki Nyman, rev. Alois Pichler, trans. Peter Winch (Oxford: Blackwell, 1998), 4e. As I note elsewhere, one could suggest—somewhat mischievously—that in the wake of Wittgenstein's work a Wittgensteinian "community of ideas" has developed, "of

which there are many citizens." But as I also observe in that article, if there is such a community, it comprises "idiosyncrats rather than ... doctrinaire conformists" (Mikel Burley, "Approaches to Philosophy of Religion: Contemplating the World or Trying to Find Our Way Home?," *Religious Studies* 51, no. 2 [2015]: 221–39, 227).

11 Ludwig Wittgenstein, *Philosophical Investigations*, 4th ed., trans. G. E. M. Anscombe, P. M. S. Hacker and Joachim Schulte (Malden, MA: Wiley-Blackwell, 2009), § 126; cf. § 124.

12 D. Z. Phillips, *Religion and Friendly Fire: Examining Assumptions in Contemporary Philosophy of Religion* (Aldershot: Ashgate, 2004), 55.

13 James Conant, "Putting Two and Two Together: Kierkegaard, Wittgenstein and the Point of View for Their Work as Authors," in *Philosophy and the Grammar of Religious Belief*, ed. Timothy Tessin and Mario von der Ruhr (Basingstoke: Macmillan, 1995), 248–331, 280.

14 Mulhall, "Wittgenstein's Temple," 23, 26.

15 Phillips, *Philosophy's Cool Place*, 43–4.

16 "Let us be human," Wittgenstein writes in a notebook from 1937 (*Culture and Value*, 36e). As one commentator has recently proposed, "Wittgenstein's later thought can be seen as working out the implications of [this] request" (Lee Braver, *Groundless Grounds: A Study of Wittgenstein and Heidegger* [Cambridge, MA: MIT Press, 2012], 232).

17 Phillips, *Religion and Friendly Fire*, 55.

18 Thomas Nagel, *The View from Nowhere* (Oxford: Oxford University Press, 1986).

19 Conant, "Putting Two and Two Together," 280.

20 D. Z. Phillips, "Afterword: Rhees on Reading *On Certainty*," in Rush Rhees, *Wittgenstein's "On Certainty": There—Like Our Life*, ed. D. Z. Phillips (Malden, MA: Blackwell, 2003), 133–82, 182; idem, "Philosophy, Theology and Cultural Conflicts—A Reply to Ingolf Dalferth," in *D.Z. Phillips' Contemplative Philosophy of Religion*, 167–79, 167.

21 Phillips, "Afterword," 182.

22 Phillips, *Philosophy's Cool Place*, 166.

23 Simone Weil, *Waiting on God*, trans. Emma Craufurd (London: Fontana, 1959), 173.

24 D. Z. Phillips, *The Concept of Prayer* (London: Routledge and Kegan Paul, 1965), 70.

25 D. Z. Phillips, *Death and Immortality* (London: Macmillan, 1970), 54–5.

26 Ludwig Wittgenstein, *Remarks on Frazer's "Golden Bough,"* ed. Rush Rhees, trans. A. C. Miles, rev. Rush Rhees (Retford: Brynmill Press, 1979), 16e, translation slightly amended. For "*wir tragen es wieder*" (lit. "*we* carry it again"), the original translation by Miles and Rhees has "*we* impute it" and that by John Beverlsuis has "*we* ... ascribe them" (Ludwig Wittgenstein, "Remarks on Frazer's *Golden Bough*," in *Philosophical Occasions, 1912–1951*, ed. James C. Klagge and Alfred Nordmann

[Indianapolis, IN: Hackett, 1993], 115–55, 147). The phrase is, admittedly, difficult to render satisfactorily in English. What Wittgenstein seems to be suggesting is *not* that the perception of something deep and sinister in the ritual is a mere projection on our part, but rather that we recognize its presence in the ritual on account of the experience in ourselves that the ritual (or our learning about the ritual) evokes. We *retrieve* the sense of the ritual from within our own lives.

27 John Hick, *An Interpretation of Religion: Human Responses to the Transcendent*, 2nd ed. (Basingstoke: Palgrave Macmillan, 2004), 311.
28 Wittgenstein, *Remarks of Frazer's "Golden Bough"* (1979), 3e.
29 Maurice O'Connor Drury, letter to Rhees, June 15, 1971, quoted in Rush Rhees, *Rush Rhees on Religion and Philosophy*, ed. D. Z. Phillips and Mario von der Ruhr (Cambridge: Cambridge University Press, 1997), 100, fn. 4.
30 Rhees, *Rush Rhees on Religion and Philosophy*, 101. The passage is from Rhees's letter of reply to Drury, dated June 19, 1971.
31 Ibid., 102.
32 Ibid., 101.
33 Ibid., 102.
34 Ibid., original emphasis.
35 Rhees, "The Fundamental Problems of Philosophy," 578.
36 See esp. Phillips, *Philosophy's Cool Place*, 56–8; idem, *Religion and the Hermeneutics of Contemplation*, 181–2; idem, "Just Say the Word," 182; idem, "Locating Philosophy's Cool Place," 43–4.
37 Ludwig Wittgenstein, "Philosophy of Psychology—A Fragment," in his *Philosophical Investigations*, 4th ed., § 325, translation amended. The final sentence of this remark is rendered by Anscombe as "We cannot find our feet with them." But "We cannot find ourselves in them" is closer to Wittgenstein's German ("Wir können uns nicht in sie finden"). Cf. James C. Klagge, *Wittgenstein in Exile* (Cambridge, MA: MIT Press, 2011), 43.
38 Some relevant comments about "moral or religious incomprehension" occur in Phillips, *Religion and the Hermeneutics of Contemplation*, 323.
39 ISIS = Islamic State of (or in) Iraq and Syria [or ". . . and al-Sham"]; ISIL = Islamic State of (or in) Iraq and the Levant; see Faisal Irshaid, "Isis, Isil or Da'ish? One Group, Many Names," *BBC News*, December 2, 2015, http://www.bbc.co.uk/news/world-middle-east-27994277 (accessed December 10, 2018). The group's Arabic names include *al-Dawla al-Islamiyah fi al-Iraq wa al-Sham* ("Islamic State of Iraq and *al-Sham*"), *al-Sham* being an allusion "to the notion of Greater Syria which includes modern day Lebanon" (G. Michael Stathis, "ISIS, Syria, and Iraq: The Beginning of a Fourth Gulf War?" *Critical Issues in Justice and Politics* 8, no. 1 [2015]: 1–19, 2). This Arabic name has been abbreviated as *Da'ish* or *Daesh* by the group's detractors; see Fred McConnell, "Australian PM Says He'll Now Use Daesh

Instead of Isil for 'Death Cult'—But Why?," *The Guardian*, January 12, 2015, http://www.theguardian.com/world/2015/jan/12/tony-abbott-say-hell-now-use-daesh-instead-of-isil-for-death-cult-but-why (accessed August 7, 2015).

40 The video of the execution is available on the website of the Dutch newspaper *The Post Online*: "Video: IS verbrandt gevangengenomen Jordaanse piloot levend," February 3, 2015, http://nieuws.tpo.nl/2015/02/03/isis-verbrandt-gevangengenomen-jordaanse-piloot-levend/ (accessed July 11, 2015).

41 At the time when I first drafted this chapter, the entire film was readily accessible at *Tangent Code*: "Healing of the Believers' Chests—Islamic State," February 3, 2015, http://tangentcode.org/2015/02/03/healing-of-the-believers-chests-islamic-state/ (accessed August 23, 2015). It remains available on the *Tangent Code* website, but is now password protected. For discussion of how the film was distributed, see Abdel Bari Atwan, *Islamic State: The Digital Caliphate* (Oakland, CA: University of California Press, 2015), 22–3. The film's title is borrowed from Qur'ān 9:14: "Fight against them so that Allâh will punish them by your hands and disgrace them and give you victory over them and heal the breasts of a believing people" (*The Noble Qur'an*, trans. Muhammad Taqî-ud-Dîn Al-Hilâlî and Muhammad Muhsin Khân [Madinah: King Fahd Complex for the Printing of the Holy Qur'an, 1996 (1417 AH)], 245).

42 For a concise historical account of the practice of burning heretics in the name of Christianity, see Jeffrey Burton Russell, *Witchcraft in the Middle Ages* (Ithaca, NY: Cornell University Press, 1972), 149–51. For reports of burning as a method of execution in early Islam, see Gerald Hawting, "The Case of Ja'd b. Dirham and the Punishment of 'Heretics' in the Early Caliphate," in *Public Violence in Islamic Societies: Power, Discipline, and the Construction of the Public Sphere, 7th–19th Centuries CE*, ed. Christian Lange and Maribel Fierro (Edinburgh: Edinburgh University Press, 2009), 27–41, 36, and Joel L. Kraemer, "Apostates, Rebels and Brigands," *Israel Oriental Studies* 10 (1980): 34–73, 44–6.

43 Phillips, "Afterword," 146; Phillips, *Religion and Friendly Fire*, 86. Cf. Wittgenstein, *Philosophical Investigations*, § 523: "'A picture tells me itself' is what I'd like to say. That is, its telling me something consists in its own structure, in *its* own forms and colours." See also *Culture and Value*, 67e: "You might say: The work of art does not seek to convey *something else*, just itself."

44 A caption (printed in upper case) near the end of the film reads, "On this occasion, the Islamic State announces a reward of 100 gold dinars to whoever kills a Crusader pilot. The Diwan for state security has released a list containing the names of Jordanian pilots participating in the campaign. So good tidings to whoever supports his religion and achieves a kill that will liberate him from hellfire" ("Healing of the Believers' Chests—Islamic State," *Tangent Code* [accessed August 23, 2015]).

45 Sadly, the viewers' comments posted on some web pages that show the video of al-Kasasbeh's death demonstrate the ability of many people to be both flippant and obtuse in the face of human suffering.

46 Wittgenstein, "Remarks on Frazer's *Golden Bough*," 121.
47 I am grateful to Richard Amesbury, Christoph Ammann, and Hartmut von Sass for organizing the *Doing Ethics after Wittgenstein* conference (April 2016) and thereby enabling me to present, and receive comments on, an abridged version of this chapter. Amesbury also generously provided written comments on an earlier draft.

Works Cited

Atwan, Abdel Bari, *Islamic State: The Digital Caliphate*, Oakland, CA: University of California Press, 2015.

Braver, Lee, *Groundless Grounds: A Study of Wittgenstein and Heidegger*, Cambridge, MA: MIT Press, 2012.

Burley, Mikel, "Approaches to Philosophy of Religion: Contemplating the World or Trying to Find Our Way Home?," *Religious Studies* 51, no. 2 (2015): 221–39.

Christensen, Anne-Marie S., "Wittgenstein and Ethics," in Oskari Kuusela and Marie McGinn (eds.), *The Oxford Handbook of Wittgenstein*, 796–817, Oxford: Oxford University Press, 2011.

Conant, James, "Putting Two and Two Together: Kierkegaard, Wittgenstein and the Point of View for Their Work as Authors," in Timothy Tessin and Mario von der Ruhr (eds.), *Philosophy and the Grammar of Religious Belief*, 248–331, Basingstoke: Macmillan, 1995.

Hawting, Gerald, "The Case of Ja'd b. Dirham and the Punishment of 'Heretics' in the Early Caliphate," in Christian Lange and Maribel Fierro (eds.), *Public Violence in Islamic Societies: Power, Discipline, and the Construction of the Public Sphere, 7th–19th Centuries CE*, 27–41, Edinburgh: Edinburgh University Press, 2009.

"Healing of the Believers' Chests—Islamic State," *Tangent Code*, February 3, 2015, http://tangentcode.org/2015/02/03/healing-of-the-believers-chests-islamic-state/ (accessed August 23, 2015).

Hermann, Julia, *On Moral Certainty, Justification and Practice: A Wittgensteinian Perspective*, Basingstoke: Palgrave Macmillan, 2015.

Hick, John, *An Interpretation of Religion: Human Responses to the Transcendent*, 2nd ed., Basingstoke: Palgrave Macmillan, 2004.

Irshaid, Faisal, "Isis, Isil or Da'ish? One Group, Many Names," *BBC News*, December 2, 2015, http://www.bbc.co.uk/news/world-middle-east-27994277 (accessed December 10, 2018).

Johnston, Paul, *Wittgenstein and Moral Philosophy*, London: Routledge, 1989.

Klagge, James C., *Wittgenstein in Exile*, Cambridge, MA: MIT Press, 2011.

Kraemer, Joel L., "Apostates, Rebels and Brigands," *Israel Oriental Studies* 10 (1980): 34–73.

McConnell, Fred, "Australian PM Says He'll Now Use Daesh Instead of Isil for 'Death Cult'—But Why?," *The Guardian*, January 12, 2015, online: http://www.theguardi

an.com/world/2015/jan/12/tony-abbott-say-hell-now-use-daesh-instead-of-isil-for-death-cult-but-why (accessed August 7, 2015).

Mulhall, Stephen, "Wittgenstein's Temple: Three Styles of Philosophical Architecture," in Andy F. Sanders (ed.), *D.Z. Phillips' Contemplative Philosophy of Religion: Questions and Responses*, 13–27, Aldershot: Ashgate, 2007.

Nagel, Thomas, *The View from Nowhere*, Oxford: Oxford University Press, 1986.

The Noble Qur'an, trans. Muhammad Taqî-ud-Dîn Al-Hilâlî and Muhammad Muhsin Khân, Madinah: King Fahd Complex for the Printing of the Holy Qur'an, 1996.

O'Hara, Neil, *Moral Certainty and the Foundations of Morality*, New York: Palgrave Macmillan, 2018.

Phillips, D. Z., *The Concept of Prayer*, London: Routledge and Kegan Paul, 1965.

Phillips, D. Z., *Death and Immortality*, London: Macmillan, 1970.

Phillips, D. Z., "Epistemic Practices—A Reply to William Wainwright," *Topoi* 14, no. 2 (1995) 95–105.

Phillips, D. Z., *Philosophy's Cool Place*, Ithaca, NY: Cornell University Press, 1999.

Phillips, D. Z., *Religion and the Hermeneutics of Contemplation*, Cambridge: Cambridge University Press, 2001.

Phillips, D. Z., "Afterword: Rhees on Reading *On Certainty*," in Rush Rhees, *Wittgenstein's "On Certainty": There—Like Our Life*, ed. D. Z. Phillips, 133–82, Malden, MA: Blackwell, 2003.

Phillips, D. Z., *Religion and Friendly Fire: Examining Assumptions in Contemporary Philosophy of Religion*, Aldershot: Ashgate, 2004.

Phillips, D. Z., "Just Say the Word: Magical and Logical Conceptions in Religion," in D. Z. Phillips and Mario von der Ruhr (eds.), *Religion and Wittgenstein's Legacy*, 171–86, Aldershot: Ashgate, 2005.

Phillips, D. Z., "Locating Philosophy's Cool Place—A Reply to Stephen Mulhall," in Andy F. Sanders (ed.), *D.Z. Phillips' Contemplative Philosophy of Religion: Questions and Responses*, 29–54, Aldershot: Ashgate, 2007.

Phillips, D. Z., "Philosophy, Theology and Cultural Conflicts—A Reply to Ingolf Dalferth," in Andy F. Sanders (ed.), *D.Z. Phillips' Contemplative Philosophy of Religion*, 167–79, Aldershot: Ashgate, 2007.

Pleasants, Nigel, "Wittgenstein, Ethics and Basic Moral Certainty," *Inquiry* 51, no. 3 (2008): 241–67.

Rhees, Rush, "The Fundamental Problems of Philosophy," *Philosophical Investigations* 17, no. 4 (1994): 573–86.

Rhees, Rush, *Rush Rhees on Religion and Philosophy*, ed. D. Z. Phillips and Mario von der Ruhr, Cambridge: Cambridge University Press, 1997.

Richter, Duncan, "Nothing to Be Said: Wittgenstein and Wittgensteinian Ethics," *Southern Journal of Philosophy* 34, no. 2 (1996): 243–56.

Russell, Jeffrey Burton, *Witchcraft in the Middle Ages*, Ithaca, NY: Cornell University Press, 1972.

Sanders, Andy F. (ed.), *D.Z. Phillips' Contemplative Philosophy of Religion: Questions and Responses*, Aldershot: Ashgate, 2007.

Stathis, G. Michael, "ISIS, Syria, and Iraq: The Beginning of a Fourth Gulf War?," *Critical Issues in Justice and Politics* 8, no. 1 (2015): 1–19.

"Video: IS verbrandt gevangengenomen Jordaanse piloot levend," *The Post Online*, February 3, 2015, http://nieuws.tpo.nl/2015/02/03/isis-verbrandt-gevangengenomen-jordaanse-piloot-levend/ (accessed July 11, 2015).

Weil, Simone, *Waiting on God*, trans. Emma Craufurd, London: Fontana, 1959.

Winch, Peter, "Doing Justice or Giving the Devil His Due," in D. Z. Phillips (ed.), *Can Religion Be Explained Away?*, 161–74, Basingstoke: Macmillan, 1996.

Wisnewski, J. Jeremy, *Wittgenstein and Ethical Inquiry: A Defense of Ethics as Clarification*, London: Continuum, 2007.

Wittgenstein, Ludwig, *Remarks on Frazer's "Golden Bough,"* ed. Rush Rhees, trans. A. C. Miles, rev. by Rush Rhees, Retford: Brynmill Press, 1979.

Wittgenstein, Ludwig, *Zettel*, ed. G. E. M. Anscombe and G. H. von Wright, trans. G. E. M. Anscombe, 2nd ed., Oxford: Blackwell, 1981.

Wittgenstein, Ludwig, "Remarks on Frazer's *Golden Bough*," in James C. Klagge and Alfred Nordmann (eds.), *Philosophical Occasions, 1912–1951*, 115–55, Indianapolis, IN: Hackett, 1993.

Wittgenstein, Ludwig *Culture and Value*, ed. Georg H. von Wright and Heikki Nyman, rev. by Alois Pichler, trans. Peter Winch, Oxford: Blackwell, 1998.

Wittgenstein, Ludwig, *Philosophical Investigations*, 4th ed., trans. G. E. M. Anscombe, P. M. S. Hacker and Joachim Schulte, Malden, MA: Wiley-Blackwell, 2009.

9

Wittgenstein and Political Theology
Law, Decision, and the Self
Richard Amesbury

Writing in 1922, Carl Schmitt declared that "all significant concepts of the modern theory of the state are secularized theological concepts."[1] Once a respected German jurist and philosopher, Schmitt went on to cast his lot with National Socialism, and in the post-war period his work fell into disrepute and comparative obscurity, especially outside the German-speaking world, where it had not been widely read to begin with. The past decade, however, has seen a resurgence of interest in Schmitt's corpus, this time largely on the part of left-leaning political theorists, including Giorgio Agamben, Jacques Derrida, Bonnie Honig, and Paul Kahn, who find in its analyses of sovereignty, decision, and the friend-enemy distinction a useful corrective to liberal political and legal theory. Borrowing the title of one of Schmitt's best-known texts, this emerging tradition sometimes goes by the name "political theology" and seeks to bring into view the sacral dimensions of contemporary political life.

That contemporary liberal states embody the sacred might seem a startling claim; is it not, after all, the singular achievement of secular modernity to have separated church and state? Perhaps, but—political theology points out—it does not follow that politics has freed itself from the sacred. "In a crisis," Kahn writes, "it remains true today that the secular state does not hesitate to speak of sacrifice, patriotism, nationalism, and the homeland in the language of the sacred. The state's territory becomes consecrated ground, its history a sacred duty to maintain, its flag something to die for."[2] By attending to the liturgies of modern political life, the new political theology aims to track the movement of the sacred across the border (the porousness of which is attested by its vigilant policing) said to separate the secular from the religious.[3]

Apart from his remark about the theological character of the modern state, the sentence for which Schmitt is most commonly remembered is this: "Sovereign is he who decides on the exception."[4] Just as a miracle has been conceived as a suspension of the laws of nature by God, so, Schmitt suggests, political sovereignty belongs to whomever is capable of suspending the positive legal order for the sake of its survival.[5] This may sound like little more than an apologia for dictatorship—and it is that[6]—but one of Schmitt's most important theoretical insights is that the exception is built conceptually into the notion of the rule of law. At one level, Schmitt clearly had in mind emergency situations in which the legal order is perceived to be under existential threat. But what is an emergency? Sovereignty, in Schmitt's account, is the power of *successfully naming the exception*. The underlying thought here is that the exception is not a lacuna in the legal order that demands a stop-gap decision (and which could, in theory, be fixed with more or better law); rather, it exists only insofar as it is "decided on" or declared. But this *de facto* power of decision, which cannot be restricted to any constitutionally-designated office (e.g., that of the President), points to a deeper insight, namely, that the *force* of law depends on an authority beyond the *formal system* of law. This authority cannot be located in an additional act of legislation, a law that says that we should obey the law; rather, it occupies what Agamben describes as a "no-man's-land between public law and political fact . . . between the juridical order and life."[7] Whereas liberalism tends to imagine that the space of sovereignty can be eliminated by extending the rule of law indefinitely in all directions—the legal analog of a closed physical universe[8]—Schmitt argued that this project is futile: the exception is a function not of any deficit in the legal order but of the interface of that order with practice.[9] The possibility of the exception cannot be legislated away: "whether the extreme exception can be banished from the world is not a juristic question."[10]

Schmitt was hostile to liberalism, and some of his skepticism carries over into the contemporary discussion. But whereas Schmitt was critical in part of the *practice* of liberalism, most contemporary practitioners of political theology limit their critique to liberal political *theory*, which they view as inadequate to lived political experience in liberal democracies like the United States. In his book *Political Theology: Four New Chapters on the Concept of Sovereignty*, Kahn engages Schmitt's similarly titled work to offer a sort of phenomenological description of the sacral dimension of American political life. Where liberal political theory emphasizes contract, discourse, and the rule of law, Kahn highlights the significance of sacrifice, violence, and the exception. American politics, according to this account, is a pursuit, not primarily of interests, but of transcendent *meaning*:

> At stake in the politics of sacrifice is participation in the mystical corpus that is the popular sovereign: a giving up the self and a living in and through the transcendent being that is the popular sovereign. Popular sovereignty in the United States is distinctly not a conception of self-government through elections that express the majority will as it emerges from constantly shifting coalitions. Political theory may give us such a process view of popular-sovereignty, but to pursue this path is like thinking that we can understand religious faith by examining church attendance statistics. The popular sovereign is a trans-temporal, omnipresent, and omniscient plural subject. It is invisible to those outside of its presence just as other forms of the sacred are invisible to those outside of the faith. It is the reified object of an experience of faith sustained through the imagination of sacrifice. This is the national narrative, endlessly repeated in film, books, and political rhetoric.[11]

If, on Robert Bellah's account, the American civil religion came across as fairly benign, Kahn's work seeks to recover something of its *mysterium tremendum et fascinans,* or as we might say today, its "shock and awe."[12] Far from an epiphenomenal embellishment on an otherwise "well ordered society," theological categories belong, on Kahn's reading, to the "deep structure of American political belief."[13]

Kahn, like a number of other contemporary thinkers who have picked up on these themes (including Derrida and Honig), emphasizes the ubiquity of decision-making. Indeed, part of the claim is that the need for decisions is not limited to those "states of exception" where it most clearly manifests itself—declarations of martial law, revolutions, black sites—but penetrates the everyday workings of government. For example, a judge asked to decide between competing understandings of a law cannot fall back on the law in question but must render a decision that affirms the law from a standpoint outside the norm whose meaning is at issue. In this view, the application of law depends crucially upon judicial decisions that serve to impose meaning on otherwise indeterminate norms. These decisions are not something *apart from* law that bear only contingently on how it comes to be understood, but belong ineliminably to the very possibility of law itself.

Although the emphasis on decision offers a potentially helpful corrective to the liberal preoccupation with norms, there is more than one way of accounting for the significance of decisions, and the way the decision is theorized has important implications for thinking about the place of law in liberal societies.

Ironically, in the contemporary decisionist critique of liberal theory, with its focus on the *meaning* of the law, it is possible to detect a liberalizing tendency: by insisting on the ubiquity of decision-making, the exception is made to seem unexceptional. In this way, Schmitt is tamed, and sovereignty is diffused into the mundane world of administrative governance. For Honig and Derrida, this move is explicit, but a similar trajectory can be detected in Kahn's writing, which tends to work at cross-purposes to his stated aim of exposing the exceptional character of American politics. By contrast, I want to resist this normalizing account, and to do so primarily on philosophical grounds: if one is to appreciate the exceptional character of the decision, it is important to retain some background of regularity with which it can be contrasted. As Schmitt put it, "For a legal order to make sense, a normal situation must exist, and he is sovereign who definitely decides whether this normal situation actually exists."[14] Mine is not a critique of political theology *per se*, or even of decisionism, but of a metaphysical *picture* that distorts the phenomenology of decision-making.

In this chapter I make constructive use of Schmitt's contemporary, Ludwig Wittgenstein, to argue against this picture of the relation between law and decision, and in favor of a more pragmatic understanding, one that situates law within wider networks of meaning and authority. Making the exception exceptional does not do away with the space of sovereignty, but—I argue—it allows us to recover a more robust conception of *the self*, and thus to hold space open for alternative theologies of the political that refuse the choice between "reason" and "will."

1 Indeterminate Law

To begin, it is helpful to consider a couple of recent statements of the view in question, which I call the *new decisionism*.[15] The first of these is from Derrida's essay "Force of Law," and the second from Kahn's *Political Theology*:

> To be just, the decision of a judge, for example, must not only follow a rule of law or a general law but must also assume it, approve it, confirm its value, by a reinstituting act of interpretation, as if ultimately nothing previously existed of the law, as if the judge himself invented the law in every case. No exercise of justice as law can be just unless there is a "fresh judgment."[16]

> Liberalism prefers to focus on norms rather than power; in place of political conflict, it would rather argue about what the law is. The problem of the "realization of law," however, is never resolved at the level of the norm itself, for

the norm is indeterminate over some range of outcomes. In law, we can't avoid the decision.[17]

Although it may be tempting to imagine legal norms as—to borrow a phrase from Wittgenstein—"rails invisibly laid to infinity," the view being advanced in these passages suggests that, by means of decisions, track is constantly being put down, contributing to the *meaning* of the norms in question.[18] The methodological claim is thus that focusing on exceptional circumstances that demand decisions can be more theoretically illuminating than taking as one's point of reference those seemingly unproblematic situations in which law appears to be humming along under its own steam.

From a liberal perspective, the Schmittian emphasis on decision can seem alarming, but both Derrida and Kahn argue that it need not be interpreted as landing us on a slippery slope to the anti-liberal political conclusions for which Schmitt remains infamous.[19] Indeed, both thinkers argue that foregrounding decision reintroduces salutary elements of freedom and responsibility into our understanding of legal reasoning, elements without which law's connection to justice becomes tenuous.[20] Moreover, many of the new decisionists argue that the exception is in reality *unexceptional*—an ordinary, if sometimes unacknowledged, dimension of governance. Honig writes:

> Simply put, then, within the rule-of-law settings that Schmitt *contrasts* with decisionism, something like the decisionism that Schmitt approvingly identifies with a dictator goes by the name of discretion and is identified (approvingly or disapprovingly) with administrators and with administrative governance.[21]

In this reading, justice requires something more than laws, even good laws; it requires decision. The decision is sometimes said, seemingly paradoxically, to be "undecidable," meaning that it must be made in the absence of "any certitude or any supposed criteriology that would assure us of [its] justice."[22] In this respect it constitutes an act of free will. "Freedom," Kahn writes, "is choice."[23] To see the legal and political order as the product of choice is to see it as an expression of autonomy, and thus as possessing legitimacy. "Politics as a performance of freedom fails when we cannot see the state itself as a product of our own acts."[24]

Conceived in this way, the new decisionism assuages some of the political misgivings associated with Schmitt's legacy, at the cost of giving rise to several theoretical worries. One is hinted at in the Honig quote above, namely, that it threatens to collapse the very distinction on which it depends for its contrast case. Derrida, for example, makes much of the alleged difference between merely following rules and making new decisions. In his view, only the latter contains the opening in which justice is possible: "no exercise of justice as law can be just *unless there is a 'fresh judgment.'*"[25] But if, as Derrida claims, *every* application of law requires decision—if in the absence of a "transcendental signified" or self-applying sign, decision is an inescapable dimension of rule-application as such[26]—it is hard to see how the "fresh judgment" he advocates can be distinguished from cases that "the rule guarantees . . . in no uncertain terms," in which the application "simply consists of applying a rule, of enacting a program or effecting a calculation."[27]

A second worry is that the new decisionism sometimes seems not to take seriously enough its own doctrine of the indeterminacy of norms. Kahn—from whose work, owing to its admirable clarity, I draw most of my examples in this chapter—frequently claims that the meaning of law awaits the decision. His point is partly negative, i.e., that norms do not apply themselves. He writes:

> [N]o norm can establish the authority of its own application.[28]
>
> On Schmitt's view, we don't know what the law is until after the decision. The decision does not follow from the law, but the law follows from the decision.[29]
>
> The meaning of the law is simply indeterminate until there is a decision.[30]
>
> [O]nly after the issue has been decided will we know what the legal principle of equality means.[31]

If norms, however, were really indeterminate absent decisions, it would seem that no decision, even that of a judge, could "establish" their meaning. No sooner would a decision be made, than another would be required. The problem to which decision is said to provide the solution would apparently recur with every successive application, thus rendering otiose the concept of law altogether. While it is true that rules, treated as abstract utterances, do not "apply themselves" (although there is something misleading about this way of putting it: what is the "rule," exactly?)[32] it is not clear that the appeal to decisions gets us very far.

2 Wittgenstein's Therapeutic Approach

Why, then, is *decision* thought to be the critical term? The answer, I suggest, is twofold. On one hand, we can point to various practical situations in which this picture is reasonably apt, including jurisprudential contexts in which the decision of a judge is required. But the attractions of the decisionist model as a general account of rule application go deeper and are rooted in a particular philosophical puzzle with which Wittgenstein wrestled. In what have come to be called his "rule-following considerations," Wittgenstein imagines an interlocutor who resembles, in certain respects, the "liberal" of whom political theology is critical. The view to which the interlocutor is committed is what Robert Brandom calls "regulism," i.e., the idea that the assessment of performance requires *explicit rules or laws*.[33] Naturally, the application of these rules is itself a kind of performance, and thus it would appear, according to the regulist account, that we require an additional set of rules to determine the application of the first set of rules. Here the interlocutor finds himself on a slippery slope. "But what does a game look like that is everywhere bounded by rules?" Wittgenstein asks. "Whose rules never let a doubt creep in, but stop up all the cracks where it might?—Can't we imagine a rule determining the application of a rule, and a doubt which *it* removes—and so on?"[34] This threat of a regress of rules for ensuring the correct application of rules is what gives rise to the hope that a way out can be provided not by reason but by will, so that what is needed is not another rule but a *decision*, unconstrained by rules. Wittgenstein writes, "it would almost be more correct to say, not that an intuition was needed at every stage, but that *a new decision* was needed at every stage."[35]

Some of Wittgenstein's interpreters have taken the latter conclusion to be the moral of the story. For instance, Simon Glendinning understands Wittgenstein to be endorsing here the view that "what 'conforming to the rule' *is*, is itself constituted on the basis of repetitions which are ungrounded or structurally abyssal. In every case the 'moment of decision' is ineliminable."[36] Yet, the hesitance with which Wittgenstein entertains the claim—"it would *almost* be *more* correct"—cautions against too hastily identifying it with his considered opinion. Indeed, a few paragraphs later Wittgenstein writes, "When I obey a rule *I do not choose*. I obey the rule blindly."[37] He is denying not that I can decide *whether* to obey a rule, but that I can ordinarily decide what "obeying" it *consists in*, i.e., which acts count as "following" the rule. Wittgenstein's point here is logical: although explicit rules do not "apply themselves," neither does it make sense to speak of rules whose meaning depends entirely on decisions.

To put it another way, what Wittgenstein is attacking is the idea that there is necessarily a *gap* between norms and applications, which renders all norms "indeterminate."

> "But then how does an explanation help me to understand" [he imagines his interlocutor worrying] "if after all it is not the final one? In that case the explanation is never completed; so I still don't understand what he means, and never shall!"—As though an explanation as it were hung in the air unless

> supported by another one. Whereas an explanation may indeed rest on another one that has been given, but none stands in need of another—unless *we* require it to prevent a misunderstanding. One might say: an explanation serves to remove or to avert a misunderstanding—one that is, that would occur but for the explanation; not every one that I can imagine.
>
> It may look as if every doubt merely *revealed* an existing gap in the foundations; so that secure understanding is only possible if we first doubt everything that *can* be doubted, and then remove all these doubts.
>
> The sign-post is in order—if, under normal circumstances, it fulfills its purpose.[38]

The picture of which Wittgenstein is attempting to disabuse us is of a gap lurking unannounced between every rule and its application, to which the skeptic calls our attention. This, he contends, is the wrong conclusion to draw from the doubts that *do* occasionally arise. *Sometimes*, to paraphrase Wittgenstein, decisions are needed to make sense of norms whose application is in question, but it is a mistake to infer that rules and laws are, as a matter of metaphysical principle, beset by a generalized indeterminacy.[39]

Recall, however, that it is precisely the latter picture that lies at the heart of what I earlier called the "new decisionism." Kahn writes, "No legal norm, no matter how clear we might think it to be, applies itself. There is a gap between norm and application always and everywhere. That we might not be aware of it in 'easy cases' just tells us that there is unanimity at this moment on the nature of the decision."[40] And similarly: "Norms remain lifeless absent the decision. To insist on the place of decision and exception in the political order is to find common ground with the theologian of creation and the modern existentialist."[41] Decision as ungrounded, creative act is presented as the only solution to the sort of skeptical worry that Wittgenstein's therapeutic approach is meant to dissolve, rather than solve.

Although Wittgenstein did not address the question of law specifically, his so-called "rule-following considerations" can be interpreted as recalling our attention to the cultural horizons within which law has its life. Only when philosophically abstracted from these does law come to seem semantically indeterminate. To be sure, we can imagine situations, such as the proceedings of a high court, in which "there must be a decision," but because the cases that end up working their way through the courts tend to be hard ones, to generalize from these can be misleading. To claim that decisions lurk always and everywhere within the quotidian application of law is simply the reverse side of the liberal error of imagining that hard cases can be decided by ferreting out a hidden meaning, imagined to be present independently of us. What both pictures omit is the culture within which law operates, the background agreements that make disagreement possible in specific cases. Judges too must draw upon the cultural resources of the wider community, and these act as conceptual constraints on the decisions judges are free to reach. Occasionally, the new decisionism appears to concede something in this direction. For instance, to claim, as Kahn does, that "the norm is indeterminate over *some range* of outcomes" is tacitly to admit the existence of certain limits, i.e., that some "decisions" could not be meaningfully construed as "applications" at all.

3 Core and Penumbra

Here it may be instructive to revisit an example posed by H. L. A. Hart:

> A legal rule forbids you to take a vehicle into the public park. Plainly, this forbids an automobile, but what about bicycles, roller skates, toy automobiles? What about airplanes? Are these, as we say, to be called "vehicles" for the purpose of the rule or not? If we are to communicate with each other at all, and if, as in the most elementary form of law, we are to express our intentions that a certain type of behavior be regulated by rules, then the general words we use—like "vehicle" in the case I consider—must have some standard instance in which no doubts are felt about its application. There must be a core of settled meaning, but there will be, as well, a penumbra of debatable cases in which words are neither obviously applicable nor obviously ruled out.[42]

In Hart's account, every legal rule consists of both a center, where its application is clear, and a periphery, within which decisions are required. "If a penumbra of uncertainty must surround all legal rules, then their application to specific cases in the penumbral area cannot be a matter of logical deduction, and so deductive reasoning, which for generations has been cherished as the very perfection of human reasoning, cannot serve as a model for what judges, or indeed anyone, should do in bringing particular cases under general rules."[43] Because objects and actions do not ordinarily come "neatly labeled, creased, and folded," Hart argued, "someone must take the responsibility of deciding that words do or do not cover some case in hand with all the practical consequences involved in this decision."[44] Penumbral cases, unlike those at law's center, open space for judicial discretion: here, judges are obliged to "legislate."

Hart draws the distinction between core and penumbra in the context of a general defense of the distinction between law and morality—"law as it is" and "law as it ought to be."[45] His aim is to carve out a middle position between a legal realism according to which all decisions are manifestations of power, explainable entirely in relation to social conditions rather than rationally assessable, and a natural law tradition according to which morality determines the content and authority of the law, such that there can be no such thing as a binding but immoral law. The debate over the relation of law to morality is beyond the scope of this essay, but it is worth taking note of Ronald Dworkin's response to Hart, if only to highlight what is distinctive about Kahn's understanding of the role played by decision. According to Dworkin, judges are properly guided in the interpretation of legal *rules* by further legal *principles*, which belong to the background of a community's political morality.[46] In Dworkin's view, law never ceases to be a rational enterprise, and judges are never required to go *outside* the law to apply it; indeed, they are required not to. Their interpretation of law is oriented normatively toward a "right answer."[47] Faced with a case like the one in Hart's example, a judge would, for instance, examine the legislative history of the statute; look to see how the term "vehicle" had previously been interpreted; and consider the political implications of rival interpretations of the law.[48] An interpretation that violated a general principle of legal reasoning would be *ipso facto* implausible. For Dworkin, there is no distinction to be made in practice between "core" and "penumbra."[49] Legal rules do not admit of "strong discretion"; even hard cases are constrained by the law, when the latter is understood not simply as rules but also as the principles by means of which rules are interpreted and applied. But if Dworkin rejects the distinction between core and penumbra on the ground that there is no penumbra, Kahn rejects it for the opposite reason: "while Dworkin argues that discretion never begins, I argue that there is no core."[50] In Kahn's account, the need for decision is not limited to hard cases: "Law is not controversial just at the margins; rather every legal claim is a subject of possible controversy. Put most simply, between legal norm and the facts, there must be a decision."[51]

Whether in practice judges are licensed to exercise discretion in so-called hard cases is a question I bracket here, because one need not endorse Dworkin's view in order to reject decisionism as a general theory of law. If the argument of the preceding section is correct, it is a confusion to generalize on the basis of "penumbral" situations. From the fact that a court may be called upon to decide whether, e.g., a bicycle counts as a "vehicle" for purposes of city ordinances, whatever resources or methods it ought to employ in such a situation, it does not follow that there are no "core" cases in which the statute forbidding vehicles in the park could unambiguously (even willfully) be violated. The alternative for which I have been arguing, and with which Hart's example is consistent, is pragmatic rather than Cartesian: doubt is not the default position, and the decisions of a judge presuppose situations in which decisions are not required. In the Wittgensteinian view advocated above, everything is not equally and simultaneously indeterminate; indeterminacy presupposes a background of much that is unproblematic. This is in no way to deny the precarity of the "agreements in form of life" that sustain our various practices of rule-following and language use generally. Difficulties can and sometimes do arise, and what at one point appears to belong to the "core" of a norm can later be shifted to the periphery, and vice versa. This, however, is a matter of contingency, not necessity: there is no *general* problem of indeterminacy, only particular ones. Penumbral situations cast a revealing light on law precisely because of their distinctive character, not because they are typical. The courtroom is a special context, an inescapable *dimension* of law, but not a paradigm of it generally. Generalizing from the periphery, from "hard cases," is what creates the impression that there is no core. To quote Hart: "Of course, it is good to be occupied with the penumbra. Its problems are rightly the diet of the law schools. But to be occupied with the penumbra is one thing, to be preoccupied with it another. And preoccupation with the penumbra is, if I may say so, as rich a source of confusion in the American legal tradition as formalism in the English."[52]

Indeed, when it comes to sovereignty, a preoccupation with courts and judges in general can divert attention from the sort of examples of the exception in which Schmitt himself was primarily interested. Part of what makes the new decisionism *new* is its focus on *meaning*.[53] Whereas Schmitt pointed to a distinction between what Agamben calls "public law and political fact," the new decisionism posits a gap at the level of interpretation: the judiciary, rather than the executive, constitutes the paradigmatic site of sovereignty. I have argued that Wittgenstein provides useful tools for resolving the confusion inherent in the picture of ineliminable shortfalls of meaning that must be overcome by interpretive acts of will. Yet, because Schmitt's account of the exception does not hinge on the semantic indeterminacy of law, the possibility to which it points is not resolvable through the sort of philosophical therapy offered above. The sovereign suspension of law need not depend on any ambiguity of meaning.

4 The Voluntarist Self

Duly limited to the contexts out of which the theory arises—regarded, for instance, as a partial account of how courts deal with "hard cases"—the new decisionism offers much that is plausible and deserving of serious consideration. But the alternative for which I am arguing departs from it with respect to a deeper question at stake in these debates, namely, the question of *the self*. According to Kahn, the point of political theology is "to criticize the understanding of the person upon which liberal theory rests. That understanding places reason at the foundation of its conception of the person as citizen. Political theology places will, not reason, at the foundation."[54] I have no interest in defending a conception of the person that places reason at the foundation, but neither do I wish to valorize will.[55] Indeed, one implication of the foregoing discussion of rules is that the choice between will and reason is generally false: decision is not required by an endemic shortfall of meaning.

The space of sovereignty does not arise primarily because law is semantically indeterminate (even if sometimes it *is* unclear, and judicial decisions *are* required). Rather, Schmitt's point is that no number of laws, however meaningful, can imbue law with the authority it is ordinarily taken to possess. (Imagine, for example, a regress of rules enjoining obedience to the rules.)[56] To put it another way, the space of will in politics is not simply that left vacant by reason. What is ordinarily interrupted in a state of exception is not law's meaning but its *force*. Sovereignty haunts law, not because law is everywhere ambiguous, but because, as Schmitt recognized, no amount of reason can finally close off the space of will. Whether law can be suspended is, however, always an empirical question. Sovereignty resists being walled up within legally prescribed offices—for why could not these laws and offices (including that of the judge) also be suspended?—but, in the event, not everyone is sovereign.

Kahn suggests that his criticism of the liberal conception of politics as fundamentally rational mirrors the earlier "communitarian" critique of the Rawlsian self.[57] Part of the latter critique, however, was directed against an underlying current of *voluntarism*, which so-called communitarians like Sandel and MacIntyre claimed to detect in Rawls and the liberal tradition he represented. For instance, Sandel read Rawls to be committed to a conception of the self who *chooses* his or her ends and is not constituted by them. Since such a "choice," Sandel argued, could amount to little more than an arbitrary exercise of will, it is difficult to understand the importance that liberalism places on freedom.[58] Similarly, MacIntyre criticized the "emotivist self" he claimed to find lurking beneath the incessant debates he regarded as characteristic of modern moral discourse.[59] What both writers oppose is not reason but, on the contrary, an *impoverished understanding* of reason that requires will to take up the slack.

The attractions of voluntarism, it should be noted, are theological and can be traced to late medieval nominalism, which attempted to safeguard divine freedom by denying any normative order in nature that could constrain God's creative decisions.[60] Divine sovereignty admits of no external limit. This theological argument would eventually be anthropologized in modern accounts of morality that locate its origins in the autonomy of the human will. Far from being alien to liberalism, voluntarism belongs to its moral foundations. To the extent that a valorization of will circulates through both liberalism and some of its seeming alternatives, the new decisionism remains caught within the very logic from which it seeks to free us.

5 Conclusion

Kahn claims that political theology "places will before reason, the act before the norm."[61] He is speaking not simply of the secularized theology of liberal theory, but of political theology as an academic discipline. I suggest, by contrast, that these claims, far from constituting the necessary methodological premises of political theology, are "secularized theological concepts," which belong among the political imaginaries such a discipline properly takes as its *object*. Just as MacIntyre held that the emotivism of A. J. Ayer and C. L. Stevenson, though mistaken if regarded as a normative moral theory, nevertheless offered a perceptive descriptive account of the moral crisis in which they found themselves, so I would contend that the masculinist conception of the citizen as essentially an embodiment of will, though inadequate generally, may indeed capture something important about the individualistic self-understanding central to certain political imaginaries.[62] Thinking with Wittgenstein about rules suggests that political theology's critique of liberal political theory may benefit from being folded back on itself, opening conceptual space for alternative (theo-)political anthropologies. This, however, is a further task that exceeds the modest philosophical ambition of this chapter, which is simply to point out that when it comes to law, we need not choose between reason and will, between an abstract rule that "applies itself" and a will that heroically, if arbitrarily, decides. A third possibility is to understand law within the contexts of its use, to view it as, among other things, a cultural practice. Voluntarism may be especially attractive when social practices break down, when they are no longer sustained by what Wittgenstein called "agreements in form of life," but such situations are the exception and not the rule.

Notes

1. Carl Schmitt, *Political Theology: Four Chapters on the Concept of Sovereignty*, trans. George Schwab (Cambridge, MA: MIT Press, 1985), 36.
2. Paul W. Kahn, *Political Theology: Four New Chapters on the Concept of Sovereignty* (New York: Columbia University Press, 2011), 23.
3. Note that the sacred derives its power partly from its invisibility. Because its name cannot be uttered, we must look for the sacred indirectly, by tracing its influences in the social world. One way to get at what is sacred, unblinkered by the distinction between the secular and the religious, may be to ask what can be profaned. Burning a national flag arouses strong emotions because it is an assault on an object that, for many, has more than merely symbolic status. It is significant that the flag of a nation state is nevertheless typically regarded as a secular and not a religious symbol. Whereas Kahn calls attention to the use of theological language by the state in times of crisis, Carolyn Marvin and David W. Ingle have argued that, under ordinary circumstances, the state maintains its sacral power partly by denying it: "[O]vert efforts to deify the flag as sacred place it in competition with sectarian faiths, and cause the state to speak the forbidden name of God. Denying the sanctity of the flag honors the ancient command not to speak God's name." Carolyn Marvin and David W. Ingle, *Blood Sacrifice and the Nation: Totem Rituals and the American Flag* (Cambridge: Cambridge University Press, 1999), 28. In other words, one of the functions of the religious-secular distinction is to shield the state from competition by positioning it above, rather than alongside, alternative conceptions of the sacred. The point to appreciate is not, as some commentators have claimed, that the secular is really "religious," or (as Kahn sometimes says) that it is not in fact secular, but rather that "religion" does not monopolize the sacred (understood functionally, rather than substantively). Indeed, insofar as religion is subordinated to the state, the sacred necessarily resides outside it, in the blind spot of liberal theory.
4. Schmitt, *Political Theology*, 5.
5. Note, however, that the concept of miracle here is itself a distinctively modern one, which presupposes an otherwise mechanistic understanding of nature. To borrow a phrase from Charles Taylor, we might say that such an understanding belongs to the *immanent frame*—i.e., to the universe conceived as a self-sufficient order permitting but not requiring reference to something "transcendent." Charles Taylor, *A Secular Age* (Cambridge, MA: The Belknap Press of Harvard University Press, 2007), 542. The theology from which, according to Schmitt, the modern theory of the state borrows its concepts would appear to be already a rather "secularized" one.
6. In light of its intentions and uses, Schmitt's corpus must be handled with caution. But it is possible to appreciate some of Schmitt's criticisms of liberal political theory, and of liberalism, while strenuously rejecting Schmitt's preferred alternatives.

7 Giorgio Agamben, *State of Exception*, trans. Kevin Attell (Chicago: University of Chicago Press, 2005), 1.
8 Schmitt argued that "[t]he idea of the modern constitutional state triumphed together with deism, a theology and metaphysics that banished the miracle from the world." Schmitt, *Political Theology*, 56.
9 Agamben noted that "the lacuna does not concern a deficiency in the text of the legislation that must be completed by the judge; it concerns, rather, a *suspension* of the order that is in force in order to guarantee its existence.... The lacuna is not within the law [*la legge*], but concerns its relation to reality, the very possibility of its application." Agamben, *State of Exception*, 31.
10 Schmitt, *Political Theology*, 7.
11 Paul W. Kahn, "Sacrificial Nation," *The Utopian* (March 29, 2010), http://www.the-utopian.org/post/2340099709/sacrificial-nation
12 See Robert N. Bellah, "Civil Religion in America," *Daedalus* 96 (Winter 1967): 1–21.
13 Kahn, "Sacrificial Nation."
14 Schmitt, *Political Theology*, 13.
15 Although this view is commonly associated with political theology, I do not want to *identify* it with political theology. The latter, I argue, need not endorse decisionism in the forms discussed here. My aim, in other words, is to argue not against political theology, but against a particular interpretation of it.
16 Jacques Derrida, "Force of Law: The 'Mystical Foundation of Authority,'" trans. Mary Quaintance in *Deconstruction and the Possibility of Justice*, ed. Drucilla Cornell, Michael Rosenfeld, and David Gray Carlson (New York: Routledge, 1992), 23.
17 Kahn, *Political Theology*, 74.
18 Ludwig Wittgenstein, *Philosophical Investigations*, trans. G. E. M. Anscombe (Englewood Cliffs, NJ: Prentice Hall, 1958), §218.
19 The view in question might be taken precisely the other way around, as an apology for so-called "liberal judicial activism." It is this charge to which, for example, Drucilla Cornell seeks to respond in "The Violence of the Masquerade: Law Dressed Up as Justice," in *Working Through Derrida*, ed. Gary B. Madison (Chicago: Northwestern University Press, 1993), 77–93.
20 Derrida writes: "[N]ever to yield on this point, constantly to maintain an interrogation of the origin, grounds and limits of our conceptual, theoretical or normative apparatus surrounding justice is on deconstruction's part anything but a neutralization of interest in justice, an insensitivity toward injustice. On the contrary, it hyperbolically raises the stakes of an exacting justice; it is sensitive to a sort of essential disproportion that must inscribe excess and inadequation in itself and that strives to denounce not only theoretical limits but also concrete injustices, with the most palpable effects, in the good conscience that dogmatically stops

before any inherited determination of justice." Derrida, "Force of Law: The 'Mystical Foundation of Authority,'" 20.
21 Bonnie Honig, *Emergency Politics: Paradox, Law, Democracy* (Princeton, NJ: Princeton University Press, 2009), 67.
22 Derrida, "Force of Law: The 'Mystical Foundation of Authority,'" 24–5.
23 Kahn, *Political Theology*, 130.
24 Ibid., 131.
25 Derrida, "Force of Law: The 'Mystical Foundation of Authority,'" 23, italics added.
26 Derrida's earlier writings are directed against the idea of a "presence" of meaning to which the spoken word is closer than its written representation. According to this account, rules do not possess a prior meaning to which we can appeal to determine whether or not their application is correct. Martin Stone, summarizing Derrida's position, writes: "the singular, datable behavioral 'event' of judging according to a rule is to be thought of as essential to the meaning of the rule—as somehow determining and not merely following from the rule's meaning what it does." Martin Stone, "Wittgenstein on Deconstruction," in Alice Crary and Rupert Read, eds., *The New Wittgenstein* (New York: Routledge, 2000), 86.
27 Derrida, "Force of Law: The 'Mystical Foundation of Authority,'" 23.
28 Kahn, *Political Theology*, 84.
29 Ibid., 77.
30 Ibid., 80.
31 Ibid., 89.
32 I argue that a rule, like a concept in general, is better conceived not as an abstract sign or inscription, but as comprising a mode of application.
33 Robert B. Brandom, *Making It Explicit: Reasoning, Representing, and Discursive Commitment* (Cambridge, MA: Harvard University Press, 1994), 18ff.
34 Wittgenstein, *Philosophical Investigations*, I:§84.
35 Ibid., I:§186.
36 Simon Glendinning, *On Being With Others: Heidegger, Derrida, Wittgenstein* (New York: Routledge, 1998), 104.
37 Wittgenstein, *Philosophical Investigations*, I:§219, italics are mine.
38 Ibid., I:§87.
39 As David Finkelstein put it, "when rules are seen as situated within our lives, such gulfs are exceptional." David H. Finkelstein, Wittgenstein on Rules and Platonism, in *The New Wittgenstein*, 69.
40 Kahn, *Political Theology*, 88. Cf. "There will always be a gap between form and judgment." Kahn, *Political Theology*, 64.
41 Kahn, *Political Theology*, 48.
42 H. L. A. Hart, "Positivism and the Separation of Law and Morals," *Harvard Law Review* 71, no. 4 (1958): 607.

43 Ibid., 607–8.
44 Ibid., 607.
45 The particular objection to which he is responding is the claim that, in interpreting the law, a judge necessarily falls back on moral aims that are "latent" in the law conceived broadly, obliterating any distinction between law and morality. Against this, Hart insists that not *all* applications of law, but only penumbral cases, are open to resolution in relation to social policy. Moreover, he holds that moral aims are not the only relevant purposes by which penumbral cases can be decided.
46 See Ronald Dworkin, *A Matter of Principle* (Cambridge, MA: Harvard University Press, 1985).
47 Ronald Dworkin, *Law's Empire* (Cambridge: The Belknap Press of Harvard University Press, 1986), 80. Dworkin discusses his thesis in relation to an example that in some respects resembles Hart's vehicle case: "Suppose the legislature has passed a statute stipulating that 'sacrilegious contracts shall henceforth be invalid.' The community is divided as to whether a contract signed on Sunday is, for that reason alone, sacrilegious. . . . Tom and Tim have signed a contract on Sunday, and Tom now sues Tim to enforce the terms of the contract, whose validity Tom contests. Shall we say that the judge must look for the right answer to the question of whether Tom's contract is valid, even though the community is deeply divided about what the right answer is? Or is it more realistic to say that there simply is no right answer to the question?" Dworkin, *A Matter of Principle*, supra note 45, at 119.
48 See, e.g., Dworkin's description of the methods employed by his ideal judge, Hercules. Dworkin, *Law's Empire*, 313ff.
49 According to Dworkin, this distinction "is just an expository device." Dworkin, *Law's Empire*, 351. Hercules "does not need one method for hard cases and another for easy ones. His method is equally at work in easy cases, but since the answers to the questions it puts are then obvious, or at least seem to be so, we are not aware that any theory is at work at all." Dworkin, *Law's Empire*, 354.
50 Kahn, *Political Theology*, 88.
51 Ibid., 77.
52 Hart, "Positivism and the Separation of Law and Morals," 615.
53 To be sure, this interest was not altogether alien to Schmitt, who argued that "a transformation takes place" whenever a "concrete fact" is subsumed under a "legal principle in its general universality." Schmitt, 31. Schmitt's primary concern, however, was with the authority required to enact such a transformation. Questions of sovereignty arise because "[a] distinctive determination of which individual person or which concrete body can assume such an authority cannot be derived from the mere legal quality of a maxim." Schmitt, *Political Theology*, 31. To the extent that Schmitt can be read as positing a metaphysical gap between every norm and its application, the Wittgensteinian critique above would apply. I tend not to

read Schmitt this way, however, because it appears to be in tension with his claim that sovereignty is the power to decide *whether* an exception exists. What I am arguing against is not that decisions about meaning can be moments of sovereignty, but that such decisions are required everywhere.

54 Kahn, *Political Theology*, 124–5.
55 Kahn shares with Foucault an emphasis on power, but he notes, "Against Foucault's position, I argue for the need for a decision. Power remains an attribute of subjects." Kahn, *Political Theology*, 89. Recall that for Foucault, power is also *generative* of subjectivity: there is no "self" anterior to the law. The function of law is not simply to control or protect persons but to form them. "[R]ather than ask ourselves how the sovereign appears to us in his lofty isolation, we should try to discover how it is that subjects are gradually, progressively, really and materially constituted through a multiplicity of organisms, forces, energies, materials, desires, thoughts etc." Michel Foucault, *Power/Knowledge: Selected Interviews and Other Writings 1972-1977*, ed. Colin Gordon (New York: Pantheon, 1980), 97. Following Foucault, I would want to balance Kahn's emphasis on sovereignty vis-à-vis law with a corresponding recognition of law's role in the formation of citizens. As Foucault put it, "The individual is an effect of power, and at the same time, or precisely to the extent to which it is that effect, it is the element of its articulation. The individual which power has constituted is at the same time its vehicle." Foucault, *Power/Knowledge*, 98.
56 It was precisely to put a stop to such a regress that Hans Kelsen had posited a *Grundnorm* or basic norm. "The basic norm is the answer to the question: how—and that means under what condition—are all these juristic statements concerning legal norms, legal duties, legal rights, and so on, possible?" Hans Kelsen, *General Theory of Law and State*, trans. Anders Wedberg (Cambridge, MA: Harvard University Press, 1945), 116–17. Kelsen's view is one of the principal targets of Schmitt's *Political Theology*.
57 Kahn, *Political Theology*, 124–5.
58 See Michael J. Sandel, *Liberalism and the Limits of Justice*, 2nd ed. (Cambridge: Cambridge University Press, 1998), ch. 1.
59 See Alasdair MacIntyre, *After Virtue: A Study in Moral Theory*, 3rd ed. (Notre Dame, IN: University of Notre Dame Press, 2007), ch. 3.
60 In John Milbank's reading, "In the thought of the nominalists, following Duns Scotus, the Trinity loses its significance as a prime location for discussing will and understanding in God and the relationship of God to the world. No longer is the world participatorily enfolded within the divine expressive *logos*, but instead a bare divine unity starkly confronts the other distinct unities which he has ordained." John Milbank, *Theology and Social Theory: Beyond Secular Reason* (Malden, MA: Wiley, 1993), 14.

61 Kahn, *Political Theology*, 62.
62 Macintyre, *After Virtue*, 14.

Works Citied

Agamben, Giorgio, *State of Exception*, trans. Kevin Attell, Chicago: University of Chicago Press, 2005.

Bellah, Robert N., "Civil Religion in America," *Daedalus* 96 (Winter 1967): 1–21.

Brandom, Robert B., *Making It Explicit: Reasoning, Representing, and Discursive Commitment*, Cambridge, MA: Harvard University Press, 1994.

Cornell, Drucilla, "The Violence of the Masquerade: Law Dressed Up as Justice," in Gary B. Madison (ed.), *Working Through Derrida*, 77–93, Chicago: Northwestern University Press, 1993.

Derrida, Jacques, "Force of Law: The 'Mystical Foundation of Authority,'" Mary Quaintance trans., in Drucilla Cornell, Michael Rosenfeld, and David Gray Carlson (eds.), *Deconstruction and the Possibility of Justice*, 3–67, New York: Routledge, 1992.

Dworkin, Ronald, *A Matter of Principle*, Cambridge, MA: Harvard University Press, 1985.

Dworkin, Ronald, *Law's Empire*, Cambridge, MA: The Belknap Press of Harvard University Press, 1986.

Finkelstein, David H., "Wittgenstein on Rules and Platonism," in Alice Crary and Rupert Read (eds.), *The New Wittgenstein*, 53–73, New York: Routledge, 2000.

Foucault, Michel, *Power/Knowledge: Selected Interviews and Other Writings 1972–1977*, ed. Colin Gordon, New York: Pantheon, 1980.

Glendinning, Simon, *On Being With Others: Heidegger, Derrida, Wittgenstein*, New York: Routledge, 1998.

Hart, H. L. A., "Positivism and the Separation of Law and Morals," *Harvard Law Review* 71, no. 4 (1958): 593–629.

Honig, Bonnie, *Emergency Politics: Paradox, Law, Democracy*, Princeton: Princeton University Press, 2009.

Kahn, Paul W., "Sacrificial Nation," *The Utopian* (March 29, 2010), http://www.the-utopian.org/post/2340099709/sacrificial-nation

Kahn, Paul W., *Political Theology: Four New Chapters on the Concept of Sovereignty*, New York: Columbia University Press, 2011.

Kelsen, Hans, *General Theory of Law and State*, trans. Anders Wedberg, Cambridge, MA: Harvard University Press, 1945.

MacIntyre, Alasdair, *After Virtue: A Study in Moral Theory*, 3rd ed., Notre Dame, IN: University of Notre Dame Press, 2007.

Marvin, Marvin and David W. Ingle, *Blood Sacrifice and the Nation: Totem Rituals and the American Flag*, Cambridge: Cambridge University Press, 1999.

Milbank, John, *Theology and Social Theory: Beyond Secular Reason*, Malden, MA: Wiley, 1993.

Sandel, Michael J., *Liberalism and the Limits of Justice*, 2rd ed., Cambridge: Cambridge University Press, 1998.

Schmitt, Carl, *Political Theology: Four Chapters on the Concept of Sovereignty*, trans. George Schwab, Cambridge, MA: MIT Press, 1985.

Stone, Martin, "Wittgenstein on Deconstruction," in Alice Crary and Rupert Read (eds.), *The New Wittgenstein*, 83–117, New York: Routledge, 2000.

Taylor, Charles, *A Secular Age*, Cambridge, MA: The Belknap Press of Harvard University Press, 2007.

Wittgenstein, Ludwig, *Philosophical Investigations*, trans. G. E. M. Anscombe, Englewood Cliffs, NJ: Prentice Hall, 1958.

10

Wittgenstein Does Critical Theory

Alice Crary

1 The Idea of Widely Rational Critique

It is plausible but by no means uncontroversial to suggest that liberating social criticism needs to be conceived so that it is capable of harnessing the cognitive power of critical gestures that shape our sense of what is important, inviting us to see social phenomena in new moral and political lights. Here we might think of the sorts of changes in our sense of significance that are sometimes affected by consciousness-raising, social movements, counter publics, or political art. There is, admittedly, nothing contentious about the suggestion that activities, forms of social upheaval, images, utterances, or inscriptions that alter what strikes us as important, and that as a result change our conception of the social world, can affect our understanding of social situations in accidental or external ways. But suppose that what interests us is not merely a suggestion on these lines. Suppose that we are interested in the idea that the kinds of critical interventions that thus adjust our sense of significance can as such internally inform our understanding of decisive features of the social world. Then it will appear to us that, if we are to approach the task of criticism in a morally and politically responsible manner, we need critical methods and resources that take this possibility seriously.

Consider, as an initial example of the kind of critical exercise in question, the work of the legal scholar Kimberlé Crenshaw and, more specifically, portions of Crenshaw's work in which she undertakes to shed light on harms done to Black women in the United States who are victims of sexual violence. Crenshaw has written with great insight about, for instance, the case of Anita Hill, who in 1991 was subpoenaed to testify at the US Senate hearings for Clarence Thomas's nomination to the Supreme Court because she told the FBI that, when she was working under Thomas at the Department of Education and the Equal Employment Opportunity Commission, he repeatedly subjected her to unwanted sexual attention.[1] Somewhat more recently, Crenshaw has discussed the case of Daniel Holtzclaw, a former Oklahoma City police officer, who while on the force systematically sought out women who were poor, Black, and had criminal records or legal troubles, sexually assaulting and raping them.[2]

One notable presupposition of Crenshaw's treatments of these and other cases is that—in order to appreciate the awfulness of unwelcome sexual behavior visited upon women—we need to have a vivid image of how, in our society, women experience disadvantages that are substantial, structural, and pervasive, and how women therefore have vulnerabilities that unwanted sexual activity both exploits and exacerbates. That is a theme from classic feminist accounts of rape and sexual harassment, and part of what is distinctive about Crenshaw's work is that, in addition to sounding this theme, she stresses that if we are to do justice to harms done to Black women who are victims of sexual violence, we need to have a vivid sense of ways in which antiblack racism in the United States affects Black women, interacting or—in Crenshaw's famous term of art—"intersecting" with sexism in a manner that effectively sexualizes it.[3] We need to be aware not only that rape and sexual assault have been conditions of Black women's work lives for centuries but also that today there are still institutional remnants of associated myths about Black women as "sexually voracious" and "sexually indiscriminate."[4] For instance, we need to know that Black women's words are less likely to be taken as truth and, further, that even in situations in which a conviction is secured for a sex crime against Black women, the sentence is likely to be less severe than sentences imposed on men who commit the same crime against white women.[5]

A guiding motif of Crenshaw's work in this area is that our sense of ways in which these aspects of US history continue to shape social life need to inform our social vision if we are to be able to recognize and register the gravity of the harms done to Black women who are victims of sexual violence. Crenshaw accordingly proceeds as a critic by trying to get us to appreciate forms of social exposure produced by intertwined systems of racism and sexism. At the same time, she presents herself as, in this way, internally contributing to our ability to understand real aspects of social life (viz., specific injuries done to Black women). That is the sort of thing at stake in the claim that critical gestures that shape sense of salience or importance can as such directly inform genuine or objective understanding.

However unsurprising this claim may sound to feminists and critical race theorists,[6] there are philosophical circles in which it is taken to verge on heresy. At issue is a claim about how critical exercises that direct our attitudes may as such be rationally authoritative. To accommodate the claim we have to challenge an entrenched philosophical understanding of rationality on which our ability to make the connections of a rational line of thought cannot essentially depend on our possession of any particular routes of feeling. We need to expand—or "widen"—this familiar and, arguably, overly "narrow" conception so that bits of discourse that encourage us to look at things from new cultural or evaluative perspectives may as such have rational power. We might speak here of a move away from a *narrower* and toward a *wider* conception of rationality.[7] Similarly, we might speak of a transition from *narrowly rational* to *widely rational* modes of critique.

A widely rational conception of critical social thought has a clear moral and political appeal. By its lights, social criticism is conceived so that critics can't antecedently exclude the possibility of needing to explore and perhaps embrace cultural or ethical values, or historical perspectives, that shape the social settings they are investigating. It follows that efforts at social criticism need not be vulnerable to charges—of sorts sometimes leveled at Kantian-formalistic or consequentialist modes of social criticism—of an *elitist* or *ethnocentric* tendency to impose unacknowledged values cherished by other, possibly hegemonic societies while being insensitive to the local values at hand. (E.g., consider how Crenshaw and other anti-racist feminists call on us to revise our understanding of what counts as grossly unjust and coercive treatment so that it includes some forms of sexual behavior that weren't previously classified as such; it is essential to these theorists' procedures that they give us a feel for structurally produced social susceptibilities of women socially identified as nonwhite, specifically with a view opening our eyes to harms that aren't otherwise visible.) Further, to the extent that what is at issue is an understanding of social criticism as wholeheartedly rational, particular efforts at social criticism need not be vulnerable to charges—of sorts sometimes leveled at poststructuralist or other anti-universalistic modes of social criticism—of a *merely partisan* willingness to affirm whatever attitudes happen to be regarded as liberating at a given place and time. (E.g., there is no obstacle to taking Crenshaw and other feminist anti-racists who talk about sexual violence against Black and other nonwhite women in a similar manner, that is, in a manner that essentially presupposes the mobilization of specific evaluative attitudes, to be thereby speaking with rational authority.)

Despite its evident moral and political interest, a widely rational conception of social criticism often goes missing from discussions about what social criticism is like. It's not that theorists routinely consider and then reject as untenable widely rational accounts of social criticism. More commonly, the possibility of such accounts simply goes unregistered, and it is suggested that we are confronted with a choice between, on the one hand, conceptions of social criticism on which it is essentially in the business of exploring the perspective and values of specific social contexts—and on which it is in this strong sense "context-bound"—and, on the other, conceptions on which it is rationally authoritative. For an illustration of this trend, consider the distinction that the Kantian moral and political philosopher Onora O'Neill draws between critique that is "weakly normative" and critique that is "strongly normative."[8] When O'Neill discusses weakly normative critique, she has in mind critique that as she sees it cannot help but represent "normative claims as . . . more limited and less deeply justified" because it is anchored in the "conceptions, obligations and agreements of actual ethical codes as well as in the political institutions of a people."[9] When, in contrast, she strongly talks about normative critique, she has in mind critique that eschews the kind of context-groundedness characteristic of its weakly normative counterparts and can, in her view, thus lay claim to "norms that have cosmopolitan reach and that supply the ground of the action of all people" (720). The very terms in which O'Neill discusses these kinds of critique reveal that there is for her no prospect of social criticism that is both essentially grounded in particular values and rationally authoritative and that is thus capable of combining the respective virtues of social criticism in what she describes as its competing weakly and strongly normative instantiations. The very terms that she uses reveal, that is, that there is for her no prospect of widely rational social criticism. Nor is O'Neill alone in overlooking the possibility of such social criticism.[10] Among other things, the past several years have witnessed the emergence of a new set of debates about ideology and liberating critique within analytic philosophy that likewise mostly neglect the possibility of critique that uses widely rational resources.[11]

2 Widely Rational Critical Theories

One place to look for calls for widely rational social criticism is the philosophical tradition, associated with the University of Frankfurt-based Institute for Social Research and placed under the heading of "Critical Theory," that aims to promote emancipatory politics by offering a special kind of theoretical image of society. It was in the late 1930s that affiliates of the institute began to think that what united them was the pursuit of such an image or—as Max Horkheimer first put it—a *critical theory* of society.[12] Critical theories have generally been understood to possess the following elements. They are, to use a formulation of Raymond Geuss's, essentially capable of serving as "guides to human action" in that they both reveal to the agents who hold them "what their true interests are" and emancipate agents by "free[ing them] from a kind of coercion which is at least partly self-imposed." Thus understood, critical theories are supposed to have a kind of "cognitive content" that is nonscientific.[13] They are conceived in opposition to the "positivist" idea that the kind of self-understanding that would free us from oppressive strictures is something we achieve by transcending all ethically loaded perspectives and adopting the standpoint of scientific experts.[14] This hostility to a scientific model is of a piece with a conception of critical theories as charged with exploring values embedded in particular social contexts and reflecting perspectives "immanent in human work."[15] But a commitment to the exploration of immanent values is taken to be consistent with a theoretical vision possessed of context-transcendent rational authority. It is characteristic of critical theorists to summarize these desiderata by saying that they aim to do justice to the *dialectics of immanence and transcendence*. More succinctly, critical theorists sometimes say that they aspire to a satisfactory conception of *immanent critique*.

There is a striking measure of disagreement among critical theorists today about what a tenable account of what immanent critique is, or should be, would look like. A significant number accept the constraints of a philosophically orthodox, narrower conception of rationality. Indeed, it is possible to arrive at a reasonable classification of many of the accounts currently on offer by representing them as different strategies for achieving the core aims of immanent critique while respecting or at best modestly challenging these narrowly rational constraints. But it is not clear that early members of the Frankfurt school took themselves to be bound by similar restrictions, and any fair description of recent accounts of immanent critique should mention that there are critical theorists who, sometimes harking back to critical theory's origins, issue calls for widely rational modes of social criticism.[16]

The contours of these widely rational projects emerge when they are considered against the backdrop of their more narrowly rational counterparts. The most high-profile forays into critical theory that operate with narrower assumptions about what rationality is like are projects that their cue from Kant's moral theory. The original model for these endeavors is Jürgen Habermas's approach to inheriting from Kant, an approach that has inspired a number of subsequent, in some respects quite different, Kantian accounts of immanent critique.

The roots of Habermas's Kantian strain lie in his inheritance, from members of the Frankfurt school's first generation, of the Marxian idea that a signature ill of modern capitalist societies is the takeover of political discourse by instrumental or "purposive-rational" reason. One of Habermas's signature ambitions, already very early in his career, is defending the authority of noninstrumental "communicative" or "interactive" forms of reason that are, he believes, capable of reviving the political sphere.[17] By the 1970s, Habermas is pursuing this goal by appealing to resources from John Searle's version of Austinian speech-act theory and, more specifically, by appealing to the idea that individual utterances may have different illocutionary forces.[18] Starting from this idea, Habermas goes on to insist that speech acts with different illocutionary forces raise validity claims that, although comparably authoritative, are established in different ways. While the validity claims of the sorts of theoretical or "cognitive" utterances that we rely on in the instrumental realm are established objectively, in terms of their adequacy to how things stand in the world, the validity claims of the sorts of "interactive" utterances that are decisive for the moral realm are established intersubjectively, in a manner aptly captured by Kant's conception of the categorical imperative in its universal law formulation. Habermas's Kantian thought is that the question of the truth of moral beliefs is one we settle by asking, not theoretical questions about whether the beliefs do descriptive justice to the world, but rather practical questions about whether the maxims they encode are universalizable in the formal sense of being such that everyone could in principle consent to them.[19] Notice that, in thus borrowing from Kant's moral theory, Habermas is introducing a clear value-norm split. He is avoiding commitment to the idea of objective ethical values and construing norms as objective only in a formal or procedural sense.[20]

Consider now how Habermas uses these Kantian resources in arriving at a distinctive account of immanent critique. Habermas tends to distance himself from the monological aspect of Kant's categorical imperative procedure, representing normative rightness as achieved not by the in principle universalizability of practical maxims but by the concrete universalization of such maxims considered "from the perspective of real-life argumentation," when subject to idealizing conditions.[21] The critical exercises Habermas describes— and that are pivotal for his mature "discourse ethics"—respect a demand for "immanence" insofar as they in this way involve normative claims that arise from and are adjudicated within actual conversational contexts. But Habermas assumes that it would be right to worry that this institutionalization of Kant's transcendental moral project cannot by itself be relied upon to yield rationally authoritative conclusions, and so cannot be relied upon to qualify as critique in a full-blooded, context-transcendent sense. Because, as Hilary Putnam once put it, ethical values are for Habermas "as noncognitivist as they are to positivists,"[22] it appears to Habermas that we need grounds for holding that it is possible to reason from our ethical starting points to rationally defensible conclusions. He addresses the putative problem by representing moves toward more reflective, post-traditional societies as moves toward progress. He embraces a philosophy of history on which, in his parlance, "there is progress in the de-centering of our perspectives when it comes to viewing the world as a whole."[23] Habermas takes this philosophy of history to provide a teleological perspective from which "we" reflective moderns can be confident that we are moving from our ethical starting points to authoritative conclusions. That is how he mobilizes narrowly rational, Kantian resources in trying to demonstrate his entitlement to represent the discourse-based critical maneuvers he champions not only as immanent but also as rationally authoritative and hence as cases of full-blooded critique.

Habermas's project has inspired other narrowly rational, Kantian accounts of immanent critique. This includes contributions to critical theory that proceed along more orthodox Kantian lines, such as, notably, the work of Rainer Forst. Like Habermas and other Kantian moral philosophers, Forst steers clear of endorsing the idea of objective ethical values and adopts a strictly practical, formal approach to accounting for the universal authority of normative claims.[24] But, unlike Habermas, Forst thinks it is possible to tell a tenable story about immanent critique in standard—transcendental—Kantian terms. He believes he can satisfy the demand for appropriate immanence by allowing for essential context sensitivity in nonmoral spheres of thought and action and, additionally and more importantly, by underlining that even moral demands—that is, demands for universal justification—arise in concrete conversational contexts in which individuals make them.[25] The result is supposed to be a "contextualist universalism" that, in addition to having a claim to rational authority, has a good claim to immanence in virtue of its context-situatedness.[26] Forst thus endeavors to use familiar Kantian materials to accommodate the "dialectics of immanence and transcendence."

Suppose we speak generally of Kantian contributions to critical theory that aim to satisfy the conditions of a narrower conception of rationality. There is a notable political worry that arises in reference to these critical approaches. To say that the approaches are designed to satisfy narrowly rational constraints is to say that they take it for granted that we can make the connections internal to rational lines of thought apart from an even imaginative appreciation of any particular cultural or evaluative perspectives. This strategy is politically problematic insofar as it antecedently imposes substantial limits on the critical interest that exploration of such perspectives can have, excluding the possibility that we may need to enter into particular cultural perspectives in order to recognize the correctness of specific critical inferences. (E.g., it leaves no room for the possibility—insisted on by several generations of feminist theorists—that we need to look at society from a perspective informed by an appreciation of systematic and pervasive forms of sex-based discrimination in order to recognize that the concepts "objectification" and "harassment" apply to forms of some sexual behavior that have historically been regarded as at worst tasteless or annoying.[27]) So, despite the liberating aims of the thinkers who espouse them, narrowly rational critical approaches veer toward being dismissive of local values in a manner that pushes them irretrievably toward elitism or ethnocentrism.

A prominent topic of conversation among critical theorists today is how best to combat such ethnocentrism.[28] A recognizable cohort of theorists contest what they see as the tradition's ethnocentric tendencies by taking their cue from strands of poststructuralist and postcolonialist thought.[29] It is possible to give a rough sketch of the stance that unites many of these theorists by referring to the basic theory of signs that at the heart of poststructuralist thought. At the core of the theory, which receives a classic treatment in Derrida's writings, is the idea that expressions acquire the status of signs as a result of being used in different contexts and that, when thus used, their meanings invariably suffer a displacement reflecting language users' sense of the importance of similarities between previous contexts and the new context.[30] It is characteristic of the theorizing of self-avowed poststructuralists not merely to conclude from considerations along these lines that a value-neutral standpoint for thought about the world is forever beyond our grasp but also to take it for granted that neutrality is a necessary condition of true universality—and that the loss of a neutral standpoint is therefore tantamount to the loss of any claim to universal, rational authority. This skeptical conclusion depends for its apparent force on the coherence of the very—narrower—conception of rationality that poststructuralists typically represent as an unattainable ideal. It is only if we assume, in accordance with the conception, that rational moves of thought must be recognizable as such from a dispassionate standpoint that our invariable reliance on particular perspectives or attitudes seems to threaten the universal, rational authority of thought.

This inverted narrowly rational logic informs some of the signature political moves of poststructuralist theorists. A striking—and strikingly valuable—contribution of poststructuralist and postcolonialist thinkers has been to bring out how colonialist and racist violence often takes the form of the imposition of false universals, and it is certainly possible to accept this observation without being guided by any narrower assumptions about what rationality is like. But it is typical for poststructuralists to make a further pair of political-theoretical moves that are shaped by such assumptions. One of their characteristic gestures is insisting, in a manner that takes for granted that rationality is properly construed in narrower terms, that our very willingness to represent our critical reflections as aspiring to universal or rational authority is inseparable from a slide into politically dangerous forms of ethnocentrism.[31] A second closely connected gesture is urging us to abandon our faith in narratives of "progress, right, sovereignty, free will, moral truth [and] reason" and to promote an emancipatory agenda without imagining that we can think and talk about the social world in a universally authoritative voice.[32]

One ambitious recent attempt to use this basic strategy to inherit the mantle of critical theory is Amy Allen's *The End of Progress: De-colonizing the Normative Foundations of Critical Theory*. Allen's de-colonizing efforts specifically target contributions to critical theory that she regards as Eurocentric and incapable of overcoming political sins of Europe's colonial past.[33] This is an undeniably important project. Allen should be credited with underlining how a number of prominent critical theorists' commitment to narrowly rational conceptions of the authority of their guiding normative ideals prevents them from recognizing forms of racism and ethnocentrism written into those ideals.[34] But Allen goes on from making this important point to making questionable theoretical moves that bear the imprint of an unacknowledged debt to a narrowly rational logic. She takes this logic for granted in calling on us to reject any sort of clearly universalist politics.[35] A central preoccupation of *The End of Progress* is developing this claim in connection with the notion of *progress*. While Allen is happy to avail herself of talk of progress insofar as it is forward-looking and used to underwrite efforts to identify and agitate for liberating forms of social life, she wants to distance herself from any suggestion that this stance commits her to allowing that particular social changes might rightly be established as progressive once and for all. This is because, however unwittingly, she tends to operate with the narrowly rational view that a given change could only be recognized as progressive as a matter of fact if, per impossible, it was considered from an ideally dispassionate standpoint or "God's eye view".[36] Thus swayed by theory, Allen forfeits the very idea of progress (and its regressive opposite) as a fact. She tries to avoid the political dis-ease likely to be occasioned by this posture by denying that, in adopting her distinctive view of progress, she is committing herself to a "first-order moral relativism" that would disallow *talk* of truth or rationality.[37] Yet, insofar as she depicts moral and political assessments as capable only of a type of "truth" or "rationality" that is a mere reflection of specific cultural values, it is fair to disregard the form of linguistic self-presentation she takes to be permissible and to insist that her preferred critical posture cannot avoid sliding into a politically and philosophically disempowering form of relativism. The resulting outlook is, in Allen's view, our best hope for achieving critical theorists' aspiration to liberating immanence and hence, as she sees it, the most satisfactory outcome of critical theory's pursuit of immanent critique.[38]

The political limitations of Allen's outlook are not trivial. Whereas Allen can consistently claim that it is open to us to employ nonrational methods to persuade people to adopt new perspectives, thereby bringing about liberating social changes, she is obliged to add that any such changes will fail to qualify as unequivocally progressive. She leaves herself vulnerable to the charge that she is advocating social remedies that, far from having an unambiguously emancipatory character, merely happen to seem emancipatory to particular groups of people at particular times. That is, she leaves herself open to the complaint that she is using theory to bully us into qualifying even our most careful critical conclusions.[39] (Suppose, for example, that we affirm, as we should, Crenshaw's claim that Holtzclaw's selection of socially vulnerable victims made his actions especially pernicious. According to Allen's main line of reasoning, theoretical considerations oblige us to weaken our critical judgments by relativizing them, implicitly appending a disclaimer about how this is just how things appear in the cultural context in which we find ourselves.)[40] Reflection on the political pitfalls of an Allen-style approach to critical theory suggests the need to confront questions along the following lines. In trying to avoid the ethnocentric tendencies of accounts of immanent critique that strive to satisfy constraints of a narrower conception of rationality, are we obliged to relinquish any claim to the rational authority of our conclusions? Are we obliged to maneuver, as cleverly as possible, within a narrowly rational conceptual space, endeavoring somehow to avoid both the Scylla of ethnocentrism and the Charybdis of skepticism about our critical conclusions' rational authority?

There is good reason to believe that this is not how members of the Frankfurt school's first generation conceived the project of giving a satisfactory account of immanent critique. It is possible to find suggestions of a quite different theoretical strategy in the work of leading figures in the early history of the Institute for Social Research. Already in the *Dialectic of Enlightenment*,

Horkheimer and Adorno were taking their cue from the lesson of the method of Hegel's *Phenomenology of Spirit*, a book that tells the story of the education of consciousness in a manner that repudiates, with rigorous consistency, the idea of an external standpoint on the rapport between mind and world. Properly understood, this methodological precept has substantial implications for how we think about the nature of values, and of our mental contact with them. To get the basic idea, suppose that we understand social concepts as "thick" in the sense that an appreciation of particular cultural and evaluative perspectives is essential to the ability to authoritatively describe the patterns the concepts trace out. If we now reject in a thoroughly consistent manner the idea of a transcendent standpoint from which to determine that our modes of appreciation have an essential tendency to distort our view of the world, then we won't be in a position to insist that such thickness betokens a cognitive deficit. We will be in a position to allow that thick social concepts are real or metaphysically transparent concepts, and we will also be in a position to sanction, in reference to such concepts, an idea of objective values. That is, we will find ourselves wanting to sanction, in reference to social phenomena, an idea of objective values. This means that we will be in a position to allow—in a widely rational manner—that we may require specific sensitivities in order to recognize the correctness of intellectually respectable lines of thought about these values. Having arrived at this widely rational point, it will strike us as a relatively uncomplicated matter to produce an account of immanent critique. For now there is no tension between conceiving such critique as immanent, in the sense of being internally informed by specific cultural and historical perspectives, and conceiving it as possessing unqualified rational authority.

Today this sort of straightforward route to an account of immanent critique strikes many critical theorists as closed-off. In the decades after the Institute for Social Research's post–Second World War return to Frankfurt, it became common for critical theorists to reject the idea of objective ethical values and the closely related idea of a conception of rationality wide enough to accommodate thought about a worldly landscape featuring such values.[41] It would not be unreasonable to trace the willingness of thinkers to make this twofold gesture of rejection, at least in significant part, to critical theory's encounter with Anglophone philosophy in the 1960s and, perhaps above all, to the so-called positivism disputes in which, for all their hostility to positivism, some representatives of critical theory took on board significant commitments of analytic metaethics.[42] Nevertheless, there are contributions to critical theory that clearly make use of widely rational resources.

This is true—to mention one significant recent example—of the image of immanent critique developed in Rahel Jaeggi's *Critique of Forms of Life*.[43] Jaeggi follows Horkheimer's and Adorno's leads in inheriting the method of the *Phenomenology of Spirit*, and, from the opening moments of her book, she makes it clear that she will contest narrowly rational strictures. She announces her interest in a construal of immanent critique on which its object is "forms of life," which for her is a label for those portions of our lives in which we develop and respond to ethical values. The guiding thesis of Jaeggi's book is that forms of life are constitutively ethical and such that there is no question of bringing them empirically into view while abstaining from ethical evaluation. Jaeggi sets out to show that the critique of forms of life is in this sense unavoidable. She is aware that many liberal political theorists take an openness to criticizing individuals' conceptions of the good to be inseparable from paternalism or even authoritarianism. In addition to attacking this posture as politically misconceived,[44] she argues that it reflects a philosophical confusion about what our relation to forms of life is like.

Jaeggi's core account of forms of life starts with the claim that they are made up of social practices.[45] This matters, she maintains, because social practices are constituted by steps that are only authoritatively recognizable as such in terms of sensitivities that we come to possess in the process of learning to participate in the practices in question. So, learning a practice is inseparable from getting a feel for the practice's point, and—Jaeggi adds—this lesson bears not only on individual practices but also on the constellations of practices that, for her, are constitutive of forms of life. It is possible to succinctly formulate these observations by saying that forms of life have ends. (To be sure, Jaeggi stresses that we are simply thrown into—without arriving at the point of thematizing—a fair number of our own practices and forms of life. Insofar as our explanations of our practices are thus not infrequently post hoc rationalizations, it follows that our forms of life may involve disorganized clusters of—acknowledged and unacknowledged—ends.[46]) When Jaeggi observes that forms of life have ends, she is noting that there is a sense in which, in reference to these ends, they can succeed or fail. That, very succinctly, is how she defends the view that, in our efforts to get forms of life in focus, we cannot help but concern ourselves with their normative happiness or unhappiness.[47]

This view is pivotal for Jaeggi's preferred conception of immanent critique. To say that, in thinking and talking about forms of life as such, it is necessary to use irredeemably ethical categories is to allow that it makes sense to describe forms of life as enterprises of dealing with "problems" and, more specifically, as enterprises of dealing with problems that—since, far from being brutely given, they are articulated in our practices—are appropriately described as "second order." To conceive forms of life as thus problem-involving is in turn to make room for conceiving the bundles of practices of which they are composed as susceptible to crises. For Jaeggi, criticizing forms of life is grappling with these sorts of internally arising crises, a task that, for her, we can only undertake by employing immanent, irreducibly ethical categories. When she characterizes the relevant categories as irreducibly ethical, she is, as noted above, suggesting that we can only authoritatively project them insofar as we enter into particular cultural perspectives. But she does not take it to follow that the concepts in question are therefore cognitively limited.

It is at this point in the presentation of her social theoretic vision that we see the significance of her reliance on the method of the *Phenomenology of Spirit* and, more specifically, of her reliance on its author's thoroughgoing attack on the idea of a God's eye view from which to antecedently determine that ethical perspectives as such veer toward hampering our ability to follow rational lines of thought.[48] One of Jaeggi's typical ways of formulating her preferred conception of immanent critique is to say that such critique is not merely "internal" (i.e., in being somehow limited to determining the consistency of "practices and institutions with existing values and beliefs").[49] In presenting a notion of critique that counts as immanent without somehow needing to be disparaged as merely "internal," she is allowing that particular cultural and historical perspectives may directly contribute to our ability to make wholeheartedly rational inferences, a step she justifies by using the aforementioned gesture of Hegel's to introduce a relevantly wide conception of rationality. A wider conception is thus pivotal for her effort to straightforwardly accommodate the "dialectics of immanence and transcendence."

Now we have before us an illustration of how, instead of working within a narrowly rational space to address apparently opposed worries about ethnocentrism and mere nonrational partisanship, one contemporary critical theorist orients herself in a widely rational space in which addressing both kinds of worries simultaneously is unproblematic. (Notice, to return to this article's guiding example, that the position thus equips us to accept on its own terms of the work of a social critic like Crenshaw—work that, taken at face value, seems to have rational power in virtue of provoking us to look at things from new, ethically laden, historical or cultural perspectives.) We have an illustration of one current contribution to critical theory that is dedicated to the sympathetic elaboration of widely rational modes of social criticism.

A Jaeggi-style account of immanent critique depends for its plausibility on a wider conception of rationality (i.e., a conception on which our sensitivities are internal to our rational abilities). Because this conception represents an affront to the current philosophical climate, we have good reason to suspect that, in the absence of a thoroughgoing defense, any theorist who helps herself to its resources will be perceived by many to be advocating critical exercises that fall short of rational authority. Despite the clear risk of misunderstanding along these lines, Jaeggi herself consistently, and quite deliberately, places greater emphasis on bringing out the political importance of her views than on mounting a defense of the philosophically unorthodox conception of rationality that animates them.[50] Granted that she does not present a philosophical argument for this conception, we should expect that some readers of her work will complain that she is not entitled to depict immanent critique, as she understand it, as a rational enterprise. And this has in fact happened.[51] If we are committed to following up on contributions to critical theory, like Jaeggi's, that make use of widely rational resources, we ought to be able to tell a story about why we are entitled to a wider conception of rationality. A reasonable place to turn is a core contribution to Anglo-American analytic philosophy of the social sciences that takes as one of its organizing themes a question about whether it is possible to overcome antecedent obstacles that may seem to prevent us from conceiving rationality on wider lines.

3 A Widely Rational Reading of Winch

Consider Peter Winch's landmark 1958 book *The Idea of a Social Science and Its Relation to Philosophy*.[52] Although one of Winch's goals in this work is to defend a nonrelativistic, widely rational account of social understanding, there has been a great deal of debate about whether he succeeds. Today it is not uncommon to find Winch represented as advocating a version of the very sort of culturally relativistic outlook he claimed to be avoiding.[53] To be sure, there is a small and vocal set of readers who maintain that we should credit Winch with an anti-relativistic outlook that is capable of accommodating rationally authoritative modes of social criticism.[54] This interpretative dispute, which has now run on for over half a century, is vexed and involved, and it makes sense to simply bypass it. Without getting distracted by exegetical questions about details of Winch's exposition, it is possible to isolate a pivotal strand of thought in *The Idea of a Social Science*—a strand of thought that develops themes from Wittgenstein's later philosophy and that is dedicated to motivating a view of the understanding of social phenomena on which such understanding is both objective and ineradicably ethical. Winch tends to formulate this view by saying that, as he conceives it, social understanding resists assimilation to the natural sciences. In connection with this reference to "the" natural sciences, some commentators have argued that Winch takes for granted a now discredited, positivistic claim about the unity of the sciences.[55] It is worth avoiding this further exegetical dispute except to observe that Winch's argument for his preferred view of social understanding can be run without any such unacceptable claim.[56] More important for the issues considered here, it is possible, by following up on his argument for this view, to outline a defense of the sort of nonrelativistic and widely rational account of social criticism that is pivotal for politically liberating critical endeavors.

At the opening of *The Idea of a Social Science*, Winch announces that he is setting out not only to reject the (then venerable and today still widely held) view that to progress the social sciences must "emulate the natural sciences" (1)[57] but also to defend the different view that "any worthwhile study of society must be philosophical in character" (3). Although the latter view is questionable, it is worth considering what draws Winch to it. The view depends for its plausibility on the idea, which Winch seeks to defend in his book (and which is discussed below), that there is no such thing as a standpoint outside language from which to characterize the relationship between language and the world.[58] Suppose that, following Winch's lead, we abandon as incoherent the notion of a view on language "from sideways on."[59] Now it seems justified to represent the kinds of conceptual investigations undertaken in philosophy as capable of shedding light on what the world is like in a manner that isn't merely a matter of limning the contingent structures of the disciplines within which the concepts in question are at home.[60] Taking his cue from an observation along these lines, Winch sets out to defend a view of the relationship between language and the world that would enable him to treat an investigation of the concept of *social phenomena* as genuinely illuminating. That is what he has in mind when he calls for a rapprochement of philosophy and the social sciences. His aspiration is to show that, as he puts it, "the central problem of sociology, that of giving an account of the nature of social phenomena in general, itself belongs to philosophy" (43). This is undoubtedly an important problem for sociology, though it's worth noting in passing that it's possible to grant its significance without holding, with Winch, that *any* worthwhile study of society must be philosophical in the sense of being addressed to it.

Winch starts his philosophical account of social phenomena from the uncontroversial idea that these phenomena are as such composed of actions or, as he puts it, of "meaningful behavior" (45). He then claims that meaningful behavior is "*ipso facto* rule-governed" (52). This is a claim that, in the years after the publication of his book, he is eager to qualify. He revises it, he explains in 1990, both because he thinks it might wrongly seem to imply that all human activities are articulated in the same way and because he thinks it threatens to obscure the fact that different aspects of social life are "frequently internally related in such a way that one cannot even be intelligibly conceived as existing in isolation from others" (xv–xvi).[61] Although Winch in these ways refines his position on the rule-governed character of meaningful behavior, he doesn't abandon the plausible thought that originally led him to bring up the topic of rule-following, namely, the thought that meaningful behavior is as such (at least unreflectively) articulated in terms of concepts or universal categories and that it accordingly admits questions about what counts as going on and doing the same.[62] Since there is good reason to think that we can defend this thought on independent grounds,[63] it seems reasonable to assume that Winch is right to introduce it. He introduces it because he wants to show that, however apparently uninteresting, the conceptually structured character of social activities is of philosophical moment. It is with an eye to showing this that Winch appeals to Wittgenstein's later philosophy and, more specifically, to Wittgenstein's later remarks on rule-following.

Operating with concepts or universal categories places us in the realm of rule-following, and a name is a universal category insofar as it can be applied in an indefinite number of circumstances. So, it shouldn't surprise us that, when Winch first broaches the topic of rule-following he considers the practice of using a name, namely, the name "Mount Everest." Winch imagines a scenario in which someone who is giving him English-language instruction tries to teach him to use this name by gesturing at the mountain through the window of an airplane. There would, he claims, be nothing objectionable about saying that either this definition "lays down the meaning" or that "to use a word in its correct meaning is to use it in the same way laid down in the definition" (26). But, he adds, talk of using a term "the same way" doesn't do much work by itself. In the scene of language learning he is describing, it would be unclear whether his teacher was giving the name of the mountain or the word "mountain" and, by the same token, unclear what "using the term the same way" amounts to.[64] What interests Winch here is not so much the possibility of misunderstanding but what this possibility reveals about what "going on with a term in the same way" involves. What it reveals is that there is an element of context sensitivity in the grasp of sameness that is internal to operating with a concept. Far from being the expression of a psychological mechanism that produces correct behavior in a manner independent of our sensitivities, such a grasp is inseparable from a sense of the importance of similarities uniting the context at hand with other contexts in which a concept is used.

Winch frequently speaks of "the necessity for rules to have a social setting" (33), and when he does so he has in mind this basic view of conceptual understanding or rule-following (i.e., a construal of it as presupposing a feel for a given context). In developing this view, Winch is—as he himself stresses—inheriting from Wittgenstein's treatment of rule-following. Still borrowing from Wittgenstein, Winch goes on to suggest by means of a series of examples that the basic point he is making applies even to conceptual capacities—such as those we exercise in extending simple mathematical series—that may at first glance seem well suited to the context-independent model he rejects.[65] Winch is preoccupied with these issues because they have a bearing on how we conceive social activities. Insofar as social activities as such involve conceptuality or rule-following, it is an implication of Winch's larger argument that a certain sensitivity to context or social setting is necessary for participating in any social activity.

This account of social activities, however apparently insignificant by itself, has significant consequences for how we construe the *understanding* of such activities. To appreciate the kinds of consequences that interest Winch, it's helpful to accent an aspect of his argument that he himself doesn't underline. In defending his preferred account of social activities, he commits himself to a distinctive claim about understanding within the individual natural sciences.[66] When Winch is making a case for the account of social activities he favors, he claims that sensitivities contribute internally to all conceptual capacities. This means that, to the extent that modes of natural-scientific understanding involve conceptuality, sensitivities contribute internally to these modes of understanding.[67]

This view of understanding within the natural sciences forms the backdrop for the claims about social understanding that are the centerpiece of *The Idea of a Social Science*. Winch invites us to regard social understanding as resembling natural-scientific understanding in the following respect. Just as we require particular sensitivities to consistently apply the concepts internal to different forms of natural-scientific understanding, we require particular sensitivities to consistently apply the concepts internal to social understanding. At the same time, Winch brings out how social understanding is distinctive. He emphasizes that, in addition to resembling all other conceptual understanding in being rule-governed, social understanding takes rule-governed behavior as its object (see 87–8). If we formulate Winch's claim that rule-governed behavior necessarily draws on particular sensitivities by saying that this behavior is as such structured by practical normativity, then we can bring into relief what is noteworthy about this view of social understanding by saying that, unlike concepts characteristic of the individual natural sciences, characteristically social concepts trace out patterns in a ground that is essentially structured by practical normativity or, in other words, in a ground that is essentially ethically nonneutral.[68] This means that we require sensitivities or modes of cultural appreciation not merely to project these concepts consistently (something that is also true of mastery of concepts characteristic of individual natural sciences) but also to grasp their contents.[69] That is Winch's preferred conception of social understanding, and, as various commentators have noted, the passages in which he presents it are rightly taken to represent the climax of his early book.[70]

One of the most arresting outcomes of the book's main argument is a conception of social understanding on which it is as such ethically charged. Granted that Winch as a rule represents social understanding, conceived in this manner, as genuine—not merely subjective—understanding, it follows that he is asking us to regard such understanding as both irreducibly ethical and objective. It follows, that is, that he is giving us an image of a region of objective reality as an intrinsically ethical realm and, by the same token, that he is placing himself in opposition to the sort of engrained conception of reality on which it is in itself bereft of ethical value. He is also thereby presenting a distinctive view of what the social is, a distinctive *social ontology*. It is an ontology on which objective features of the social world are irreducibly ethical and on which, in consequence, particular ethical attitudes may contribute internally to an objective understanding of these features. Here gestures that shape our attitudes may inform objective social understanding in a manner that is internal or direct (as opposed to merely external or accidental). This is what it comes to say that Winch's ontology of the social leaves room for the wider conception of rationality at issue in this article.

To say this is not to address the vexed exegetical question of whether Winch describes such a conception of rationality in a rigorously consistent manner, or whether instead he sometimes talks about his preferred conception of rationality in a qualified and relativizing style.[71] What matters here is that it is possible to find in *The Idea of the Social Sciences* an argument for this wider conception. Having now sketched the argument, we can explore the kind of philosophical opposition that it is likely to encounter, with an eye to building on Winch's efforts.

Consider what seems, in the eyes of many thinkers, to exclude the very idea of a wider conception of rationality. This idea is in tension with the entrenched view that objective reality is as such bereft of ethical value, and, by the same token, in tension with the kinds of philosophical reflections that are standardly taken to render this view obligatory. These reflections typically begin from some version of the following image of how the mind makes contact with the world. Here our subjective makeups have an essential tendency to block our view of things, and it is only to the extent that we abstract from elements of these makeups that we can bring reality into focus. The idea is that, in trying to distance ourselves from all contributions from subjectivity, we eliminate from our conception of the objective world every quality that is "subjective" in the sense that it can only be brought into focus in reference to aspects of our subjective endowments. Starting from a suggestive picture of the relationship between mind and world, we wind up with a conception of reality that, insofar as it is intolerant of all subjective qualities, expels the ethically inflected qualities that Winch-style social understanding takes as its object.

The Idea of a Social Science is organized with an eye to resisting this basic line of thought.[72] The line of thought is driven by the idea of an obligation to abstract from all of our subjective endowments, and the book's argument is supposed to bring into question the very coherence of this idea by getting us to ask ourselves whether we have a clear notion of what satisfying such an obligation would be like. Recall Winch's reflections on Wittgenstein's view of rule-following. Winch credits Wittgenstein with showing that mastery of a concept necessarily presupposes a sense of the significance of similarities uniting its uses in different settings. As we saw, Winch brings out how this Wittgensteinian lesson applies even to those conceptual capacities—such as, say, simple mathematical ones—to which it may at first glance seem most foreign. In thus borrowing from Wittgenstein, Winch is inviting us to see that, even if we are inclined to believe otherwise, we have no clear notion of what it would be for a conceptual capacity to count as wholly abstract. Winch's thought seems to be that this conclusion counts not only against the idea of an obligation to abstract from all of our subjective endowments but also against the ethically neutral conception of reality that this idea is sometimes taken to underwrite.

This thought is bound to strike many philosophers as simply wrong. This is because today the idea of an obligation to abstract depends primarily for the influence it enjoys within philosophical circles on the assumption—not that one or another conceptual capacity meets the obligation but rather—that the obligation is satisfied by perceptual experience, where such experience is taken to be essentially a matter of the reception of content that is nonconceptual. Yet Winch doesn't criticize nonconceptualist views of perception. For this reason, both his attack on the idea of an obligation to abstract, and the case for a wider conception of rationality that he grounds in this attack, may seem unconvincing. The point is not that Winch is wrong to approach a defense of a wider conception of rationality by trying to dislodge the idea of obligatory abstraction. Nor is it that he is wrong to look for resources in Wittgenstein's later philosophy. Although Winch doesn't discuss these issues, Wittgenstein's writings do in fact contain resources for a direct assault on nonconceptualist views of perception. It follows that it is possible to employ Winch's strategy of inheriting from Wittgenstein to make a stronger case than Winch himself does against a call for abstraction, and to thereby also make a stronger case than Winch himself does for the sort of ethically permissive conception of how things really are that is the ontological counterpart of a wider conception of rationality.

One place in Wittgenstein's writings to look for expressions of the anti-nonconceptualist—or "conceptualist"—view that perception is conceptual all the way down is the discussion, in Part II, § xi of the *Philosophical Investigations*, of the phenomenon Wittgenstein calls *changes of aspect*. Wittgenstein's aim here is to illustrate how, far from being independent of what is seen, conceptuality directly informs our perception. He proceeds by presenting us with cases in which we see something new in an object (a new "aspect") while recognizing that the object has not changed. (Thus, for example, when gazing at a set of lines on a piece of paper, we may suddenly see a figure in it, although the drawing itself is unaltered.) This presentation of cases doesn't amount to an argument for a conceptualist view, but there are resources for an argument elsewhere in Wittgenstein's writings, for instance, in the passages in the *Investigations* in which he is concerned with the privacy of experience. An important goal of some of these passages is—to simplify and condense quite a bit—to get us to see that nonconceptualists place inconsistent demands on what perceptual experience is like. With an eye to summarizing these considerations, we might start by noting that perceptual thought has a normative character that allows for questions about what justifies it. We might then add, plausibly but not uncontroversially, that, with regard to noninferential perceptual thought, we can appeal to experience to answer questions about what justifies perceptual beliefs, and that we thus ordinarily treat experience as having rational significance. Yet, if, following nonconceptualists, we represent perceptual experience as merely causal and essentially nonconceptual, we construe it as shorn of what by our own lights is its rational character. Now there can be no question of being in a position to depict experience as having what we ordinarily regard as its rational character. That is a sketch of a reconstructed Wittgensteinian case for thinking that nonconceptualism is internally inconsistent.

Debates about the prospects for a conceptualist account of perceptual experience are involved, and many philosophers maintain that there are insurmountable obstacles to a viable conceptualism. But the apparently most telling objections to conceptualism (viz., objections having to do with whether it can account for the perceptual capacities of babies and animals) can be answered.[73] Granted that this is so—and granted that nonconceptualist accounts of perception are the best case for making sense of the idea of an obligation to abstract—it follows that there's a good case for abandoning this idea as bankrupt.

This conclusion is of interest insofar as the idea of obligatory abstraction is what seems to force us to whittle away from our image of the world all qualities with a necessary reference to affect—and to, by this route, arrive at an image reality as in itself bereft of ethical values. Consistently forfeiting this idea is tantamount to conceding that we don't have a coherent enough account of what ideally abstract mental access to the world would be like to appeal to such access in antecedently impugning the cognitive credentials of nonabstract modes of thought. It is tantamount to conceding that we are not in a position to determine in advance that, any time we allow nonabstract or subjectively shaped considerations to inform our thought and speech, we thereby undermine our claim to do justice to how things really are. The result of our attempt to discredit the idea of ideal abstraction is thus that we are obliged to refashion our understanding of objective reality so that it no longer excludes everything subjective. It is a short step from here to accommodating within the objective realm the ethically nonneutral qualities that Winch urges us to see as objects of social understanding.[74]

If we now allow that some objective qualities are as such ethically charged, we at the same time allow that modes of thought that shape our ethical sensibilities may as such directly contribute to our grasp of objective features of the world, thereby qualifying as rationally authoritative. By elaborating Winch's Wittgensteinian case for his suggestive and philosophically unorthodox social ontology, we accordingly equip ourselves to accommodate the wider conception of rationality that—as we have seen—we require in order to make sense of liberating social criticism, of the sort sought by contemporary critical theorists, that is rationally authoritative and capable of combating forms of ethnocentrism. By the same token, we equip ourselves to account for the rational authority of critical gestures—such as those characteristic of Crenshaw and, indeed, many other radical social critics—that essentially involve bringing us to look at our lives from new evaluative perspectives.[75]

4 Extending the Argument

There is a respect in which the foregoing account of liberating social criticism needs to be supplemented. What drives the idea that we need widely rational modes of social criticism, both in the work of some contemporary critical theorists and in a Winchian strand of thought from analytic philosophy of the social sciences, is the conviction that social phenomena are irreducibly ethical and that they therefore reveal themselves to nonneutral modes of thought that only a wider conception equips us to recognize as rational. These are not, however, the only values that responsible social criticism needs to register. There are aspects both of human lives and of the lives of nonhuman animals, that despite not qualifying as social, likewise necessarily encode values. The Winchian argument for the irreducibly ethical character of social phenomena starts from an understanding of social activities as modes of fully conceptual or rational expression, and it is possible to show that there are values necessarily encoded not only in all rational forms of animate life but also in all nonrational forms as well. Indeed, it is possible to show that the Winchian thesis about the irredeemably ethical character of rational human social life is a specific instance of a more general point about the irredeemably ethical character of animate life. We need to insist that social criticism be responsible to valuable aspects of nonrational animate life if we are to ensure that our practices and institutions are respectful both of the vulnerabilities of those human beings who (as a result of, say, congenital conditions, illness, or injury) are not fully rational as well as of the vulnerabilities of nonrational animals. Although showing this is a task for another occasion, Wittgenstein is in fact a good guide to this expansion of the realm of values that are open for immanent critical exploration.[76] This marks another noteworthy point of contact with critical theory, above all, with prominent early members of the Frankfurt school, such as Adorno and Horkheimer, who held that doing justice to the worldly circumstances of animals as well as human beings called for affectively saturated "aesthetic reflection."[77] So, even bearing in mind the need to further develop this chapter's main line of argument in the manner just adumbrated, it is appropriate to see the larger conversation in question as combining themes from Wittgenstein and critical theory.

5 Epilogue

If it is right to maintain, in accordance with sections 3 and 4 of this chapter, that Wittgenstein bequeaths to us a wider conception of rationality, then it is also fair to say that Wittgenstein gives us a straightforward method for incorporating what critical theorists call the logic of immanence and transcendence. Further, if with Habermas and his Frankfurt-based predecessors, we take as a key ill of late capitalism the overreach into the political sphere of instrumental reason, then we can add that the widely rational forms of reason Wittgenstein brings within reach are capable of countering this politically pernicious trend and reanimating the political domain. The relevant forms of reason are logically distinct from and, arguably, politically far more promising than the "communicative" forms proposed by Habermas himself.

The image of Wittgenstein that is operative here, an image of him as contributing decisively to an understanding of emancipatory criticism, is a far cry from the image many contemporary philosophers were brought up on. Since at least 1959, when Ernest Gellner published his polemical tract *Words and Things: An Examination of, and Attack on, Linguistic Philosophy*, the idea that Wittgenstein's later philosophy has an irredeemably conservative bent has enjoyed widespread acceptance. Despite the staying power of this idea, it seems clear that the push to depict Wittgenstein as a politically conservative thinker has been far stronger than any of the considerations offered in its favor.[78] There is good reason to rework our picture of Wittgenstein's philosophical and political legacy, bringing out how it is capable of directly informing our grasp of liberating social thought and how it provides support for the most promising accounts of such thought to emerge from critical theory. Or, as we might also put it, there is good reason to conclude that Wittgenstein can—help us to—do critical theory.[79]

Notes

1 See Kimberlé Crenshaw, "Whose Story Is It Anyway? Feminist and Anti-Racist Appropriations of Anita Hill," in *Race-ing Justice, En-Gendering Power: Essays*

on *Anita Hill, Clarence Thomas and the Construction of Social Reality*, ed. Toni Morrison (New York: Pantheon Books, 1992), 402–40.

2   See Amy Goodman's interview with Kimberlé Crenshaw and others, posted on www.democracynow.org on December 15, 2015, under the title "When Cops Rape: Daniel Holtzclaw and the Vulnerability of Black Women to Police Abuse." Thirteen women ultimately testified against Holtzclaw, and in 2015 he was convicted by an all-white jury of crimes (including four counts of first-degree rape) against eight of them.

3   For Crenshaw's classic discussion of the importance of attention to "intersections" among forms of bias that affect women of color, see her "Mapping the Margins: Intersectionality, Identity Politics and Violence against Women of Color," *The Stanford Law Review* 43 (1991): 1241–99.

4   Crenshaw, "Whose Story Is It Anyway?," 411.

5   See ibid., 412 and 413.

6   Cf. Alice Crary, "The Methodological is Political: What's the Matter with 'Analytic Feminism,'" *Radical Philosophy* 2, no. 2 (2018), online: https://www.radicalphilosophy.com/article/the-methodological-is-political

7   For more detailed discussion of these competing conceptions of rationality, see Alice Crary, *Inside Ethics: On the Demands of Moral Thought* (Cambridge, MA: Harvard University Press, 2016), section 6.1.

8   See Onora O'Neill, "Starke und Schwache Gesellschaftskritik in einer Globalisierten Welt," *Deutsche Zeitschrift für Philosophie* 48, no. 5 (2000): 719–28. The translations of the passages quoted from this article in this chapter are my own.

9   Ibid., 719.

10 Although it is possible to use the work of a Kantian, universalist critic like O'Neill to illustrate the tendency to overlook this possibility, it is equally possible to turn to an anti-universalist to make the same point. For an anti-universalist critic who believes we are obliged to choose between what O'Neill would call "strongly normative" and "weakly normative" critique, while differing from O'Neill in opting for the latter alternative, we could turn to the writings of Richard Rorty. See my discussion of relevant aspects of Rorty's work in my "Wittgenstein and Political Thought," in *The New Wittgenstein*, ed. Alice Crary and Rupert Read (London: Routledge, 2000), 118–45. For further examples of both universalist and anti-universalist varieties, see the text below.

11 Some of the most influential spokespeople for this emerging philosophical corpus are in effect "universalist" theorists who don't represent critique as essentially context-sensitive, even if at some level they aim to do so. This includes Miranda Fricker (*Epistemic Injustice: Power and the Ethics of Knowing* [Oxford: Oxford University Press, 2007]) (for relevant commentary on Fricker, see Alice Crary, "The Methodological is Political" and Jason Stanley, *How Propaganda Works* [Princeton: Princeton University Press, 2015]) (for relevant commentary on Stanley, see my "Putnam and Propaganda," *The Graduate Faculty Philosophy Journal* 38, no. 2

[2017]: 385–98). Not that there aren't analytically trained and engaged theorists, who are involved in new ideology debates, and who help themselves to widely rational resources. For one illuminating counterexample, see Catherine Mills, "Ideology," in *The Routledge Handbook to Epistemic Injustice*, ed. Ian James Kidd, José Medina and Gail Pohlhaus Jr. (London: Abingdon, 2017).

12 See Max Horkheimer, "Traditional and Critical Theory," in *Critical Theory: Collected Essays* (New York, NY: Continuum, 1972), 190–243.

13 The inset quotes in the last two sentences are from Raymond Geuss (*The Idea of a Critical Theory: Habermas and the Frankfurt School* [Cambridge: Cambridge University Press, 1981], 1–2). For another helpful and congenial overview of the tradition of critical theory, see Axel Honneth, "A Social Pathology of Reason: On the Intellectual Legacy of Critical Theory" (Ch. 2 of his *Pathologies of Reason: On the Legacy of Critical Theory*, trans. James Ingram [New York, NY: Columbia University Press, 2009]).

14 Opposition to this positivist idea is a guiding theme of Max Horkheimer's classic "Traditional and Critical Theory," esp. 198–9 and 232.

15 Ibid., 213.

16 It would have been possible to frame this as a discussion about how to conceive the nature of *ideology critique*. The standard umbrella term for the theoretical images of society that critical theories aim to challenge is *ideology*, and, while in some conversational contexts "ideology" is used without any negative connotations, inside critical theory the term is typically employed pejoratively and in reference to ethically charged beliefs that are essentially woven into the fabric of, and inseparable from, social practices. For helpful remarks on how ideological beliefs are inextricably "practice-soaked," see, for example, Geuss, *The Idea of a Critical Theory*, 5–7 and Rahel Jaeggi, "Rethinking Ideology," in *New Waves in Political Philosophy*, ed. Boudewijn de Bruin and Christopher F. Zurn (Hampshire: Palgrave Macmillan, 2009), 63–86, esp. 64. Any reasonable gloss on what is insidious about ideological beliefs would have to mention both an *epistemic* aspect having to do with ways in which ideological beliefs fail to truly capture the lives of the individuals caught up in the practices and institutions that they themselves support and stabilize and a *functional* aspect having to do with how these beliefs organize us "in relations of domination and subordination" (see Sally Haslanger, "Critical Theory and Practice: Ideology and Morality," unpublished), thereby nevertheless assuming an aura of truth. Given that ideological beliefs have this sort of functional character, it seems clear that we need materially effective, nonneutral methods in order to combat them. Our answer to the question of whether these methods need to be regarded as in themselves nonrational—and hence as at best propaedeutic to ideology critique understood as a rationally respectable enterprise—or whether instead they may themselves qualify as rationally respectable ideology critique will reflect our views about the availability of a wider conception of rationality.

17 For a clear early statement of this view of Habermas's, see his "Technology and Science as 'Ideology,'" in *Toward a Rational Society: Student Protest, Science, and Politics*, trans. Jeremy J. Shapiro (Boston, MA: Beacon Press, 1987), 81–122 (originally published in 1969).
18 See, for example, Jürgen Habermas, "What Is Universal Pragmatics?," in *Communication and the Evolution of Society*, trans. Thomas McCarthy (Boston, MA: Beacon Press, 1979), 1–68.
19 See Jürgen Habermas, "Discourse Ethics: Notes on a Program of Philosophical Justification," in *Moral Consciousness and Communicative Action*, trans. Christian Lenhardt and Shierry Weber Nicholsen (Cambridge, MA: MIT Press, 1999), 43–115, esp. 64–5.
20 For a discussion of the centrality to Habermas' work of this sort of value-norm divide, see Hilary Putnam, "Values and Norms," in *The Collapse of the Fact/Value Distinction: And Other Essays* (Cambridge, MA: Harvard University Press, 2002), 111–34.
21 The inset quote is from Habermas, "Discourse Ethics: Notes on a Program of Philosophical Justification," 65.
22 Putnam, "Values and Norms," 112.
23 Jürgen Habermas, "Reply to My Critics," in *Habermas and Religion*, trans. Ciaran Cronin and ed. Craig Calhoun, Eduardo Mendieta, and Jonathan VanAntwerpen (Cambridge: Polity Press, 2013), 347–90, 360.
24 See, for example, Rainer Forst, *Contexts of Justice: Political Philosophy beyond Liberalism and Communitarianism*, trans. John M. M. Farrell (Berkeley, CA: University of California Press, 2002), 156, 176, 180–1 and 190) and idem, *Justification and Critique: Toward a Critical Theory of Politics* (Cambridge: Polity Press, 2014).
25 For Forst's own account of his inheritance from Habermas, see, for example, Forst, *Contexts of Justice*, 192–7.
26 See ibid., 1, 60, 164, 172–3 and 197–8 and Forst, *Justification and Critique*, 3, 9 and 107.
27 For insightful discussion of the inability of Kantian approaches in ethics to do justice to feminist claims about *sexual objectification*, see Nancy Bauer, *How to Do Things with Pornography* (Cambridge, MA: Harvard University Press, 2015).
28 One notable recent collection that takes up this important question is Penelope Deutscher and Christina Lafont, *Critical Theory in Critical Times: Transforming the Global Political and Economic Order* (New York, NY: Columbia University Press, 2017).
29 Perhaps it merits mention that, although most self-identified poststructuralists accepts versions of the type of skepticism about rationality sketched in this paragraph, it is in principle possible for poststructuralist theorists to reject such skepticism.

30 See Derrida's discussion of what he calls "iterability" in "Signature Event Context," in his *Limited Inc.* (Evanston, IL: Northwestern University Press, 1988), 1–23.
31 For an influential version of this view within poststructuralism, see Jacques Derrida, *Of Grammatology*, trans. Gayatri Spivak (Baltimore, MD: The Johns Hopkins University Press, 1976).
32 The inset quote in this sentence is from Wendy Brown, *Politics Out of History* (Princeton: Princeton University Press, 2001), 4.
33 See Amy Allen, *The End of Progress: Decolonizing the Normative Foundations of Critical Theory* (New York: Columbia University Press, 2016), 15.
34 For further helpful discussion of this basic point in reference to Axel Honneth's *Freedom's Right*, see Lois McNay, "Social Freedom and Progress in the Family: Reflections on Care, Gender and Inequality," *Critical Horizons* 16, no. 2 (2015): 170–86, and Karen Ng, "Social Freedom as Ideology," *Philosophy and Social Criticism* 20, no. 10 (2018): 1–24.
35 See Allen, *The End of Progress*, 2.
36 Allen, 19.
37 Ibid., 34, 65–6, 121, 212–15.
38 See ibid., xi.
39 For an elegant treatment of this theme, see Sabina Lovibond, "Feminism and Postmodernism," *New Left Review* 78 (1989): 5–28. See also my critique of Richard Rorty's view of political discourse—a view that in fundamental respects anticipates that of Allen and other poststructuralists—in Crary, "Wittgenstein and Political Thought."
40 Poststructuralist theorists often present themselves as favoring *genealogical* methods (see, for example, Allen, *The End of Progress*, Ch. 5), so it is worth accenting that the attack on poststructuralism-leaning critical theories just sketched is *not* an attack on the interest of genealogy understood—as David Owen, for example, understands it—as dedicated to freeing us from pictures of our lives that we experience as repressive; for Owen's view of genealogy, see especially his "Criticism and Captivity: On Genealogy and Critical Theory," *European Journal of Philosophy* 10, no. 2 (2002): 216–30. It is possible to place value on genealogy, understood as a method of getting us to see that our current image of the world is not obligatory (say, by shifting our sense of what matters so that things look very different to us), without suggesting—as Allen effectively does—that it is incapable of contributing internally to a rationally authoritative, liberating theory of society. This article's concern with critical theories that have this poststructuralist bent is that their reliance on a narrower conception of rationality that seems to strip genealogy of this rational power.
41 The philosophical posture in question is sometimes dignified with the label "postmetaphysical." See, for example, Jürgen Habermas, *Postmetaphysical Thinking: Philosophical Essays* (Cambridge, MA: MIT Press, 1992).
42 See esp. Habermas's contribution to Theodor W. Adorno et al. (eds.), *The Positivist Dispute in German Sociology*, trans. Glyn Adey and David Frisby (London: Heinemann, 1976).

43 It is also true of the accounts of immanent critique presented in the work of a fair number of critical theorists, including some who take their cue from Horkheimer and Adorno.
44 See, for example, Rahel Jaeggi, *Critique of Forms of Life*, trans. Ciaran Cronin (Cambridge, MA: Harvard University Press, 2018), 9–15.
45 For Jaeggi's detailed account of forms of life and the conception of immanent critique they support, see *Critique of Forms of Life* (ibid., chapters 1–6). For a helpful, compressed account of forms of life, see Rahel Jaeggi, "Lebensformen als Problemlösungsinstanzen," *Philosophisches Jahrbuch* 125 (2018): 64–89.
46 See ibid., 75.
47 See, for example, ibid., 78.
48 See, for example, Jaeggi, *Critique of Forms of Life*, 194.
49 Jaeggi, "Lebensformen as Problemlösungsinstanzen," 86, transl. mine). Although Jaeggi insists on distinguishing her preferred critical methods from "internal" modes of critique, she is too willing to sanction the coherence of the internal methods she rejects. See in this connection, see Alice Crary, "Recovering the Core of Critique: Response to Jaeggi's 'Lebensformen als Problemlösungsinstanzen,'" *Philosophisches Jahrbuch* 126:1 (2019), 109–16.
50 See Jaeggi, *Critique of Forms of Life*, 194. For discussion of this feature of Jaeggi's work, see Crary, "Recovering the Core of Critique."
51 See, for example, Andreas Niederberger and Tobias Weihrauch, "Rahel Jaeggi: *Kritik von Lebensformen*," *Notre Dame Philosophical Reviews* (2015), online: https://ndpr.nd.edu/news/kritik-von-lebensformen/.
52 Issued with a new preface in 1990.
53 This view was defended plausibly by some readers writing at roughly the same time as Winch (see, for example, Alasdair MacIntyre, "The Idea of a Social Science," *Proceedings of the Aristotelian Society*, suppl. vol. 41 [1967]: 95–132), and it still receives thoughtful defenses in the work of a number of readers today (see, for example, Cora Diamond, "Criticizing from 'Outside,'" *Philosophical Investigations* 36, no. 2 (2013): 114–32, idem, "Putnam and Wittgensteinian Baby-Throwing: Variations on a Theme," in *The Philosophy of Hilary Putnam*, ed. Douglaus Anderson and Randall Auxier (Chicago, IL: Open Court, 2015), 603–49; see also Mark Risjord, *Philosophy of Social Science: A Contemporary Introduction* (New York, NY: Routledge, 2014), esp. 65–8.
54 Lars Hertzberg defended this view as early as 1980 in "Winch on Social Interpretation," *Philosophy of the Social Sciences* 10 (1980): 151–71. For more recent efforts along the same lines, see Phil Hutchinson, Rupert Read and Wes Sharrock, *There Is No Such Thing as a Social Science* (Surrey: Ashgate, 2012), and Jonas Ahlskog and Olli Lagerspetz, "Language-Games and Relativism: On Cora Diamond's Reading of Peter Winch," *Philosophical Investigations* 38, no. 4 (2015): 293–315.

55 See, for example, Paul A. Roth, "Naturalism Without Fears," in *Philosophy of Anthropology and Sociology*, vol. 15 of *Handbook of the Philosophy of Science*, ed. Mark Risjord and Stephen Turner (Amsterdam: Elsevier, 2006), 683–708.

56 For a defense of Winch against the charges Roth (2006) levels, see Kevin M. Cahill, "Naturalism and the Friends of Understanding," *Philosophy of the Social Sciences* 44, no. 4 (2013): 460–77.

57 In his book, Winch critically examines the classic version of this view that is defended in the writings of John Stuart Mill (see *The Idea of a Social Science and Its Relation to Philosophy*, 2nd ed. [London: Routledge, 1990], part III, 66–94; page numbers in brackets above refer to this book). For a well-regarded, up-to-date defense of a view on these lines, see Arthur Rosenberg, *Philosophy of Social Science* (Boulder, CO: Westview Press, 2012). While the sort of natural science-orientated outlook that Rosenberg favors is today well received among analytic philosophers of the social sciences, it is much less well represented in European philosophy of social science.

58 Winch offers his most quoted formulation of this view, not in *The Idea of a Social Science*, but a few years later in his influential article "Understanding a Primitive Society," reprinted in Winch, *Ethics and Action* (London: Routledge, 1972), 8–49. On p. 12 of this piece, he writes, "Reality is not what gives language sense. What is real and what is unreal shows itself *in* the sense that language has."

59 This is a well-known phrase from John McDowell.

60 This is one side of the "pincer movement" that, at the outset of *The Idea of a Social Science*, Winch declares he is setting out to make. The accent here is on Winch's efforts to distance himself from classic "underlaborer" conceptions of philosophy on which it is a parasitic discipline that solves "problems thrown up in the course of non-philosophical investigations" (4). The other side of Winch's project is distancing himself from "master scientist" conceptions on which philosophy "aims at refuting scientific theories by purely a priori reasoning" (7). To appreciate this part of Winch's project, we need to see that, as Winch conceives them, conceptual investigations, while capable of giving us second-order awareness of knowledge of the world embodied in our concepts, don't result in the sort of new empirical information that would make them competitors of any of the natural sciences.

61 This quote is taken from Winch's Preface to the 1990 2nd edition of *The Idea of a Social Science*.

62 Winch might plausibly be read as trying to find exceptions to this claim in his striking paper "The Universalizability of Moral Judgments," *The Monist* 49, no. 2 (1965): 196–214. For reasons too involved to discuss here, this paper is problematic. Given that Winch doesn't mention relevant considerations in his 1990 remarks on *The Idea of a Social Science*, it seems reasonable simply to set it aside here.

63 For a discussion of relevant topics, see Alice Crary, "Freedom Is for the Dogs," in *Ethics – Society – Politics*, ed. Martin G. Weiss and Hajo Greif (Berlin: De Gruyter, 2013), 203–26.

64 That is, since using a name for a particular mountain consistently and using the general term "mountain" consistently are different things.

65 See Winch, *The Idea of a Social Science*, 29–33. Around the time of *The Idea of a Social Science*, Winch is independently concerned to stress that Wittgenstein's later remarks on rule-following represent a significant development in his philosophical outlook. See esp. "The Unity of Wittgenstein's Philosophy," Winch's introduction to his edited volume, *Studies in the Philosophy of Wittgenstein* (London: Routledge and Kegan Paul, 1969), 1–19.

66 Having already, at the opening of this section, flagged my awareness that the individual natural sciences involve different modes of understanding, it is worth stressing that the suggestion Winch is making here doesn't depend for its soundness on any failure to acknowledge differences among individual modes of natural-scientific understanding. All it depends on is the thought that all natural-scientific modes of understanding, however different in other respects, involve conceptuality.

67 It seems reasonable to suppose that Winch selects his opening example of a rule-governed social activity with an eye to making just this point. That is, he chooses an activity—viz., use of the name "Mt. Everest"—that involves concern with aspects of the physical world because he wants to impress on his readers that sensitivities are necessary prerequisites of the kind of consistent application of concepts that is internal even to various natural-scientific modes of understanding.

68 It might seem reasonable to protest that Winch's line of reasoning here entitles him to represent social categories as irreducibly normative without representing the kind of normativity in question as ethical. For considerations that effectively speak for regarding the relevant normativity as in fact ethical, see Crary, *Inside Ethics*, chapter 2.

69 A case could be made for thinking that the concepts characteristic of the part of biology, sometimes called natural history, that is concerned with the description and classification of organisms trace out patterns in a normatively structured ground. (For a defense of an account of natural history on these lines, see my commentary on Michael Thompson's work in Crary, *Inside Ethics*, 5.1.i.) But the kind of normativity in question is not practical or ethical and hence different from kind of normativity that forms the ground for projecting characteristically social concepts.

70 See, for example, Hertzberg, "Winch on Social Interpretation," 168–9, and Ahlskog and Lagerspetz, "Language-Games and Relativism," 304–5.

71 There is good reason to hold with Cora Diamond—see, for example, her "Criticizing from 'Outside'"—that there are passages in Winch's early work, and perhaps above all in "Understanding a Primitive Society," in which he effectively slides into a relativistic posture. At the same time, it seems reasonable to think that Winch's core philosophical commitments early on speak for an attractive, contextualist, and decidedly nonrelativistic account of social understanding.

72 Some interpreters who take *The Idea of a Social Science* to be propounding a relativist view arrive at this reading because they approach his work through the lens of this line of thought (see, for example, Risjord and Rosenberg). Other who recognize that Winch is hostile to the line of thought nevertheless arrive at similar readings because they think he fails to fully distance himself from it (see, for example, Diamond). There are passages in Winch's writing that might plausibly be read as expressing sympathy for the kind of relativistic position that he officially disavows. For instance, in *The Idea of a Social Science* he tells us that "criteria of logic . . . are only intelligible in the context of ways of living or modes of social life" and that, moreover, different ways of living each offer "a different account of the intelligibility of things" (*The Idea of a Social Science*, 101 and 103). Or, again, a few years later, in "Understanding a Primitive Society," he claims that different societies have different "standards of rationality" and that these standards "do not always coincide" (in *American Philosophical Quarterly* 1, no. 4 [1964]: 307–24, 317).

73 For an argument to this effect, see Alice Crary, "Dogs and Concepts," *Philosophy* 87, no. 2 (2012): 215–37. An expanded version of this materials is presented in Crary, *Inside Ethics*, Ch. 3.

74 There is an extensive literature—one focused on a disanalogy between values and perceptual qualities—that is concerned with the thought that, even if we show that the objective realm includes qualities that count as subjective because they have essential reference to perceptual responses, there are special and additional *a priori* obstacles to representing the objective realm as including values or qualities that count as subjective because they have essential references to not to perceptual but to affective responses. The idea of such obstacles is, however, suspect. For discussion, see Alice Crary, *Beyond Moral Judgment* (Cambridge, MA: Harvard University Press, 2007), Ch. 1.

75 The idea that critical gestures that mobilize evaluative perspectives can as such directly inform rational understanding is, according to the persuasive line of thought developed in Catherine Mills, "Alternative Epistemologies," in *Blackness Visible: Essays on Philosophy and Race* (Ithaca: Cornell University Press, 1998), 21–39, a common thread uniting Marxist, feminist, and Black epistemologies.

76 For a detailed treatment of these themes, see Chapters 2, 3, and 4 of my *Inside Ethics*. For further discussion of the case of cognitively disabled human beings, see Alice Crary, "Cognitive Disability and Moral Status," in *Oxford Handbook of Philosophy and Disability*, ed. Adam Cureton and David Wasserman (Oxford: Oxford University Press, 2018); for further discussion of the case of animals, see Alice Crary, "Ethics," in *Critical Terms in Animal Studies*, ed. Lori Gruen (Chicago: University of Chicago Press, 2018).

77 Theodor W. Adorno and Max Horkheimer, *The Dialectic of Enlightenment: Philosophical Fragments*, trans. Edmund Jephcott (Stanford, CA: Stanford University Press, 2002), 209.

78 See Alice Crary and Joel de Lara, "Who's Afraid of Ordinary Language Philosophy? A Plea for Reviving a Wrongly Revived Tradition," *The Graduate Faculty Philosophy Journal* 39, no. 2 (2019): 317–39.
79 This chapter is a fundamental reworking of my article "Wittgenstein Goes to Frankfurt (and Finds Something Useful to Say)," which appeared in the *Nordic Wittgenstein Review* in June 2018. That article's treatment of contemporary trends in critical theory came to me to seem unacceptably limited. After offering a set of lectures on these topics at Oxford in Hilary Term of 2019, I decided to revise the manuscript. I am grateful to the students and faculty members who attended the lectures for their provocative questions and helpful interventions. I subsequently presented versions of this material at the University of Essex as well as at the conference "Crisis and Critique: Philosophical Analysis and Current Events," in Kirchberg, and I am grateful for the productive feedback I received on those occasions. I owe special thanks to Sarah Bufkin, Patricia Cipollitti, Rebecca Duke, Matteo Falomi, Fabian Freyenhagen, Thomas Khurana, María Pía Lara, and Stella Villarmea. I am likewise thankful to Nathaniel Hupert and Hartmut von Sass for their generous and constructive comments during a final round of editing.

Works Cited

Adorno, Theodor Hans Albert, Ralf Dahrendorf, Jürgen Habermas, Harald Pilot and Karl R. Popper (eds.), *The Positivist Dispute in German Sociology*, trans. Glyn Adey and David Frisby, London: Heinemann, 1976.

Adorno, Theodor and Max Horkheimer, *The Dialectic of Enlightenment: Philosophical Fragments*, trans. E. Jephcott, Stanford, CA: Stanford University Press, 2002.

Ahlskog, Jonas and Olli Lagerspetz, "Language-Games and Relativism: On Cora Diamond's Reading of Peter Winch," *Philosophical Investigations* 38, no. 4 (2015): 293–315.

Allen, Amy, *The End of Progress: Decolonizing the Normative Foundations of Critical Theory*, New York: Columbia University Press, 2016.

Bauer, Nancy, *How to Do Things With Pornography*, Cambridge, MA: Harvard University Press, 2015.

Brown, Wendy, *Politics Out of History*, Princeton: Princeton University Press, 2001.

Cahill, Kevin, "Naturalism and the Friends of Understanding," *Philosophy of the Social Sciences* 44, no. 4 (2013): 460–77.

Crary, Alice, "Wittgenstein and Political Thought," in Alice Crary and Rupert Read (eds.), *The New Wittgenstein*, 118–45, London: Routledge, 2001.

Crary, Alice, *Beyond Moral Judgment*, Cambridge, MA: Harvard University Press, 2007.

Crary, Alice, "Dogs and Concepts," *Philosophy* 87, no. 2 (2012): 215–37.

Crary, Alice, "Freedom is for the Dogs," in Martin G. Weiss and Hajo Greif (eds.), *Ethics – Society – Politics*, 203–26, Berlin: De Gruyter, 2013.

Crary, Alice, *Inside Ethics: On the Demands of Moral Thought*, Cambridge, MA: Harvard University Press, 2016.

Crary, Alice, "Putnam and Propaganda," *The Graduate Faculty Philosophy Journal* 38, no. 2 (2017): 385–98.

Crary, Alice, "Cognitive Disability and Moral Status," in Adam Cureton and David Wasserman (eds.), *Oxford Handbook of Philosophy and Disability*, Oxford: Oxford University Press, 2018.

Crary, Alice, "Ethics," in Lori Gruen (ed.), *Critical Terms in Animal Studies*, Chicago: University of Chicago Press, 2018.

Crary, Alice, "The Methodological Is Political: What's the Matter with 'Analytic Feminism'," *Radical Philosophy* 2, no. 2 (2018), online: https://www.radicalphilosophy.com/article/the-methodological-is-political.

Crary, Alice, "Recovering the Core of Critique: Response to Jaeggi's 'Lebensformen als Problemlösungsinstanzen'," *Philosophisches Jahrbuch* 126, no. 1 (2019): 109–16.

Crary, Alice and Joel de Lara, "Who's Afraid of Ordinary Language Philosophy? A Plea for Reviving a Wrongly Revived Tradition," *The Graduate Faculty Philosophy Journal* 39, no. 2 (2019): 317–39.

Crenshaw, Kimberlé, "Mapping the Margins: Intersectionality, Identity Politics and Violence against Women of Color," *The Stanford Law Review* 43 (1991): 1241–99.

Crenshaw, Kimberlé, "Whose Story Is It Anyway? Feminist and Anti-Racist Appropriations of Anita Hill," in Toni Morrison (ed.), *Race-ing Justice, En-Gendering Power: Essays on Anita Hill, Clarence Thomas and the Construction of Social Reality*, 402–40, New York: Pantheon Books, 1992.

Derrida, Jacques, *Of Grammatology*, trans. Gayatri Spivak, Baltimore, MD: The Johns Hopkins University Press, 1976.

Derrida, Jacques, *Limited Inc.*, Evanston, IL: Northwestern University Press, 1988.

Deutscher, Penelope and Christina Lafont, *Critical Theory in Critical Times: Transforming the Global Political and Economic Order*, New York: Columbia University Press, 2017.

Diamond, Cora, "Criticizing from 'Outside'," *Philosophical Investigations* 36, no. 2 (2013): 114–32.

Diamond, Cora, "Putnam and Wittgensteinian Baby-Throwing: Variations on a Theme," in Douglaus Anderson and Randall Auxier (eds.), *The Philosophy of Hilary Putnam*, 603–49, Chicago, IL: Open Court, 2015.

Forst, Rainer, *Contexts of Justice: Political Philosophy beyond Liberalism and Communitarianism*, trans. John M. M. Farrell, Berkeley: University of California Press, 2002.

Forst, Rainer, *Justification and Critique: Toward a Critical Theory of Politics*, Cambridge: Polity Press, 2014.

Fricker, Miranda, *Epistemic Injustice: Power and the Ethics of Knowing*, Oxford: Oxford University Press, 2007.

Gellner, Ernest, *Words and Things: An Examination of, and Attack on, Linguistic Philosophy*, London: Routledge, 2005.

Geuss, Raymond, *The Idea of a Critical Theory: Habermas and the Frankfurt School*, Cambridge: Cambridge University Press, 1981.

Goodman, Amy, "When Cops Rape: Daniel Holtzclaw and the Vulnerability of Black Women to Police Abuse" (2015), online: https://www.democracynow.org/2015/1 2/15/daniel_holtzclaw:convicted_of_serial_rape (accessed May 7, 2018).

Habermas, Jürgen, "What Is Universal Pragmatics?," in *Communication and the Evolution of Society*, trans. Thomas McCarthy, 1–68, Boston, MA: Beacon Press, 1979.

Habermas, Jürgen, "Technology and Science as 'Ideology'," in *Toward a Rational Society: Student Protest, Science, and Politics*, trans. Jeremy J. Shapiro, 81–122, Boston, MA: Beacon Press, 1987 (originally published in 1969).

Habermas, Jürgen, *Postmetaphysical Thinking: Philosophical Essays*, Cambridge, MA: MIT Press, 1992.

Habermas, Jürgen, "Discourse Ethics: Notes on a Program of Philosophical Justification," in *Moral Consciousness and Communicative Action*, trans. Christian Lenhardt and Shierry Weber Nicholsen, 43–115, Cambridge, MA: MIT Press, 1999.

Habermas, Jürgen, "Reply to My Critics," in *Habermas and Religion*, trans. Ciaran Cronin and ed. Craig Calhoun, Eduardo Mendieta, and Jonathan VanAntwerpen (Cambridge: Polity Press, 2013), 347–90.

Haslanger, Sally, "Critical Theory and Practice: Ideology and Morality," unpublished manuscript, no date.

Hertzberg, Lars, "Winch on Social Interpretation," *Philosophy of the Social Sciences* 10 (1980): 151–71.

Honneth, Axel, *The Struggle for Recognition: The Moral Grammar of Social Recognition*, trans. Joel Anderson, Cambridge: Polity Press, 1995.

Honneth, Axel, *Pathologies of Reason: On the Legacy of Critical Theory*, trans. John Ingram, New York: Columbia University Press, 2009.

Honneth, Axel, *Freedom's Right: The Social Foundations of Democratic Life*, New York: Columbia University Press, 2011.

Honneth, Axel, "Rejoinder," *Critical Horizons: A Journal of Philosophy and Social Theory* 16, no. 2 (2015): 204–26.

Horkheimer, Max, "Traditional and Critical Theory," in *Critical Theory: Collected Essays*, 190–243, New York: Continuum, 1972.

Hutchinson, Phil, Rupert Read, and Wes Sharrock, *There Is No Such Thing as a Social Science*, Surrey: Ashgate, 2012.

Jaeggi, Rahel, "Rethinking Ideology," in Boudewijn de Bruin and Christopher F. Zurn (eds.), *New Waves in Political Philosophy*, 63–86, Hampshire: Palgrave MacMillan, 2009.

Jaeggi, Rahel, *Critique of Forms of Life*, trans. Ciaran Cronin, Cambridge, MA: Harvard University Press, 2018.

Jaeggi, Rahel, "Lebensformen as Problemlösungsinstanzen," *Philosophisches Jahrbuch* 125 (2018): 64–89.

Lovibond, Sabina, "Feminism and Postmodernism," *New Left Review* 78 (1989): 5–28.

MacIntyre, Alasdair, "The Idea of a Social Science," *Proceedings of the Aristotelian Society*, suppl. vol. 41 (1967): 95–132.

McNay, Lois, "Social Freedom and Progress in the Family: Reflections on Care, Gender and Inequality," *Critical Horizons* 16, no. 2 (2015): 170–86.

Mills, Catherine, "Alternative Epistemologies," in *Blackness Visible: Essays on Philosophy and Race*, 21–39, Ithaca, NY: Cornell University Press, 1998.

Mills, Catherine, "Ideology," in Ian James Kidd, José Medina, and Gail Pohlhaus Jr. (eds.), *The Routledge Handbook to Epistemic Injustice*, London: Abingdon, 2017: 100–112.

Ng, Karen, "Social Freedom as Ideology," *Philosophy and Social Criticism* 20, no. 10 (2018): 1–24.

Niederberger, Andreas and Tobias Weihrauch, "Rahel Jaeggi: *Kritik von Lebensformen*," *Notre Dame Philosophical Reviews* (2015), online: https://ndpr.nd.edu/news/kritik-von-lebensformen/ (January 25, 2015).

O'Neill, Onora, "Starke und Schwache Gesellschaftskritik in einer Globalisierten Welt," *Deutsche Zeitschrift für Philosophie* 48, no. 5 (2000): 719–28.

Owen, David, "Criticism and Captivity: On Genealogy and Critical Theory," *European Journal of Philosophy* 10, no. 2 (2002): 216–30.

Putnam, Hilary, "Values and Norms," in *The Collapse of the Fact/Value Distinction: And Other Essays*, 111–34, Cambridge, MA: Harvard University Press, 2002.

Risjord, Mark, *Philosophy of Social Science: A Contemporary Introduction*, New York: Routledge, 2014.

Rosenberg, Arthur, *Philosophy of Social Science*, Boulder, CO: Westview Press, 2012.

Roth, Paul A., "Naturalism Without Fears," in Mark Risjord and Stephen Turner (eds.), *Philosophy of Anthropology and Sociology*, vol. 15 of *Handbook of the Philosophy of Science*, 683–708, Amsterdam: Elsevier, 2006.

Stanley, Jason, *How Propaganda Works*, Princeton: Princeton University Press, 2015.

Winch, Peter, "Understanding a Primitive Society," *American Philosophical Quarterly* 1, no. 4 (1964): 307–24.

Winch, Peter, "The Universalizability of Moral Judgments," *The Monist* 49, no. 2 (1965): 196–214.

Winch, Peter (ed.), *Studies in the Philosophy of Wittgenstein*, London: Routledge and Kegan Paul, 1969.

Winch, Peter, *Ethics and Action*, London: Routledge, 1972.

Winch, Peter, *The Idea of a Social Science and Its Relation to Philosophy*, 2nd ed., London: Routledge, 1990.

Contributors

Richard Amesbury is Professor of Religious Studies and Director of the School of Historical, Philosophical and Religious Studies at Arizona State University (ASU). Before joining ASU, he served as Professor of Philosophy and Religious Studies and Chair of the Department of Philosophy and Religion at Clemson University and as Professor of Theological Ethics and Director of the Institute for Social Ethics at the University of Zurich, Switzerland. His writings include *Morality and Social Criticism: The Force of Reasons in Discursive Practice* (2005), a Wittgensteinian engagement with critical social theory.

Mikel Burley is Associate Professor of Religion and Philosophy at the University of Leeds, UK. His books include *A Radical Pluralist Philosophy of Religion: Cross-Cultural, Multireligious, Interdisciplinary* (2020) and *Contemplating Religious Forms of Life: Wittgenstein and D. Z. Phillips* (2012). He is also the editor of *Wittgenstein, Religion and Ethics: New Perspectives from Philosophy and Theology* (2018).

Alice Crary is University Distinguished Professor at The New School for Social Research in New York City and was Professor of Philosophy at the University of Oxford (2018–19). She was the New School's Philosophy Department Chair and founding co-Chair of its Gender and Sexuality Studies program (2014–2017). She is the author of *Inside Ethics: On the Demands of Moral Thought* and *Beyond Moral Judgment* (2007 and 2016). And she edited *The New Wittgenstein* (with Rupert Read, 2000), *Reading Cavell* (with Sanford Shieh, 2006) and *Wittgenstein and the Moral Life: Essays in Honor of Cora Diamond* (2007).

Hans-Johann Glock is Professor of Philosophy at the University of Zurich. Before, he held a professorship at the University of Reading, UK. His publications include *A Wittgenstein Dictionary* (1996), *Quine and Davidson on Language, Thought and Reality* (2003), and *What Is Analytic Philosophy?* (2008), as well as the editions *Strawson and Kant* (2003) and *The Blackwell Companion to Wittgenstein* (with J. Hyman; 2017).

Nora Hämäläinen is Senior Researcher at the Centre for Ethics as Study in Human Value at the University of Pardubice, Czech Republic. Before, she was teaching at the University of Helsinki and at the Swedish Collegium for Advanced

Study, Uppsala. She is the author of *Literature and Moral Theory* (2015) and *Descriptive Ethics: What Does Moral Philosophy Know about Morality?* (2016). She has coedited *Language, Ethics and Animal Life—Wittgenstein and Beyond* (with Niklas Forsberg and Mikel Burley; 2012).

Julia Hermann is Assistant Professor in Philosophy and Ethics of Technology at the University of Twente. Her current research focuses on the ethics of socially disruptive technologies. Her publications include *On Moral Certainty, Justification and Practice: A Wittgensteinian Perspective* (2015) and *Justice Everywhere: A Blog about Philosophy in Public Affairs*.

Lars Hertzberg is Professor Emeritus in Philosophy at Åbo Akademi University, in Åbo/Turku, Finland. Before he has taught at the Universities of Helsinki and Arizona. His publications include *The Limits of Experience* (1994) and, with Martin Gustafsson, *The Practice of Language* (2002). Also, he has translated some of Wittgenstein's work into Swedish (*Über Gewissheit, Vermischte Bemerkungen, Philosophische Untersuchungen*), and is cotranslator of *The Blue and Brown Books*.

Sandra Laugier is Professor of Philosophy "classe exceptionnelle" at Université Paris 1 Panthéon Sorbonne, and a senior member of the Institut Universitaire de France. She is the founder and chair of the Scientific Board of the Institut du Genre of the CNRS. Her publications include *L'Anthropologie logique de Quine* (1992), *Wittgenstein: Le mythe de l'inexpressivité* (2010), *Why We Need Ordinary Language Philosophy* (2013), *Recommencer la philosophie: Stanley Cavell et la philosophie en Amérique* (2014) and *Politics of the Ordinary: care, ethics, and forms of life*, 2020. She has edited *Le souci des autres* (2005), *Ethique, littérature, vie humaine* (2006), *Formes de vie* (2018) and has translated works by Stanley Cavell, Cora Diamond, and Carol Gilligan..

Sabina Lovibond is Emeritus Fellow and Tutor in Philosophy at Worcester College, University of Oxford. She is the author of *Realism and Imagination in Ethics* (1983), *Ethical Formation* (2002), *Iris Murdoch, Gender and Philosophy* (2011), and *Essays on Ethics and Feminism* (2015).

Hartmut von Sass is Heisenberg Research Professor at Humboldt University in Berlin. His books include *Language-Games of Faith* and *God as the Event of Being* (both in German, 2010 and 2013) as well as *Comparatively. On the Theory, Practice, and Ethics of Comparisons* (forthcoming). He is (co)editor of, i.a., *The Contemplative Spirit. Dewi Z. Phillips on Religion and the Limits of Philosophy* (with I.U. Dalferth; 2010), *Groundless Gods. The Theological Prospects of Post-Metaphysical Thought* (with E. Hall; 2014), and *Perspectivism* (2019).

Index

acknowledgment   35, 50, 51, 142
Adorno, Theodor W.   224, 225, 235
adventurousness   62–4
aesthetics   40, 103, 104, 106, 119, 235
Agamben, Giorgio   194, 195, 204
alien   3, 81, 83, 85, 153, 206
'alien visitor' analogy   84, 85
Allen, Amy   222, 223
Amesbury, Richard   8, 9
analytic ethics   27
analytic philosophy   15, 28, 217, 227, 235
anamnesis   34
Anglo-American philosophy   9, 227
animals   33–4, 41, 43, 44, 52, 235
animate life   235
Anscombe, Gertrude E. M   103
anthropological approach   104
anthropological fieldwork   43
anti-anti-realism (AAR)   5–6, 100, 109–10, 112–20, 123 n.40, 128, 130, 132, 139–41
anti-consequentialism   153, 154, 162
anti-descriptivism   105, 113, 116
anti-formalism   113, 115
anti-metaphysics   133
anti-non-cognitivism   109
anti-realism   1, 100, 104–7, 119, 120, 130, 140, 156
anti-realists   78–9, 81, 84
applied ethics   147
Archeology of Knowledge (Foucault)   42
Aristotelianism   103, 104
Aristotle   100
art   35
assertions and commands   17, 18
attitude   6, 17, 34, 42, 55–7, 80–3, 87, 99, 104, 107, 117, 129, 141, 157, 161, 173, 185, 216, 231
Austin, John L.   37, 39–43, 51, 52, 59, 64–6, 107
autonomy   138, 198, 206
Ayer, Alfred J.   103, 206

bedrock practices   84
beliefs   7, 75, 77–80, 86, 88, 89, 99, 110, 116, 117, 141, 149, 153, 157–60, 179, 184, 219, 238 n.16
Bellah, Robert   196
Blackburn, Simon   100, 107
Black women   215, 216
bolshevism   100
Bourdieu, Pierre   43
Bouveresse, Jacques   58
Brandhorst, Mario   87
Brandom, Robert   200
Burley, Mikel   7, 8

Carnap, Rudolf   102, 103
Catholicism   100
causal independence   79, 80, 82
Cavell, Stanley   1, 2, 4, 33–5, 37, 38, 50–58, 60, 63, 64, 66–8
Chiang Kai-shek   181, 182
Christian faith   178
Cities of Words (Cavell)   52
Claim of Reason, The (Cavell)   53, 57
Coetzee, John M.   33
cognitivism   104, 105, 108, 183
Collingwood, Robin G.   37
communication   3, 16, 25, 25, 43, 86, 130, 202, 219, 236
communitarian critique   205
communitarianism   130
Conant, James   176, 177
concept-formation   155, 156, 158, 160
conceptual analysis   103, 108
conceptual justice   8, 175, 177–9, 182–5
conscience (*Gewissen*)   20, 154
consensus   110, 118, 119, 133, 134, 136–40
consequentialism   7, 152–5
conservatism   2, 3, 9, 236
contemplative ethics   6, 148, 161
contemplative philosophy   6–8, 148, 150, 151, 155, 160, 174, 175, 179, 182

contextualist universalism 220
core and penumbra 202–4
Cornell, Drucilla 208 n.19
cosmopolitanism 217
Couch, Stuart 22, 25
Crary, Alice 9, 28, 46 n.6
Crenshaw, Kimberlé 214–16, 223, 226, 235
critical theory 2, 6, 9, 134, 214–27, 236, 238 n.16
"Criticizing from 'Outside'" (Diamond) 243 n.69
Critique of Forms of Life (Jaeggi) 225
culture
    practice 9
    theory 142

Daesh. *See* Islamic State (IS)
Davidson, Donald 110, 130
"deep and sinister" nature 8, 175, 179–82, 189–90 n.26
deflationism 80, 110–15
de Mesel, Benjamin 38, 75
deontological ethics 152
Department of Education 214
Derrida, Jacques 194, 197–9, 208 n.20, 209 n.26, 221
description 4, 7, 16, 30, 52, 55, 61, 106, 113, 114, 136, 156, 183, 184
descriptive discourse 118
descriptive methodology 3
descriptive philosophy 148, 150, 155–61
descriptivism 104, 105, 116
Despret, Vinciane 43, 44
Dewey, John 37, 63
Dialectic of Enlightenment (Horkheimer and Adorno) 223–4
dialectics 137, 218, 220, 226
Diamond, Cora 1, 4, 26 n.7, 28, 32–5, 44, 46 n.6, 50, 54, 56–64, 66, 68, 130
disagreement 1, 17, 58, 135, 147, 202, 218
discourse ethics 219
disposition (*Gesinnung*) 154
disquotational equivalence (DE) 111, 112
Drury, Maurice O'Connor 180, 181, 185
duty 58, 59, 99, 135, 186, 194

Dworkin, Ronald 203

ecumenical method 9
education 64, 89, 129
effective speech 17, 18, 25
elementary proposition 111
elitism 221
Elizabeth Costello (Coetzee) 33
Emerson, Ralph Waldo 63
emotivism 107, 128, 206
"emotivist self" 205
empirical objects 43
End of Progress: De-colonizing the Normative Foundations of Critical Theory, The (Allen) 222
"endorsement independence" 80, 81
Enlightenment 151
epistemology 1, 6, 46 n.4, 134, 147
Equal Employment Opportunity Commission 214
error theory 86, 87, 105
essentialism 101
ethical discourse 14, 19
Ethical Formation (Lovibond) 21
ethics 1, 162. *See also individual entries*
    conception of 53, 57, 58
    definition 106
    Deweyan 58
    and moral thinking 149–52
    nature of 120
    ordinary 64
    and perception 59–62
    post-Wittgensteinian 45
    redefinition 4, 50, 61
    statements 107, 117, 132
    theory 128
    transformation 51
    value 105
    Wittgensteinian 50, 56, 58
ethnocentrism 221–3, 226, 235
excuses 39–42
existentialism 104, 136, 201
experience 4, 25, 28, 29, 32, 36, 38, 39, 53–6, 63–7, 84, 102, 134, 137, 181, 195, 215, 233–4
experimental philosophy 78
explicit rules/laws 200
expressivism 5, 117, 139, 141

Index

fairness 58, 59, 155
false dichotomy 82–3, 85–6, 90
family resemblance 58, 59, 75, 76, 107, 108, 153
"Father Sergius" (Tolstoy) 21
feminism 215, 216, 221
field work 39–44
film criticism 60
Foot, Philippa 6, 103, 104, 108, 152–5
"Force of Law" (Derrida) 197
forms of life 39, 44, 45, 59, 61–3, 130, 138, 179, 225–6
  and differences 64–6
  moral practices and 86–8
Forsberg, Niklas 35
Forst, Rainer 220
Forster, Edward M. 67
Foucault, Michel 37, 42, 43, 211 n.55
Frankfurt school 2, 218, 219, 223, 235
Frazer, James 179
freedom 20, 198, 205, 206
Frege, Gottlob 16, 54, 58

Gaita, Raimond 29, 33
Geach, Peter 108
Gellner, Ernest 236
general ethics. *See* normative ethics
Gestalt approach 59, 60
Gestalt shifts 33, 34
gestures 4, 32, 51, 61, 62, 77, 153, 154, 156, 214, 215, 222, 224, 226, 231, 235
Geuss, Raymond 218
Gibbard, Allan 81
Glendinning, Simon 200
Glock, Hans-Johann 5–6, 128–30, 132–4, 136–41, 143 n.8
God 151, 158–60, 178–9, 195, 206, 211 n.60
Golden Bowl, The (James) 68
grace 55
grammar and logic of assertions (GLA) 110, 112

Habermas, Jürgen 218–20, 236, 238
Hacker, Peter M. S. 150
Hacking, Ian 43
Hämäläinen, Nora 3
Hare, Richard M. 103, 107–9

Hart, H. L. A. 103, 202–4, 210 n.45
"Having a Rough Story of What Moral Philosophy Is" (Diamond) 32
Healing of the Believers' Chests (2015) 184
Hegel, Georg W. F. 224, 226
Hemingway, Ernest 3, 23
Hermann, Julia 4, 5
Hertzberg, Lars 3, 13–26, 38
Hick, John 180
Hill, Anita 214
"Hills Like White Elephants" (Hemingway) 23–4
Holland, Ray 148
Holtzclaw, Daniel 215, 223
Honig, Bonnie 194, 197, 198
Hopster, Jeroen 78–81, 83
Horkheimer, Max 217, 224, 225, 235
human sacrifice 179–83, 185
Humean antirealism 82
Humean constructivism 82

"ideally coherent Caligula" 81–6, 90
"ideally coherent eccentrics" 5, 76, 81, 82, 85
Idea of a Social Science and Its Relation to Philosophy, The (Winch) 9, 227, 228, 230–2, 242 nn.55–6, 58, 242 n.58, 244 n.70
ideology critique 238 n.16
imaginative sympathy 32
immanence 218–20, 223, 226, 236
immanent critique 218–20, 223–7, 235
importance 51–2, 60, 63, 68
  attention to 68
  of film 4, 60–1, 67
  moral texture of 56–8
"The Importance of Being Human" (Diamond) 50
indeterminate law 197–9
individual ethics 154, 155
Ingle, David W. 207 n.3
inquiry 29, 36, 41, 42, 44, 45, 80
  empirical 41
  metaethical 78
  moral 79
  philosophical 37–41
Institute for Social Research 217, 223, 224

intellectual authority-relations 6, 133
internalism 153
internal realism 156
intuitionism 108, 109, 131, 137
Islamic State (IS) 184–6, 189 n.39
It Happened One night (Capra) 51–2

Jaeggi, Rahel 225–7
James, Henry 58, 62–4
Jesus 32, 180

Kahn, Paul 194–9, 201–3, 205, 206, 207 n.3, 211 n.55
Kant, Immanuel 100, 101, 154, 218–20
Kierkegaard, Soren 151, 154, 176, 177
Kirchin, Simon 86
Knausgaard, Karl Ove 3, 19, 26 n.5

Laboratory Life (Latour and Woolgar) 43
language 1, 5, 6, 14, 15, 41, 57, 64, 76, 101–3, 106, 107, 130
  conception of 115, 118, 132, 139
  philosophy 35, 39
language-games 16, 77, 85, 104, 114, 115, 132–9, 141, 156
Language Lost and Found (Forsberg) 35
Latour, Bruno 43
Laugier, Sandra 4
law and morality 203–4, 210 n.45
legal discourse 103
legal norms/rules 8, 198, 202, 203
legitimate philosophy 101, 102
liberalism 195, 197, 205, 206, 207 n.6
liberal judicial activism 208 n.19
liberal model 8
liberal theory 197, 205, 206
Limits of Experience, The (Hertzberg) 38
linguistic phenomenology 65
literary texts 19, 29, 33, 36, 43
literature 2, 3, 19, 29, 31, 32, 35, 36, 44, 57, 61, 151
Little Did I Know (Cavell) 67, 68
logical grammar rules 101, 102
logical syntax. *See* logical grammar rules
"the logic of science" 102, 103
logico-linguistic analysis 102, 103
Lovibond, Sabina 1, 5, 6, 21, 26 n.7, 100, 109, 110, 114, 115, 118, 128, 129, 131–3

Luke, gospel of 159

McDowell, John 1, 5, 100, 108, 109, 118, 128, 131, 133, 136, 138, 140
MacIntyre, Alasdair 205, 206
Mackie, John L. 105, 109
Magee, Brian 35
Marvin, Carolyn 207 n.3
Marx, Karl 100
mentalism 157
metaethics 1, 28, 78, 81, 100, 117, 118, 119, 147–9, 151
  analytic 5, 75, 89, 224
  approach 160
  debates 75
  rise and fall 101–4
  theory 85
meta-philosophy 6, 7, 100, 103, 104, 149
metaphysics 101, 102, 133, 151
  favouritism 139, 141
  principle 201
  theories 141
Milbank, John 211 n.60
military massacres 180, 181, 183
Mind, Value, and Reality (McDowell) 128
Moaz al-Kasasbeh 184, 185
Moore, Andrew 106, 108
moral agents 83–5
moral concepts 55, 59, 60, 63, 100, 103–5, 108, 117
"Moral Differences and Distances" (Diamond) 62
moral discourse 16, 80, 86, 87, 108, 116–18, 130, 139, 147, 205
moral error theory 5, 75, 76, 86–90
moral expressiveness 60, 62
moral injunctions 21, 22
"Moral Integrity" (Winch) 21
morality 5, 28, 29, 76, 77, 85, 87–90, 100, 104, 107, 108, 116, 136, 153, 162, 183, 202, 203, 206
moral judgment 59, 75, 78–81, 86, 89, 105, 108, 110, 129, 130, 137, 149, 183
moral language 21, 75
moral life 4, 28, 50, 57, 64
moral normativity 86, 88
moral norms 5, 80, 82, 83, 87–90

Index

moral objectivity 4, 75, 76, 78–81, 89
moral particularism 108
moral philosophy 1, 3–5, 9, 13, 28, 36–9, 45, 50, 58, 61, 75, 100, 103, 104, 106, 129, 173
    analytic 5, 28, 33, 46 n.4
    Anglophone 46 n.3
    "neo-intuitionist" 130, 131
    post-Wittgensteinian 28, 29, 31, 33, 35, 41
moral practices 77, 83, 86–8, 90, 148
moral reasons 5, 77, 84–6, 88–90
moral relativism 1, 118, 223
moral statements 75, 78, 105, 108, 110–12, 115, 116, 133
moral theory 1, 28, 206, 218, 219
moral thinking 149–52
moral value (MV) 5, 99, 104, 109, 115, 116, 119, 140, 141, 154, 162
moral wrongness 5, 76, 83–4, 86, 90
Mulhall, Stephen 76, 175–7
Murdoch, Iris 35, 37, 58, 60, 61, 103
"Must We Mean What We Say" (Cavell) 37
My Struggle (Knausgaard) 19–20

Nagel, Thomas 176
National Socialism 8, 194
natural history 243 n.67
natural science 78, 79, 101, 118, 228, 230, 231, 243 n.64
neo-behaviorist semantics 155
new decisionism 197, 199, 201, 202, 204–6
Nietzsche, Friedrich 100, 150
non-cognitivism 104, 105, 107–9, 116–17, 129, 133, 135
nonconceptualism 233, 234
noncontemplative contemplation 149
non-ethical concepts 103
nonfoundational epistemology 6, 134
non-metaphysics 102, 137
nonrealism 157, 158, 160
nonsense 13–15, 52, 136
    sense *vs.* 14
Nordic Wittgenstein Review 245 n.77
normative ethics 100, 103, 147, 152
normative reason 5, 76, 82–6, 90
Nussbaum, Martha 28, 57, 68

obligation 84, 99, 103, 116, 217, 232–4
O'Neill, Onora 32, 217, 237 n.8, 10
"On Really Believing" (Phillips) 156–7
ontology 59, 109, 231, 234
ordinary concepts 50–56, 64
ordinary language 35, 39, 40, 59, 64–5
ordinary lives 4, 50, 51, 56, 58, 66, 68
ordinary realism 155–61
ordinary use of "true" (OUT) 110, 112
Owen, David 240 n.38

Parfit, Derek 81
Penelhum, Terence 157
perception 4, 33, 51, 59–66, 68, 69, 81, 108, 131, 140, 233, 234
Pfizer 26 n.8
Phenomenology of Spirit (Hegel) 224–6
Philadelphia Story, The (1940) 51, 52, 63
Phillips, Dewi Z. 2, 6–8, 28, 46 n.6, 147–62, 173–9, 181, 185, 186
philosophy. *See also* moral philosophy
    Anglophone 36, 46 n.3, 224
    approach 7
    British 108
    ethics 1, 57
    of history 220
    of language 5, 109, 128
    of law 103
    normativity 28
    vs. personal 175–7
    practical 103
    problem 30, 102, 150
    of religion 160
    solipsism 99
    theory 40, 83, 129
physiognomy 131, 136
Plato 135–6
Platonist objectivism 78, 79, 82, 89
Platts, Mark 110, 131, 135
"A Plea for Excuses" (Austin) 39–42
Polanyi, Michael 163 n.10
political discourse 219
political theology 2, 8, 194, 195, 197, 200, 205, 206, 208 n.15
Political Theology: Four New Chapters on the Concept of Sovereignty (Kahn) 195, 197
political theory 2, 103, 195, 196, 207 n.6
Portrait of a Lady, The (James) 69

positivism disputes 224
postcolonialism 221
poststructuralism 216, 221–2, 240 n.38
post-Wittgensteinian procedure 33, 37
Prichard, Duncan 108
primitive reactions 77, 156, 158, 159
projectivism 105, 109, 119, 139, 140
prudential reasons 5, 88, 90
psychology 28, 56, 104
punishment 89, 184
purity 7, 8, 21, 173, 174, 177–9, 181, 182, 185
Purity of Heart (Kierkegaard) 154
Pursuits of Happiness (Cavell) 51, 52, 63
Putnam, Hilary 57–9, 220

quasi-realism 107
Quinean naturalism 101

Rabinow, Paul 43
racism 215, 222
radical transformation 55
Ramsey, Frank 113
rape 215
rational interaction 16
rationality 9, 28, 58, 102, 216, 218, 220–4, 226, 227, 231–4, 236, 238 n.16, 239 n.29
Rawlsian self 205
realism 1, 5, 6, 55, 59, 60, 79, 92 n.19, 100, 104, 105, 107–10, 120, 128–30, 156–8
Realism and Imagination in Ethics (Lovibond) 6, 26 n.7, 109, 128–30, 132, 142
realists 1, 5, 75, 78, 79, 81, 82, 84, 87, 90, 104, 105, 109, 114, 128–30, 134, 137, 138, 140, 157, 159–61
recognition 35, 45, 62, 68, 131, 136, 137, 142
redemption 55
Reflections on Fieldwork in Morocco (Rabinow) 43
regulism 200
religious rituals 184–6
Remarks on the Foundations of Mathematics 144 n.29
responsibility 20, 58, 59, 128, 155, 198, 202

Rhees, Rush 7, 8, 148, 150, 156, 174, 175, 178–86
Ripstein, Arthur 79–81
robust realists 92 n.19
Rorty, Richard 143 n.8, 237 n.10
Rose, Nikolas 43
Ross, William D. 108
rule-following 108, 134, 150, 200, 201, 204, 229, 230, 232
Russell, Jeffrey Burton 58

Sandel, Michael J. 205
Schmitt, Carl 8, 9, 194, 195, 197–9, 204, 205, 207 n.6, 210–11 n.53
Schopenhauer, Arthur 99
Searle, John 62, 108, 219
secondary quality (SQ) 119, 140
second-order philosophy 103, 226
secular modernity 194
seeing aspects and "seeing as" 3, 33–4, 36, 131
self 107, 117, 177, 178, 196, 197, 204–6
self-reflective contemplation 7, 149
semantic naturalism 155, 156, 162
semantics 7, 130, 133, 160, 162
sense 5, 7, 13, 14, 16, 18, 22, 36, 59, 63, 84, 85, 87, 106, 111, 114, 115, 134, 158, 160, 177, 181, 185, 186, 214, 215, 219, 224, 225, 232
Sex and Character (Weininger) 99
sexual behavior 215, 216, 221
sexual harassment 215
skepticism 64, 68, 69, 142, 195, 223, 239 n.29
Slahi, Mohamedou Ould 22
slavery (American) 167 n.61
social activity 135, 229, 230, 235
social criticism 9, 214, 216–18, 226–8, 234, 235
social phenomena 214, 224, 228, 229, 235
social practices 206, 225
social sciences 9, 227, 228, 235
soteriology 178
sovereignty 8, 194–7, 204–6, 210–11 n.53
speech act theory 219
Stevenson, Leslie 103, 107, 108, 206
Strawson, Peter F. 87

Street, Sharon   81–5, 93 n.65
Stroud, Barry   87
subjectivism   105, 109
subjectivity   109, 232

"tacit knowing"   163 n.10
Taming of Chance, The (Hacking)   43
Tarantino, Quentin   167 n.61
Tarski, Alfred   108
Taylor, Charles   37, 207 n.5
terminological-cum-conceptual
   prolegomena   104–5
texture   60–2, 64, 67
theoretical egoism   99
therapeutic approach   199–202
thinking for oneself   32
Thomas, Clarence   214
Thomism   103
Thoreau, Henry D.   53
thoughtlessness   66–9
Tiefe und Finstere   179
Tolstoy, Leo   21, 177
torture   5, 22, 82–4, 86, 90, 112, 113
totalitarianism   142
transcendence   176, 218, 220, 226, 236
Trigg, Roger   157
true propositions   14, 86, 139
true scientific propositions   14
truth   5, 52, 53, 57, 68, 79, 86, 102,
   109–15, 118–20, 130, 132, 134,
   136, 137, 139, 219, 223
Truth (Austin)   52

"Understanding a Primitive Society"
   (Winch)   243 n.69
United States   214, 215
universalizability   219
universal prescriptivism   107
universal reason   142
University of Frankfurt   217
utilitarianism   103, 110, 154

values and secondary qualities
   (VSQ)   139, 140
Vienna Circle   102
virtue ethics   153
"Vision and Choice in Morality"
   (Murdoch)   60
voluntarism   204–6

von Sass, Hartmut   6, 7
von Wright, Georg H.   103, 104
vulnerability   4, 61, 66, 67

Waismann, Friedrich   61, 112
Warnock, Geoffrey J.   108
Washington Post   62
Weil, Simone   177, 178
Weininger, Otto   99
What Maisie Knew (James)   62
Wiggins, David   108, 109
Williams, Meredith   83–4
Wilson, Hobart   62
Winch, Peter   2, 9, 21, 28, 32, 148, 156,
   159, 227–35, 242 nn.55–6, 58,
   60, 243 nn.64–6, 69, 244 n.70
Wittgenstein, Ludwig   1, 36, 37, 40, 50,
   53, 54, 58, 59, 61, 62, 64, 69, 75,
   99–100, 118–19, 128–32, 134,
   136, 138, 141, 142, 143 n.8, 150,
   154, 157–9, 175, 178–86, 188–9
   n.26, 227, 229, 230, 232–6
 anti-realism   105–7
 Blue Book   57
 On Certainty   76
 conception of moral objectivity   78–
   81, 89
 concerns about "ideally coherent
   Caligula"   81–6, 90
 deflationism   112–15
 ethics, metaethics and   3–7, 173–5
 Lecture on Ethics   1, 3, 5, 13–15, 25,
   106, 115, 116
 method   30–31
 non-cognitivism of   116–17
 objections to moral error
   theory   86–9
 perspectives   76–8
 Philosophical Investigations   3, 15, 16,
   30, 33, 42, 44, 53, 114, 130, 134,
   134, 143 n.8, 149, 150, 233
 philosophy   2–3, 39, 42, 45, 101–4
 realism   107–8
 *Remarks on Frazer's "Golden
   Bough"*   179, 180, 183,
   189 n.26
 Tractatus Logico-Philosophicus   1, 3,
   5, 15, 16, 101, 102, 105, 111, 112,
   115, 149

"Wittgenstein, Ethics, and Fieldwork in
    Philosophy" (Hämäläinen)   3
women exploitation   215
Woolgar, Steve   43

*Words and Things: An Examination of, and
    Attack on, Linguistic Philosophy*
    (Gellner)   236
World Viewed, The (Cavell)   68

www.ingramcontent.com/pod-product-compliance
Lightning Source LLC
Chambersburg PA
CBHW072137290426
44111CB00012B/1900